The Military Career of Field Marshal Jeffery Amherst

JEFFERY AMHERST

The Military Career of Field Marshal Jeffery Amherst

The War of Austrian Succession, The French &
Indian War, The Ohio Indian War and The
American War of Independence

ILLUSTRATED

Jeffery Amherst: A Biography
Lawrence Shaw Mayo

The Last Siege of Louisburg
C. Ochiltree Macdonald

LEONAUR

The Military Career of Field Marshal Jeffery Amherst
The War of Austrian Succession, The French & Indian War, The Ohio Indian War
and The American War of Independence
Jeffery Amherst: A Biography
by Lawrence Shaw Mayo
The Last Siege of Louisburg
C. Ochiltree Macdonald

ILLUSTRATED

FIRST EDITION

Leonaur is an imprint of Oakpast Ltd

Copyright in this form © 2022 Oakpast Ltd

ISBN: 978-1-915234-50-6 (hardcover)
ISBN: 978-1-915234-51-3 (softcover)

http://www.leonaur.com

Publisher's Notes

Contents

CHAPTER 1

Birth, Family, and Environment

Jeffery Amherst was born at Riverhead, a pleasant village in the parish of Sevenoaks, Kent, on January 29, 1717. He was the second son of Jeffery Amherst and Elizabeth Kerril, both of whom came of Kentish stock. The family was well-to-do and lived in an old mansion called "Brook's Place." In this house Jeffery was born and grew up. His ancestors had lived and died in Kent ever since the days of Runnymede and the Magna Charta, and from the reign of Richard II the genealogy is easily traced to a Reverend Jeffery Amherst who was the rector of Horsemonden—a parish near Tunbridge Wells—in the time of the Commonwealth. (Ritchie and Evans's *Lord Amherst*.) The rector was the great-great-grandfather of our Jeffery; he died in 1662. His grandson, another Jeffery Amherst, was a member of Parliament just after the Glorious Revolution, and both he and his son, the grandfather and the father of our Jeffery, were barristers.

Of the nine or ten children born to Jeffery Amherst and his wife, Elizabeth Kerril, five grew to maturity—Sackville, Jeffery, John, William, and their sister Elizabeth. Sackville, the eldest, led an obscure life, but his name is interesting for it indicates the long association of the Amherst family with the Sackvilles, Earls of Dorset, who had belonged to the peerage since the first decade of the reign of Elizabeth. The first Earl of Dorset, when Lord Treasurer of England, had employed one Richard Amherst as his steward. In later times our Jeffery Amherst's father was a neighbour of Lionel Cranfield Sackville, the first Duke of Dorset, whose seat, "Knole," was very near Riverhead. This proximity of residence led to an intimacy between the families which became a large factor in the rise of Jeffery the son, and was also an influence in the career of the duke's notorious offspring, Lord George Germain.

John Amherst, who was about a year younger than Jeffery, turned his energies to a naval life with no small amount of success. He began his career as a midshipman in the Mediterranean fleet under Admirals Haddock and Mathews, became a captain before he was thirty, and at the outbreak of the Seven Years' War was in command of the *Deptford* of 48 guns, one of the fleet with which the unfortunate Admiral Byng sailed to attempt the relief of Minorca in the spring of 1756. Two years later he was in American waters where his ship formed part of the squadron under Boscawen which made possible his brother's first great achievement, the capture of Louisburg. Towards the end of his life, he was made Vice-Admiral of the Blue, and Rear-Admiral of the White.

Probably Jeffery's favourite brother was William, who was his junior by about fifteen years. During the French and Indian War, he was one of Amherst's *aides-de-camp*, and distinguished himself in America by recapturing Newfoundland from the French in 1762. After his return to England, William commanded a fort on the Channel for a while and then was elected to Parliament. His military training, combined with his brother's influence, brought him numerous sinecures. In the army he attained the rank of lieutenant-general; and when, in 1774, the office of lieutenant-governor of Newfoundland became vacant, it was appropriately given to him who had regained the island for the British Empire twelve years before.

The England into which Jeffery Amherst was born was the England of George I. In northern Europe the meteoric Charles XII of Sweden, at whose name the world turned pale, plunged into war with Norway in 1717 and a year later fell dead before the fortress of Fredriksten. At home the ascendancy of the Whigs had already been established by the Elector of Hanover who so miraculously acceded to the English throne without domestic or foreign disturbance. The Old Pretender, to be sure, landed in Scotland in the winter of 1715-16; but soon afterwards returned discomfited to France.

The Whigs, to secure their control of the ship of state, had passed the Septennial Act, whereby they continued themselves as members of Parliament for four years more than their electors expected, and securely fortified the Protestant succession. As George I was but a puppet in their hands—understanding the English Constitution about as much as he understood the English language—this meant the establishment of the Whig oligarchy as the real power in England. For twenty years this power was personified in Walpole.

In literature the England of 1717 witnessed the sunset of the Augustan age. Addison's course was almost run, while Steele and Swift still plied their powerful pens. Defoe was turning his thoughts from

48TH REGIMENT OF FOOT, 1751

44TH REGIMENT OF GRENADIERS, 1751

politics to adventure, and Pope busied himself with the last volume of his translation of the *Iliad*. It was the end of the period which preceded the reign of Thomson's *Seasons* and Young's *Night Thoughts*.

In 1721 Walpole became Prime Minister of England and began his wise policy of conserving the country's wealth and energy until a sufficiently valid cause demanded their expenditure in a vigorous and profitable war. But England was neither as wise nor as patient as the great man at the helm, and after twenty years of peace and prosperity the country followed the counsels of less sagacious ministers and became involved in the inglorious War of the Austrian Succession.

Though Walpole fell and though his simple truth was miscalled simplicity, the good that he had done lived after him, for in those two decades of patient service he laid the financial foundation upon which Pitt was destined to erect an empire. Of this empire Pitt was to be the architect and Amherst and Clive the master builders.

Looking forward for a moment we see that during the period of Walpole's supremacy Jeffery Amherst was growing to manhood; during the fifteen years of mediocrity that followed, he assisted in one ignominious campaign after another; and it was only when William Pitt came into his own that Amherst knew the joys of victory and fame culminating in the conquest of Canada in 1760.

CHAPTER 2

Early Campaigns

Social usage of eighteenth-century England prescribed the profession of arms as the only proper pursuit for a second son, and in accordance with this law, Jeffery Amherst was predestined for a martial career. His first employment, however, was of a different nature, for at an early age he was a page in the house of the Duke of Dorset who lived but a short distance from the Amherst homestead at Riverhead. Such service was regarded as a social and educational privilege in those days and in this case, it led directly to the boy's entrance into the army. In 1735 Jeffery's noble patron was Lord-Lieutenant of Ireland and through his influence Amherst, although only eighteen years old, was appointed an ensign in the First Regiment of Foot Guards. (Sir Frederick William Hamilton's *Origin and History of the First or Grenadier Guards*, iii.)

An ensign in the British Army of the old regime was a commissioned officer of the lowest rank, corresponding to a second-lieutenant of today, (1916). The Foot Guards were an ancient institution, which traced its origin to the two regiments of King's Guards that were organised just before and just after the Restoration. (*Ibid.*) These two military bodies were merged into one by Charles II in 1665, and the combination became known as the King's Regiment of Guards, a designation which gave way twenty years later to the more familiar name of the First Regiment of Foot Guards.

In time of peace, it was usually quartered in London, sending occasional detachments to Windsor or elsewhere to attend upon members of the royal family; but in time of war this regiment was usually to be found where the fighting was most severe. At Blenheim, Ramillies, and Malplaquet it had shown itself worthy of its colonel, who in those early campaigns was no other than the invincible Marlborough.

The first seven years of Ensign Amherst's service were years of peace, for in spite of the war with Spain which broke out in 1739, Walpole's peace policy was practically maintained until his downfall three years later. During this period the Guards formed the garrison of London, guarded the sovereign at Windsor, and performed whatever occasional services naturally fell to the lot of the Household Troops.

Besides these duties, and occasionally awing a turbulent public, or aiding the customs officers in the suppression of smuggling, the regiment had little to do except to submit to an annual review, an event which is interesting chiefly from the description of the uniform of a Guardsman, which it affords. A brigade-order preceding one occasion of the kind stipulated the following requirements:

"The officers to appear in their new regimental clothes, gaiters, square-toed shoes, gorgets, sashes, buff-coloured gloves, regimental laced hats, cockades, the button worn on the left side, and twisted wigs, according to the pattern. The men to appear perfectly clean and shaved, square-toed shoes, gaiters, their hats well cocked and worn so low as to cover their foreheads and raised behind, with their hair tucked well under and powdered, but none on the shoulders, the point of their hats pointing a little to the left, their arms perfectly clean." (Hamilton's *Grenadier Guards*, ii.)

Such was the appearance of the English fighting-man of Amherst's youth, and the uniform continued to be cruelly conspicuous until the sound good sense of Lord Roberts put an end to such absurdities after the Boer War. For Continental wars, in which the great factor was standing one's ground in a battle, the scarlet coat and other accoutrements were not so great a handicap as they might seem, but it is still difficult for the American mind to comprehend their employment in wilderness warfare, for one hundred and fifty years after Braddock's disaster in 1755.

If we care to picture Amherst at this time, we must imagine a tall, thin youth with brown hair, a ruddy face, eyes of steel grey, and a nose decidedly aquiline. (Sir Nathaniel William Wraxall's *Historical and Posthumous Memoirs*—edited by H. W. Wheatley: also, Sir Joshua Reynolds' portrait of Amherst at "Montreal.") To this young man the declaration of war against Spain in 1739 must have been welcome, after the dull monotony of year after year of garrison life and reviews; and still more grateful must have been the prospect of a general war on the Continent, for two years previous to this it had been decided that in case of hostilities the First Regiment was to be at once ordered on foreign service.

The War of the Austrian Succession was caused by the violation of a scrap of paper known as the Pragmatic Sanction. By this document, which was assented to by all the important states of Europe, the Emperor Charles VI thought he had secured the succession of his daughter Maria Theresa to his whole Austrian domain, but after his death in 1740 the guaranteed heiress was not long in doubt as to the good faith of princes.

Prussia struck the first blow when Frederic II poured 30,000 men over the frontier and demanded the province of Lower Silesia. France followed his ignoble example, then Sardinia, Saxony, Spain, and Poland did likewise, and the partition of Austria seemed inevitable. English statesmen regarded the situation with grave concern, for Britain had guaranteed the Pragmatic Sanction and was likely to fulfil her engagement. In 1741 Parliament subsidised the plucky Austrian Archduchess, and in the following year 16,000 English troops were sent to Flanders as auxiliaries to her forces.

Among the regiments thus despatched to the Continent was the First Regiment of Foot Guards in which Amherst was still a minor commissioned officer. The chief command of all these troops was given to the veteran Earl of Stair, among whose major-generals was John Ligonier. The latter's name was originally Jean Louis Ligonier. He had fled from France as a Protestant refugee, after the Revocation of the Edict of Nantes, and, enlisting in the British Army, fought under Marlborough at Blenheim, Ramillies, Oudenarde, and Malplaquet, and proved himself a splendid soldier.

At Malplaquet, Ligonier had twenty-three bullets shot through his clothes and yet emerged from the battle unhurt. His rise in the service was as rapid as it was deserved, and it was a piece of great good fortune for Jeffery Amherst that the veteran commander chose him for one of his *aides-de-camp* in the present campaign. The selection was made in the previous year when Amherst was twenty-four years old, but whether it was based upon an acquaintance with the young lieutenant or upon the recommendation of the Duke of Dorset remains a mystery. At any rate, Amherst went to Flanders in the summer of 1742 in the capacity of *aide-de-camp* to General John Ligonier.

If Jeffery was impatient for active service after his long and uninteresting apprenticeship in and about London, the first campaign was disappointing. In fact, the operations of the British Army on the Continent in 1742 can hardly be called a campaign; they consisted mainly in waiting for the Dutch allies to arrive. The Netherlanders, although under the same obligations to maintain the Pragmatic Sanction, were diffident about taking any active part in its support. Their forms of procedure were slow and their temper averse to the remonstrances of Lord Stair; even Carteret, by going in person to the Hague, failed to stir them out of their apathy. In the meantime, the British troops remained in Flanders, "idle, unemployed, and quarrelling with the inhabitants." (Mahon's *History of England*, iii.)

In 1743 events assumed a more cheerful aspect, and towards the end of June the English and their Hanoverian and Hessian allies defeated a large French Army at Dettingen. This battle is usually remembered as the last in which an English king actually commanded his troops in person. Curiously enough it was also the first field upon which Amherst saw active service, and although it would be interesting to know his impressions of his first battle, for these we have no source of information. All we know is that in the campaign as a whole he acquitted himself well, for in the autumn of the same year Lord George Sackville alluded to him with genuine enthusiasm in a letter to the Duke of Dorset:

> You cannot imagine how well everybody speaks of Jeff. Amherst. He is of great use to General Ligonier and the general is very sensible of it. He cannot be long before he is promoted in his turn, for he is now the eldest lieutenant in the regiment and there can be no danger of anybody's being put over his head. (Historical Manuscripts Commission's *Report on the Manuscripts of Mrs. Stopford-Sackville, i.*)

Lord George was in a position to know because he was with the army during the summer of 1743, first as Lieutenant-Colonel of the Twenty-Eighth Regiment of Foot, and after Dettingen, as *aide-de-camp* to the king.

This battle was also the first action for at least three other soldiers, who were to distinguish themselves in the conquest of Canada before many years. One of these was James Wolfe, a youthful ensign of sixteen years, who was doing the duty of an adjutant. (Beckles Willson's *Life and Letters of James Wolfe*.) Wolfe's entrance into active service was hardly propitious, as the horse he rode was shot in the leg at the very outset of the battle, and the future hero of the Plains of Abraham pitched headlong from his saddle. (*Ibid.*) For Robert Monckton, who was second in command before Quebec and upon whose shoulders

Wolfe's mantle fell on that eventful day in 1759, Dettingen was also an initiation into a martial career.

Monckton was only a year older than Wolfe and, on this occasion, served on the King's Guard. The last of the trio was George Townshend to whom Quebec surrendered, and who hurried home to England soon after the capitulation in order to steal for himself as much as possible of Wolfe's glory. (Francis Parkman's *Montcalm and Wolfe,* ii, both volumes republished as *Musket & Tomahawk* by Leonaur:2007.) Townshend graduated from St. John's College, Cambridge, with the degree of M.A. in 1742, and instead of indulging in the "grand tour" of Europe which in the eighteenth century was the usual method of spending the first year after one's college days, he wished to join in the Continental campaign as a volunteer. As his father was Viscount Townshend and his uncle the Duke of Newcastle, a post on the staff of Lord Dunmore, who commanded a division under Lord Stair, was found for George Townshend, then eighteen years old. (C.V. F. Townshend's *Life of Field-Marshal George Townshend,* republished as *A British Soldier of the 18th Century,* Leonaur:2012.)

Thus, it was that the future conqueror of New France, and the first, second, and third officers in command on the Plains of Abraham, had their first taste of real war at the Battle of Dettingen, June 27, 1743.

The next great conflict of the war occurred almost two years later at Fontenoy. In the meanwhile, the command of the British contingent of the allied army had been given to William Augustus, Duke of Cumberland, a younger son of George II, who was not more than twenty-four years old at the time of his appointment. In spite of his youth Cumberland was a born leader of men and his personal bravery and enthusiasm were an inspiration to the rank and file. Had he commanded an harmonious army the Battle of Fontenoy, which was fought on May 11, 1745, might have been a victory for England, but lack of co-operation between the British, Hanoverians, Austrians, and Dutch prevented any such happy outcome.

Jeffery Amherst was present with his chief, General Ligonier, and had a busy day of it, dashing hither and thither over the field carrying important messages to the Duke and to his subordinate generals. (J.W. Fortescue's *History of the British Army,* republished as *Sir John Fortescue's 'A Collision of Giants',* Leonaur: 2015; F. H. Skrine's *Fontenoy,* republished as *Fontenoy, Britain & The War of Austrian Succession, 1740-1748,* Leonaur: 2017.)

More than once the French Army seemed to be defeated, but finally it was the British who were obliged to retreat. Retiring to a position, north of Brussels, they spent the rest of the spring and summer in helplessly watching Flanders fall completely into the hands of the enemy.

While in this interesting situation, the duke received word that Charles Edward Stuart, better known as the Young Pretender, had arrived in Scotland to attempt the recovery of the English throne. As Britain was drained of troops by the European war, Cumberland was instructed to send home ten battalions with Sir John Ligonier, as soon as possible. Temporarily the scene of the war was to be changed and battles were to be fought in the north of England and in Scotland. Wherever Ligonier went, his *aide-de-camp* accompanied him. Accordingly, Captain Amherst left the main army in late September and arrived in London in the first week of the following month.

The Young Pretender was the grandson of James II and was well suited to the romantic part he chose to play, for he was youthful, handsome, and blessed with a magnetic personality. At first success attended him at every hand. He marched through Scotland and down into England before the troops recalled from the Continent could be landed and put in motion against him.

When real opposition appeared upon the horizon, however, Charles Edward Stuart, having given London a good fright, turned his face northward and hurried back across the border. The English forces were divided into three small armies, one of which was entrusted to Sir John Ligonier. With this division Amherst left London in the last week of November and advanced into the Midlands to prevent the Pretender from making a dash into Wales, where Jacobite sympathies were supposed to be strong.

A week later in the heart of Staffordshire, Ligonier and the Stuart found themselves in close proximity and the latter suddenly chose Scotland, rather than London or Wales, as his objective. When the Duke of Cumberland, who was with Ligonier, got wind of the retreat of the rebels, he caught up four thousand men and started in hot pursuit. Over the border into Scotland, he harried the enemy, and on and on until the decisive victory at Culloden, in the following April, crushed the rebellion at a blow, and extinguished forever all hope of a restoration of the Stuarts.

Jeffery Amherst remained with his chief, and so did not witness the wholesale butcheries which are ever associated with the names of Cumberland and Culloden. On the contrary, life must have been quite uninteresting for the young *aide-de-camp*. Soon after the duke's departure, a rumoured invasion of the south of England by the French, brought Ligonier and his army back to London, where they arrived about Christmas time. Here the winter was spent, and though England kept a vigilant eye upon Dunkirk, the threatened expedition never took place.

Promotion in the service, however, compensated Amherst for lack of excitement in this dull period. On Christmas Day in 1745, he was given a company in the First Battalion of the First Regiment of Foot Guards, and his rank was raised to that of lieutenant-colonel. (*Army List for 1754.*) This meant not only a higher rank and the title of colonel, but also brought with it a pecuniary increase. As a captain, Amherst had received sixteen shillings and sixpence per day. In his new rank the pay was one pound, eight shillings, and sixpence—a substantial difference of twelve shillings. (Fortescue's *History of the British Army*, ii, republished as *Sir John Fortescue's 'A Collision of Giants'*, Leonaur: 2015.)

In June, 1746, Colonel Amherst accompanied Ligonier back to the Netherlands, where the French had made great progress during the absence of the British troops. Though George II was keenly desirous of revenge upon France for the suspicious part she had played in the Forty-five, his hopes were not realised in this campaign, for no battle worthy of the name was fought. Inaction and occasional compulsory retreat were the characteristics of the year's operations on the Continent. In the following winter, however, when the Duke of Cumberland was appointed commander-in-chief of the Allied Army, there was more prospect of co-operation and enterprise.

The military family which the duke adopted to help him in the campaign of 1747 is interesting. Of his seven *aides-de-camp* three were destined to win renown in America. The first of these was the ever-memorable Lord Howe, who was killed near Ticonderoga eleven years later, the idol of Americans and British alike. The second was none other than Colonel Jeffery Amherst, who, according to Horace Walpole, had been "the favourite *aide-de-camp* of Ligonier." The third was George Townshend, who, as has already been stated, commanded under Wolfe on the Plains of Abraham, and in later years became a Field Marshal of the British Army. For Amherst, who was just thirty years old, the appointment was flattering and was doubtless due to the representations of his old chief, Ligonier.

In spite of all his energy and enthusiasm, Cumberland was not a match for the enemy, and the odds against him were increased by the lack of harmony which marked the councils of the Allies. On July 2, 1747, a battle was forced upon him at Laffeldt, a tiny village near Maestricht. The British and the Hessians made a gallant stand, but when retreat became necessary, heroic measures were required to prevent it becoming a rout. Accordingly, Ligonier, with characteristic bravery, led three regiments of cavalry straight into the pursuing French horse. Before this terrific onslaught the enemy fell back in temporary confusion and gave the allied army time to make good its escape. Amherst's erstwhile chief paid dearly for his achievement: his horse was shot under him, and he himself was captured by the French. Although from a military point of view the battle of Laffeldt was unimportant, it led directly to the ending of the war.

At last King George was heartily sick of the conflict which, since Dettingen, had been one defeat after another on the Continent. Apparently, the victorious Louis XV was equally bored by the prospect of more campaigns in the Netherlands, for he availed himself of the presence of Ligonier, now his prisoner, to make overtures for peace. These were gladly transmitted to the Duke of Cumberland and when he, in turn, conveyed them to his father, George II, the tidings were received with joy by the king and his ministers. Consequently, a Congress to arrange the terms of a peace assembled at Aix-la-Chapelle in January, 1748, and the preliminary articles establishing practically the *status quo ante bellum*, were signed a few months later.

What had the six years of war meant to Amherst? For him the long and costly struggle had been an excellent training-school replete with moving accidents by flood and field, and the experience gained in the War of the Austrian Succession was destined to yield fruit in the Seven Years' War a decade later; but equally important were the friendships Colonel Amherst formed at this time. Of these his acquaintance with Sir John Ligonier was to lead directly to the prominent part awaiting him at Louisburg. Hardly less valuable was his association with the Duke of Cumberland, although the latter fell from grace at the precise moment when Amherst's real career was about to begin.

In time of peace the soldier's life is indeed dull. Jeffery Amherst returned to the monotonous routine of an officer of the Guards whose duties during the next few years consisted chiefly in assisting the civil magistrates of London to preserve the peace. There were smugglers and highwaymen to be escorted to Newgate, and there were excited crowds to be kept in order at public executions; also, there were the

BRITISH AND HESSIAN SOLDIERS

less lugubrious periods of service at Windsor, or at Hampton Court, or wherever the sovereign might choose to reside. Fortunately, the monotony of this life was somewhat relieved in Amherst's case by his appointment as Groom of the Bedchamber to his royal companion in arms, the Duke of Cumberland. Besides whatever *éclat* this membership in the ducal household brought, it also meant personal attendance upon His Royal Highness for two or three weeks at a time every year; and thus, the intimacy which had grown up between the two men during their service abroad was kept alive in time of peace.

Another friendship formed during the war appears to have been continued during these dull days, for in a letter from Wolfe to his father, written in April, 1750, the future captor of Quebec mentions having "writ" to Amherst, and "said everything that I thought could engage him to use his influence with Sir John Ligonier" to procure a provision for the son of one Mrs. Scott. (Beckles Willson's *Life and Letters of James Wolfe*.) To what extent Amherst troubled himself about the matter is not known, but a few weeks later Wolfe asserted his conviction that his friend had done his part, and gave still further evidence of confidence in his "sincerity and good inclinations." Although it is well known that the future conquerors of Canada saw their first service in the previous campaigns in the Low Countries, this is the earliest evidence of their actual acquaintance.

In the autumn of the same year, 1750, occurred the death of Jeffery Amherst, the father, at the age of seventy-three years. By his decease the family estate at Riverhead passed to Sackville, the eldest son. Eighteen months later Amherst's mother followed her husband, and was buried at Sevenoaks. These breaks in the family circle were perhaps contributing causes of the colonel's first matrimonial venture, for in May, 1753, Jeffery Amherst married his second cousin, Jane Dalison. (William Berry's *County Genealogies, Kent*.) The bride, who was thirty-one years old, and hence five years younger than her husband, came of a good Kentish family which had been established for many years not far from Riverhead. The marriage took place in Gray's Inn Chapel in London, but of this Mrs. Amherst we know little else except that she died twelve years later, leaving her husband without heirs.

Domestic events and military routine so occupied the colonel at this time that even his old friends and patrons, the Sackvilles, lost track of him, and one of them wrote to the future Lord George Germain, asking "What is become of Amherst and his General Ligonier?" (*Stopford-Sackville Manuscripts*, i.) Indeed, it seems as if the colonel shared the sentiments of Shakespeare's Henry V,—

In peace there's nothing so becomes a man
As modest stillness and humility.

But he was not to remain long in obscurity, for the clouds of war, that were to encircle the globe, already darkened the western horizon, and there was promise of a conflict which had been inevitable ever since the signing of the universally unsatisfactory Peace of Aix-la-Chapelle.

CHAPTER 3

The Seven Years' War

It is usually asserted that the Seven Years' War broke out in America and spread to the Old World. Certainly, that is the most convenient way to distinguish this upheaval from those of the preceding half-century of conflict. Whether or not conditions in Europe would have led to a general war irrespective of the clash between two empires in the New World, American developments may properly be regarded as the long, slow fuse which at length ignited the magazines of all central Europe.

Heretofore the reverse of this process had been true; European hostilities were merely echoed in America by the raids of the French and Indians upon frontier towns, or by organised attacks on the part of the British against the strongholds of New France. Colonial warfare was a display of loyalty to the mother country rather than a primary quarrel, and seldom accomplished much in the interests of either empire at large. Now the tables were turned, for when Washington encountered the French near Great Meadows in May, 1754, shots were exchanged which preluded a great European struggle. The renewal of hostilities meant that two empires spreading out over North America had at last run afoul of each other west of the Alleghanies, and the question of right of way must be settled by force of arms.

From the beginning of her American colonisation France devoted her main efforts to Canada and founded in that region a feudal state known as New France. Pushing constantly westward, up the St. Lawrence River and through the Lakes, the French established a good claim to the entire valley, a process which culminated in the pageant of Saint-Lusson in 1671. On that occasion Daumont de Saint-Lusson, in the presence of the representatives of fourteen Indian tribes formally took possession of the great inland basin at Sault Ste. Marie, and thus defined the northern boundary of England's colonial empire in the New World.

A decade later, La Salle sailed down the Mississippi from the Illinois to the Gulf of Mexico and, in April, 1682, assumed title to the entire Mississippi Valley in the name of the King of France, in whose honour he named the vast wilderness Louisiana. If his exploration was the basis of true ownership France had succeeded already in setting a western limit to the English colonies at the watershed of the Alleghanies; but as yet these ramifications of New France failed to disturb the Anglo-Saxons on the seaboard. Except in the Connecticut and Hudson valleys they still clung to the tidewater regions and cared little about the activities of French explorers in the remote hinterland.

The first check to French expansion was administered when the Iroquois, or Five Nations, and their territories were taken under the protection of the King of England. This was accomplished in 1684 by Governor Dongan of New York and it was destined to be an event of infinite importance for the future of England in America. The League of the Iroquois was a confederation of the most civilized and intelligent Indians on the continent. Their domain proper was practically that of the State of New York today, (1916), but tributary tribes were to be found throughout the Ohio Valley, and it is obvious that the friendship of the Iroquois was the key to the inland country north of the Ohio and east of the Mississippi.

The French had forfeited all possibility of true amity with the Five Nations when Champlain unadvisedly took the side of their enemies, the Ottawas, and delighted the latter by thoroughly terrifying and dispersing a band of Iroquois which he encountered near the head of Lake Champlain.

That misstep occurred in 1609 and Iroquois hostility for the French might have been overcome in time had it not been for the fact that French brandy was scarce and expensive, while English rum was always available for no great consideration. The Jesuit Fathers did their utmost not only to convert the bloodthirsty natives to Christianity of the French type, but also to suppress drunkenness among the redskins with whom they laboured. But French blandishments were wasted upon the Iroquois, and their friendship for the English was consummated at Albany in 1684 when, as we have seen, they declared themselves subjects of the King of England and placed their territory under his protection.

By one of the provisions of the Treaty of Utrecht in 1713, the King of France acknowledged the Iroquois to be English subjects. Was this not equivalent to an admission of England's title to the Ohio Valley? It must seem so, and was doubtless regarded as such by the parties to the instrument; but when France was once more upon her feet, she did everything in her power to evade the treaty obligations forced upon her in 1713.

The Treaty of Utrecht not only secured the recognition of the Iroquois as subjects of the English Crown, and thus excluded New France from expansion south of the Great Lakes, but it also lopped off Newfoundland and Nova Scotia from the Gallic empire in America. This pruning of New France in the northeast was soon balanced by the founding of New Orleans in Louisiana, near the mouth of the Mississippi, and by the middle of the century there were perhaps three thousand whites and two thousand negro slaves in the southern colony. Scattered settlements grew up along the river, extending northward from New Orleans. They dotted the banks of the Mississippi at Natchez and in the vicinity of the modern St. Louis, and there were also numerous hamlets in the Illinois country.

Thus in 1750, France held the gates to the boundless interior of North America, while the English were practically walled up by the Alleghanies, not more than two hundred miles from the Atlantic seaboard. Furthermore, as France in America had now two heads, one at Quebec, the other at New Orleans, policy dictated the connecting of these capitals by the actual possession of the Ohio Valley. The first steps in this process which aimed at the establishment of France as the predominant power in North America led to the Seven Years' War, a struggle whose outcome spelt quite the reverse of French colonial aggrandisement in the New World. In the short space of ten years the Gallic peril was not only averted, but so thoroughly annihilated that France was wiped off the continent of North America.

Quietly ignoring the limits forced upon New France by the Treaty of Utrecht and disregarding the fact that English traders abounded in the country west of the Alleghany Mountains, the governor of Canada, the Marquis de la Galissonière, sent out a party of about two hundred white men, escorted by a few Indians, to take possession of the Ohio Valley. This was in June, 1749; the leader of the expedition was Céloron de Bienville. The Frenchmen proceeded across Lake Erie, carried to Chautauqua Lake, and then floated down the Allegheny to the Ohio, depositing here and there leaden plates inscribed with a legend to the effect that Céloron was taking possession "of the aforesaid

River Ohio, of all streams that fall into it, and all lands on both sides, to the source of the aforesaid streams as the preceding Kings of France have enjoyed, or ought to have enjoyed, it, and which they have upheld by force of arms and by treaties, notably by those of Ryswick, Utrecht, and Aix-la-Chapelle." (Parkman.)

All this was very impressive, but unless followed by settlement it could in no way secure the region for France. To facilitate future expeditions and possible colonisation, the Frenchmen made themselves as agreeable as possible to the Indians, ordered a group of English traders to withdraw from the country, and then returned to Canada by the way of the Great Miami, the Maumee, and Lake Erie. From the French point of view the Ohio Valley was now indisputably French.

To realise how the two empires were destined to jostle each other in the immediate future, we need only to note the formation and activity of the Ohio Company. In the same year in which Céloron took possession of the valley of the Ohio, some Virginia gentlemen, among them Lawrence and Augustine Washington, procured a grant of two hundred thousand acres from the King of England. Roughly speaking, the land granted must lie in the northern part of the present state of West Virginia, and in 1750 the Ohio Company sent an Indian trader, Christopher Gist by name, across the mountains to spy out the land and after exploration to select a desirable tract for them.

Gist carried out instructions and explored the Ohio from its most northern point at Logstown to the Great Miami, where, a scant year and a half before, the French, under Céloron de Bienville, had preceded him. A collision between the two frontiers was now inevitable, and that collision became more immediate when, in 1752, the Marquis Duquesne de Menneville, a man with an aggressive policy, was appointed governor of Canada.

The French Government did not give any great amount of support to the ambitious schemes of the new governor. He was reminded that the expenses of the colony were already enormous and that they had doubled since the peace; but the Marquis Duquesne, seeing that it was a case of now or never, determined to occupy the upper waters of the Ohio and to strengthen that occupation by forts and garrisons. Early in the spring of 1753, an expedition of about fifteen hundred men set out for the disputed country. Instead of carrying from Lake Erie to Chautauqua Lake, as Céloron had done four years before, the present invaders landed at Presqu' isle, the site of the modern city of Erie, which they found to be an advantageous point with an excellent harbour.

At this place they constructed a fort, and then cut a road through the woods to the Rivière aux Boeufs, the nearest tributary of the Ohio. There they built another fort, which was named Fort Le Boeuf; but dysentery and discouragement put an end to further operations for the year. Leaving three hundred men to garrison the two new posts, the rest of the expedition, much the worse for exposure and fatigue, returned to Montreal.

The garrison at Fort Le Boeuf had settled down for a long winter in the wilderness, when, on the evening of the eleventh of December, the monotony of their solitude was broken by the arrival of a young Virginian, accompanied by Christopher Gist and a few other white men and Indians. The unbidden guest was Major George Washington, Adjutant-General of the Virginia militia, and he brought with him a letter from Governor Dinwiddie, expressing surprise that the French troops should fortify lands "so notoriously known to be the property of the Crown of Great Britain." The letter also demanded the peaceable departure of the intruders. The commander at Fort Le Boeuf forwarded Dinwiddie's missive to the Marquis Duquesne and Washington returned to Virginia unmolested.

One discovery which the young Virginian made while on this mission deserves especial notice. At the confluence of the Allegheny and the Riviere aux Boeufs, some sixty miles from Fort Le Boeuf, stood an English trading-house. Washington found the building converted into a French military outpost over which the invaders had raised their flag. The property had changed hands in the previous August when members of Duquesne's expedition seized the house and carried off its inmates. This aggression on the part of the French, small in itself, was the first overt act of the Seven Years' War, and it is small wonder that Governor Dinwiddie, when informed of what had occurred, arose in his wrath and determined upon energetic measures for the next year.

In February, 1754, Captain Trent, an English fur trader, crossed the mountains with a band of backwoodsmen to build a fort at the point where the Allegheny and the Monongahela unite to form the Ohio— a spot which Washington had wisely judged the best for the purpose. Hardly had Trent and his men commenced constructing the outpost when a swarm of canoes and *bateaux*, bringing about five hundred Frenchmen, descended upon the position of the English. Planting cannon in front of the embryonic fortress, the invaders forced the officer in charge to surrender, and then allowed him to depart with his men. While the vanquished English recrossed the mountains to

Virginia, the French destroyed the captured works at the forks of the Ohio and began the construction of a much larger and better building which they named Fort Duquesne.

To Dinwiddie and Washington this step towards open hostilities resembled a declaration of war, and they acted accordingly. The governor, although at odds with the Virginia Assembly, succeeded in raising a few hundred men whom he hurried through the wilderness to the scene of action. This so-called Virginia Regiment was commanded by Colonel Joshua Fry, an English gentleman, but Washington was at the head of the advance. Towards the end of May the latter had penetrated to a place called Great Meadows on the western slope of the Alleghanies, and learning that a party of Frenchmen were in the immediate vicinity, Washington determined to surprise them before they could set a trap for him.

Advancing into the forest, the Virginians came upon the French in a rocky hollow, and a short battle ensued. The commander of the enemy's force and about ten others were killed; the rest were captured, and Washington returned to the camp at Great Meadows where he awaited reinforcements. While there he erected a rude protection against the French which he called Fort Necessity, a name it very soon justified, for on July 3, 1754, he was surrounded and attacked by the enemy. After nine hours of stubborn and discouraging fighting, Washington surrendered upon conditions of marching out with drums beating and all the honours of war. In the early morning of July 4, the retreat began, and a few days later not an English flag waved beyond the Alleghanies.

Clearly, war between England and France had begun in North America, but, as in the days of Hawkins and Drake, one code of international law obtained in the Old World, another in the New. Hence hostilities on the American frontier although recognised and abetted by the home governments did not necessarily mean war between the two states in Europe. Furthermore, France needed time to increase her navy and to strengthen her garrisons in America, while England was equally unprepared with a reduced army of only eighteen thousand men. It behoved both powers to simulate peace at home while bending every energy to get the upper hand in the wilderness across the water.

In 1755, the English undertook various operations against the enemy with incidental success, but all their petty victories were more than offset by the hideous defeat of Braddock's expedition against

Fort Duquesne, in which officers and men were done to death by the French and their Indian allies. Nevertheless, Britain by no means relinquished her claim to the hinterland, nor her intention, if necessary, to fight for it. In May, 1756, she declared war against France. Thus began the most terrible conflict of the eighteenth century.

In view of the discouraging events that were taking place in America it was only natural that George II turned a worried eye towards his hereditary possessions in Germany, for in the impending European war the Electorate of Hanover could scarcely help falling into the hands of the French, particularly if Prussia took the side of Louis XV. To guard against such an event the British Government took 8,000 Hessians into England's pay and, in February, 1756, sent Colonel Jeffery Amherst to Germany to take charge of their commissariat. The appointment entailed duties of an administrative kind only, and was very likely due to the influence of the Duke of Cumberland, who still stood high as a military adviser to the Cabinet.

At first Amherst's headquarters were in the quaintly attractive town of Cassel, the capital of the old electorate of Hesse-Cassel, but hardly had the colonel arrived at the scene of his duties when he received hurried orders from home to return to England with a portion of the Hessian subsidiaries, for the island trembled at the prospect of an invasion by the French. This meant not only the task of supplying the troops, but also the engineering of their assembly and transportation, a feat which Amherst seems to have accomplished with success. Leaving Cassel in the first week in April, he went to Hanover and thence to Stade, the fortified port of the Electorate on the estuary of the Elbe.

There he remained three or four weeks, awaiting the arrival of the transports which should convey him and his Germans across the North Sea. By the eleventh of May all were on shipboard, and the imported mercenaries, escorted by their commissary on H. M. S. *Queenborough*, turned their faces toward England. The voyage was not a short one, even for those days, but Amherst and his charges arrived in good order at Southampton on the evening of May 15. (*State Papers Foreign, Military Expeditions*, vol. 27.) There the Hessians were immediately divided into two camps, one at Farnham, the other at Winchester—both sufficiently near the coast to insure its protection. (Hamilton's *Grenadier Guards*, ii.)

During the busy days when he was occupied with the landing and disposition of the Hessians, Jeffery Amherst was appointed colonel of the 15th Regiment of Foot, (Willson's *Wolfe*), an event in which Wolfe rejoiced so much that he wrote to his father:

> I hear with pleasure today, that my friend Amherst has got a regiment; nobody deserves the king's favour better than that man. (*Army List for 1757.*)

The new appointment was practically a sinecure and in no way interfered with his duties as commissary to the foreign subsidiaries, but as a recognition of his ability and services the colonelcy was decidedly significant.

In January, 1753, the eyes of Frederick of Prussia had been opened to the existence of an ill-natured secret treaty between Russia and Austria, aiming at the restitution of Silesia and the partition of the kingdom of Prussia. Saxony, too, was in the plot, and all that was necessary to ensure success was the neutrality—if not the assistance—of France. Well might even Frederick be concerned when confronted with such a hostile coalition and he looked about for a strong ally with whom to stem the threatening tide. For his royal uncle, the King of England, Frederick had little affection and less respect, but in the face of the gathering storm his practical mind discovered in Britain a much-needed source of strength.

When George II was confident of the sincerity of the Prussian king's advances, he gladly closed with him in an alliance to resist any invasion of Germany by foreign powers, for such an arrangement insured the safety of Hanover. This diplomatic move resulted in the Treaty of Westminster in January, 1756, and led France to abandon her traditional policy and to join with Austria against Prussia. The standard international cleavage of Europe was radically changed and the line-up for the oncoming struggle showed Austria, Russia, France, the Catholic German states, and finally Sweden on one side, against England and Prussia on the other. Of this inevitable European explosion, it is evident that the clash of empires in America was but the sputtering fuse.

By the Second Treaty of Versailles in May, 1757, France joined Russia and Austria in their conspiracy for the partition of Prussia, and in anticipation of that event, two French armies aggregating 100,000 men were poured across the Rhine. Then indeed was Hanover threatened with an invasion, and George II urged the Duke of Cumberland to take command of the troops of the Electorate, and of the Hessians whom he had hired for just such an emergency. Evidently age and experience had staled Cumberland's desire for foreign service.

Lacking confidence in himself he made difficulties, particularly about being under the direction of Pitt, whom he hated as much as did his father. (Corbett's *England in the Seven Years' War*, i.) When that minister, refusing to resign, was peremptorily dismissed by the king, the duke's last excuse was removed, and early in April, the Butcher of Culloden reluctantly departed for the Continent.

Meanwhile Colonel Amherst, who had sojourned in England for the past nine months with his Hessian charges, was despatched once more to Germany. Early in March, 1757, he was again in Cassel with its parks and palaces, and he remained in that vicinity for several weeks, attending to the Hessian contingent resident there. In May the commissary's duties called him to Stade to superintend the disembarking of the German troops, who, having defended Britain for a year, were now returning to the Continent to fight under the Duke of Cumberland. By the middle of the month, they were safely landed and sent on their way to the camp at Hameln on the Hanoverian frontier, a town more famous for its Pied Piper and its rats than for this military establishment. Thither Amherst followed them shortly and placed himself under the command of his royal friend. (*State Papers Foreign, Military Expeditions*, Vol. 27.)

The forces of which the duke took command numbered about 50,000 men, mostly Hanoverians and Prussians with a generous admixture of Hessians, Brunswickers, and other German levies, and with them he was expected to protect the electoral dominions. This Army of Observation, as it was appropriately called, was concentrated at Bielefeld, late in April. Cumberland's task, however, was an ungrateful one: in the first place the troops were ill-assorted; secondly, they were devoid of anything resembling *esprit de corps*; and worst of all, they believed themselves over-matched by the French, and predestined to defeat. (Torrens' *History of Cabinets*, ii.) The unhappy commander manoeuvred indecisively until the French general, Marshal d'Estrées, forced a battle upon him at Hastenbeck, on the north bank of the Weser.

This engagement took place on July 26, 1757, and Jeffery Amherst, who was present with the Hessian mercenaries in his charge, once more saw his chief go down to defeat before the enemy. Although the Duke of Cumberland was Amherst's junior by four years, he had grown old and unwieldy before his time. At Hastenbeck his failing sight compelled him to depend upon other eyes than his own, and the result was disastrous. With a loss of 1,500 men, Cumberland retreated

BATAILLE d'HASTEMBECK, Gagnée Sur les Alliés par Mr. le Mal. d'Estrées le 26.e Juillet 1757.

Corps des Alliés

HAMELEN

Echelle

N. en se marquer les bois que par en B. dans l'Endroit ou l'Action s'est passée pour ne point embrouiller les manœuvres.

steadily down the course of the Weser to Verden, which lies in the heart of the Electorate. His defeated army was completely demoralised. Rations were short and the soldiers left the ranks to pillage and to indulge in all kinds of excesses. (Richard Waddington's *La Guerre de Sept Ans*, i.)

In the meanwhile, the French swept over Hanover unresisted, plundering and pursuing, until Cumberland on the twenty-first of August proposed a suspension of hostilities. But Richelieu, who had succeeded d'Estrées as commander-in-chief of the enemy's forces, only laughed at the overture of his downcast opponent, and the chase continued across the moors towards Stade, near the mouth of the Elbe. There the archives and other valuable effects of the conquered Hanover were stored, and there, also, was the refugee Council of Regency of the Electorate. To Amherst this uninterrupted retreat into a Serbonian bog was incomprehensible, (P. C. Yorke's *Life and Correspondence of Philip Yorke, Earl of Hardwicke*, iii.); but the duke's position on the rounded peninsula between the estuaries of the Weser and the Elbe was not unlike that of Cornwallis at Yorktown.

If he could maintain a strong base upon the coast, there was hope of reinforcements from England, or at least of transports for his beleaguered army, and knowledge of this possibility was among the causes which induced Richelieu to grant his victim the amazingly lenient terms that marked the ensuing Convention of Kloster Zeven.

While Cumberland was retiring under the guns of Stade, the King of Denmark awoke to a diplomatic difficulty which presented itself owing to the recent military operations. By a treaty of forty years' standing, Denmark guaranteed Bremen and Verden to the Elector of Hanover, undertaking to maintain this obligation within six weeks by an army of 8,000 men. Now Bremen and Verden were in the hands of the enemy, and Frederic V was confronted with the choice of a profitless war, or of effecting some sort of pacification between the belligerents—some arrangement whereby the duchy and the principality might be retained by the Elector of Hanover.

Negotiations, with this in view, were opened in the last days of August, and on September 8, 1757, the Convention of Kloster Zeven was concluded. Both parties to the arrangement rushed headlong into the pacification, with the result that only its general provisions were reduced to black and white, leaving many questions to be settled at leisure—in other words, open to controversy. The Duke of Cumberland agreed to send home to their respective countries the subsidised troops from Hesse, Brunswick, and Saxe-Gotha, while about one-half of the Hanoverian army was to be interned in cantonments around Stade; the remainder returned beyond the Elbe, leaving the French in full possession of Hanover.

Years after this time Napoleon characterised the terms of the Convention of Kloster Zeven as "inexplicable" on the part of the French, and from every point of view it must appear that for the duke it was an easy way out of a very difficult situation. Returning to England, however, the unfortunate commander was received with cutting silence by his royal father, who exclaimed to the courtiers about him: "Here comes my son who has ruined me and disgraced himself." It is not surprising that on the following day William Augustus, Duke of Cumberland, once the idol of the nation, threw up all his military employments and retired forever from a career which had proved singularly unfortunate.

When the Convention was signed, Colonel Amherst very naturally began to march the Hessian troops under his jurisdiction back to their native heath. (*Amherst to Da Costa*, Sept. 10, 1757, *Emmett Collection*, MS. A, in the New York Public Library.) Then word came from England that the king did not consider himself bound by the Convention, whereupon the army recently commanded by Cumberland was speedily prepared for a fresh campaign under the leadership of Prince Ferdinand of Brunswick, a warrior who had attained high distinction in the Prussian service. Of him Colonel Amherst wrote in glowing terms to his old friend Joseph Yorke, then England's minister at the Hague: "The prince is indefatigable and with his manner with the troops gains their love and confidence; all I see and hear foretells success." (*Amherst to Yorke*, Dec. 21, 1757. *Additional MS.* No. 32876, Fol. 449, in the British Museum.)

The soldiers who three months before this time were dispirited and demoralised now bristled with impatient vigour, and almost immediately the restored army won several small advantages over Richelieu. Then, content with having started the war on a new tack, Ferdinand went into winter quarters at Lüneburg, whence he intended to resume the offensive in February.

In the meantime, there occurred in the life of Jeffery Amherst an event of inestimable importance. Early in January, 1758, while wintering at Stade, he received an order signed by Lord Holdernesse, requiring his immediate presence in England. From there he was to proceed to America with the rank of major-general in command of an army of over 11,000 men to capture the French island-stronghold at Louisburg in Cape Breton. This order came as a complete surprise, and the causes which led to it present a sequence of events too interesting and too important to be neglected. Leaving Amherst to make hurried preparations for his departure from Germany, let us turn to the men and events responsible for the sudden promotion which changed the scene of his activities from the Old World to the New.

CHAPTER 4

William Pitt

When Amherst left England for Germany in the early part of 1756, William Pitt had broken with the head of the ministry, the Duke of Newcastle, and was in open opposition to the administration in which he had enjoyed the remunerative post of Paymaster of the Forces. The occasion of his dismissal was an attack upon the policy of the government on the trite charge that Britain was subservient to Hanover, but Pitt's real reason for taking up arms against his old colleagues was his conviction that in the fall of Newcastle lay the sole prospect of his own advancement.

Long had he waited and watched for an opportunity to display the extraordinary power which he knew to be his and at last he was convinced that so long as the government was dominated by "one too powerful subject"—as he stigmatised his chief—those abilities would be under a bushel. The splendour of Pitt must rise from the ruins of Newcastle. Nor was this attitude discreditable from a broad point of view. Extremely desirous of power and fame though he was, the insurgent member was chiefly actuated by a consciousness of phenomenal ability, which in this period of military decadence could render incomparable service to his country.

His own phrase, "that sense of honour which makes ambition virtue," was exemplified in the Great Commoner, for he possessed both qualities and yet combined them successfully. Upon the ground that England needed the full strength of this one man's extraordinary powers, and upon such ground alone, we can justify Pitt's rebellion in 1755, a rebellion which was destined to make Britain the foremost power of the world.

The Newcastle constellation, rid of its unruly star, sank slowly and inevitably towards the horizon. The year 1756 brought nothing but discouragement and defeat for England abroad, while at home Britain trembled at the rumour of a French invasion. The old Duke of Newcastle felt his power in the Commons rapidly diminishing, and in November the "universal minister" resigned.

The obvious successor to the primacy was William Pitt, but though the Great Commoner was backed by the thinking part of the nation he could not count more than sixteen followers in the House of Commons. To remedy this difficulty the good-natured Duke of Devonshire accepted the nominal headship of the government, while Pitt, more capable, if less powerful, achieved his ambition, becoming actual prime minister as Secretary of State for the Southern Department. In this capacity he controlled the movement of armies in the New World and in India, as well as in southern Europe, and, as a matter of fact, determined the whole course of the war, for his strong intellect easily carried before it the mediocre mind of Holdernesse, his colleague for the Northern Department.

Politically the new administration was as weak as its worst enemy could have wished. The House of Commons, that changing tide upon which ministries rise and fall, was practically in the hands of the fallen Newcastle and his allies. Morally the Devonshire ministry was strong as the Rock of Gibraltar, for behind Pitt was the nation—not the riffraff of democracy nor the debauched Whig aristocracy, but "that unenfranchised England which had little representation in Parliament," (Parkman), that unromantic but sterling middle class, which has always made England England. But circumstances and politicians combined to shorten the life of his first attempt at administration.

In five months' time, the Newcastle-ites proved themselves supreme in Parliament, while their opponent flew in the face of both king and people in a desperate effort to save an unfortunate commander from an unjust execution. The last straw was added when Cumberland refused to take command of the Army of Observation if Pitt were to exercise authority over his actions. The king, who hated his greatest minister, no longer hesitated. On April 6, 1757, William Pitt, refusing to resign, was summarily dismissed.

The moment was a critical one for England, and it became evident at once that the work of the powerful opposition had been purely destructive. Pitt's first administration had fallen, but no one dared undertake the formation of a new ministry. On the other hand, addresses of condolence poured in upon the Great Commoner. In Horace Walpole's happy phrase "for some weeks it rained gold boxes," for in such encasements came the freedom of the cities of London, Bath, Worcester, Chester, and Exeter, besides the same honour conferred by other corporations.

It was apparent that the nation stood behind him, but the dismissed Secretary of State well knew that he could not maintain himself without the support of the unrepresentative House of Commons. The king was in despair, and for nearly three months England was without a government. There was but one thing which could save the country—a coalition between Pitt and Newcastle; in other words, an alliance of nation and Parliament. The duke hesitated to head a ministry in which he realised that he would be far outshone by the Secretary of State.

Newcastle hated Pitt as cordially as the latter despised the duke, but a combination was brought about by which each gained what he most desired; Newcastle as First Lord of the Treasury was to dole out the offices, a pleasant occupation free from all responsibility for the conduct of politics and of war, while Pitt, to use his own language, would borrow the duke's majorities to carry on the government. The cabinet meetings promised to be gatherings as congenial as those which marked Washington's first administration with Hamilton and Jefferson seated at the same table, but the arrangement was practical in a high degree, as subsequent events proved. In the last week of June, 1757, the new ministry kissed hands (Albert von Ruville's *William Pitt, Earl of Chatham*, ii.), and England thus took a necessary step on the highroad to victory.

Now that the reins of power have been securely placed in the hands of the Great Commoner, let us pause to study the character and qualities of this extraordinary man, to whom Jeffery Amherst owed much.

William Pitt was primarily a genius: secondarily he was a very great man. The genius of Pitt lay in his eloquence; his greatness in his mastery of men.

In England, the eighteenth century was an age when legislation was determined more by speechmaking than by party or policy, a phenomenon which was due to the fact that when the government and its placemen were confronted by a numerous and well-organised opposition in the House of Commons, the balance of power was held by a comparatively small group of independents. To hold these members to the government, or to carry them over to the Opposition was the aim of the party leaders, and to accomplish this end, persuasive speaking was essential. As an orator, Pitt was incomparable.

His diction was simple but poetic, calculated to imprint his intelligent ideas clearly and indelibly upon the minds of his hearers. Majestic in declamation, blasting in invective, he awed and thrilled the most fastidious audience. Nor was this all, for he united with these attributes the qualities of a great actor. A contemporary of Garrick, he rivalled in look, gesture, and tone, that greatest histrionic genius of all time. He held his adherents spellbound by his utterances, and with the lightning of his flashing eye struck terror to the hearts of those who opposed him.

Like all orators of the eighteenth century, the Great Commoner spoke with a freedom which the political speaker of today, (1916), may not enjoy, for in those days the reporting of speeches in Parliament was fitful and sporadic. Then the statesman spoke to the House of Commons and not to the proletariat, and he spoke with a personality and an art which are entirely lost in the printed page. His whole idea was to carry the House with him, and he did not need to consider the misrepresentations which might be the fruit of his words when conned in cold print by hostile critics in the country at large. With such lack of restraint Pitt uttered his trenchant aphorisms and memorable phrases. As Lyttelton said:

> His words have sometimes frozen my young blood into stagnation, and sometimes made it pace in such a hurry through my veins that I could scarce support it. (Lecky's *England in the Eighteenth Century*, ii.)

Such was the eloquence of the man, an eloquence which was but the ornament of a scholar's mind and a statesman's intellect. The divine spark of Pitt's oratory was his patriotism: first, last, and always he was an Englishman, whether defending the American colonists, when they, as Englishmen, claimed the rights of other subjects of the Crown, or casting them out of the realm of conciliation because they had joined in an alliance with Britain's hereditary enemy. As with Webster, so with Pitt, love of country was the Promethean heat which kindled extraordinary eloquence and stirred to their deepest depths the hearts of his hearers. Such was the genius of this paragon of public speakers.

Pitt was not merely scholar and orator. He was a monarch of men. His instructions to the commanders under his jurisdiction, and his letters to the colonial governors, sound like the edicts of a king. Expressed with marvellous clearness and force, his missives were calculated to bring forth the greatest efforts from those who understood the tasks, however Herculean. Generous with commendation, yet firm in reprimand, the great War Minister displayed at all times an appreciation of the difficulties attending the campaigns as well as the results which might justly be expected. His knowledge of the detail of every situation, amazing as it was, accounts for much of the efficiency of his administration. So inspiring was his personality that every commander who entered his closet came out of it a braver man and carried away with him new courage and faith.

Scarcely less admirable was his standard of political honour. Moving in an age when offices were sought more for their remunerative contingencies than for the power or even the fame which they brought the incumbent, a period when every arm of the service was festered with rottenness and honeycombed with graft, William Pitt inaugurated an entirely new system of morals. Upon coming into the Pelham administration in 1746, he was given the notoriously lucrative post of Paymaster of the Forces. Every occupant of this office before his time had availed himself of the opportunity to invest the large floating balance in government securities, appropriating the interest for his own purse, as well as receiving one-half per cent of all subsidies voted by Parliament to foreign princes.

Although Pitt was probably the poorest man who had ever held this office, he refused from the first to accept these perquisites which seemed to him illegal; and when the King of Sardinia endeavoured to make him a gift of no mean proportions, the Paymaster of the Forces refused it as he would a bribe. To us any other course than that which Pitt pursued in this matter would seem more surprising than that which he chose. To eighteenth-century England, however, such an honourable conviction, with the courage to support it, was astounding. The general run of office-holders shrugged their shoulders, while the nation, long-suffering under the corruption of its representatives and weary of the selfish deeds of placemen, "feeding at the public crib," recognised the greatness of William Pitt, and from that hour he was its idol.

Genius usually sets limitations to greatness, and this was conspicuously the case with Pitt. Until his accession to power under the Pelhams in 1746, one is little attracted to the violent spitfire who assailed with the fury of a madman, the wise administration of Walpole. The Whig statesman at the helm was attacked at every point by "this terrible cornet," as Walpole dubbed him, and even after 1742, Pitt continued his hostility, insisting upon an impeachment. The succeeding administration pursued an entirely different policy, but Pitt, finding himself as far from power as before, continued his venomous assaults upon the government.

He even went so far as to insult the king by calling Hanover a "despicable electorate." One cannot but feel that, as a rule, Pitt in opposition was actuated more by a desire to overthrow the existing ministry in the hope of acquiring power through its downfall, than by any sincerely patriotic motive. Hence it came about that his career was replete with inconsistencies. Measures he abhorred when others were in control of the affairs of state, William Pitt was often entirely ready to adopt or to continue, when he found himself in the seats of the mighty.

For instance, the cornerstone of his vehement opposition in 1743, was the folly of subsidising Hanoverian troops to defend the king's electoral dominions, but three years later he quietly acquiesced in the continuance of that scheme by a ministry in which he held office. He never murmured against the Pelhams when they closely followed in Walpole's steps, in spite of the fact that his own speeches, not long before, had condemned absolutely the policies of the great Whig. Wise men change their minds, we are told; but in Pitt's case one cannot help feeling that opposition was for opposition's sake, and only when he was on the political bridge did the man take a statesmanlike view of the situation.

Another concomitant of his genius was Pitt's nervous irritability, a misfortune which sometimes amounted almost to insanity. Lord of others, he was not always master of himself, and in disciplining his own party he was frequently so imperious and dictatorial that one would have thought his invectives were directed against the Opposition. Often, too, that dramatic power which served him so well in flights of eloquence or bursts of scorn led to excesses which made the Great Commoner ridiculous and wellnigh contemptible. A great sufferer from gout, that bane and torture of the eighteenth century, Pitt made the most of his ill-health.

Displaying rather than concealing, his painful malady, he delighted to appear the heroic patriot whom no amount of suffering could keep from the performance of his duties. Swathed in flannel and supporting himself upon the familiar crutch, he was well aware of the fact that he presented a piteous spectacle in the Commons or among the Peers. This ostentation was part and parcel of his delight in being theatrical:

although many of his deeds were noble and disinterested, William Pitt never lost sight of the effect which they might produce. Like Disraeli he was always acting a part in the drama of life, and was ever conscious of his audience.

Finally, Pitt's love of pomp and show proclaimed him a parvenu. Royalty dazzled him to an incredible extent. One of his contemporaries declared that at the levee he bowed so low one could see the tip of his hooked nose between his legs. (Lecky's *England in the Eighteenth Century*, ii.) Although he had spent half of his career railing at the Court, when actually brought into the presence of royalty he was almost unmanned; and when at the height of his power Pitt received a few words of commendation from George III—a pygmy in comparison with this giant—the world-famous minister burst into tears. This last event was doubtless due to Pitt's physical condition, for at that moment he was on the verge of a nervous disorder which soon after laid him prostrate; but it is certain that he never possessed the unconscious majesty of a Washington or a Wellington.

Such was William Pitt, who, in spite of his faults and weaknesses, was a very great man—towering above his contemporaries as a mammoth pine rises conspicuously above the restless tree-tops of the forest. His eloquence has become proverbial; his patriotism was matchless; and as a war minister, he displayed a genius and efficiency which made the Bourbons tremble for their possessions the world over. Take him for all in all, he was a man, and England was not to look upon his like again.

Although Pitt was now securely established where he could govern the course of the war, the first six months of his administration saw little indication of the victorious era upon which Britain was about to enter. In Germany, as we have seen, the Duke of Cumberland laid down his arms in an ignominious capitulation. On the French coast, an expedition to capture Rochefort—the War Minister's pet project—failed because of lack of co-operation between army and navy. From America came even worse tidings.

The Marquis de Montcalm, who had succeeded to the command of the French forces in the New World, captured Fort William Henry at the southern end of Lake George, while Lord Loudon, the British commander-in-chief, made an unsuccessful attempt to take the enemy's stronghold at Louisburg on Cape Breton Island.

The autumn of 1757 was indeed a season of depression for Pitt, relieved only by the news of Clive's astounding victory over the natives

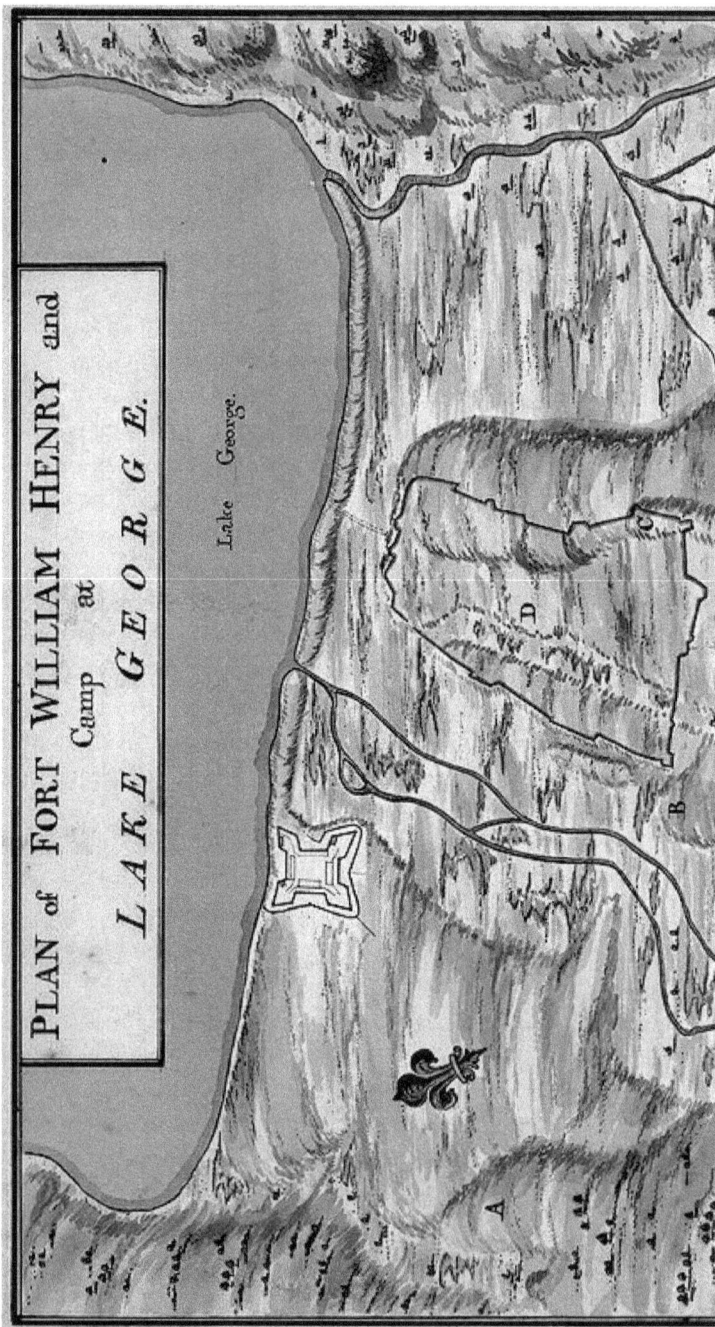

PLAN of FORT WILLIAM HENRY and Camp at LAKE GEORGE.

Lake George.

Lake George.

A

B

C

D

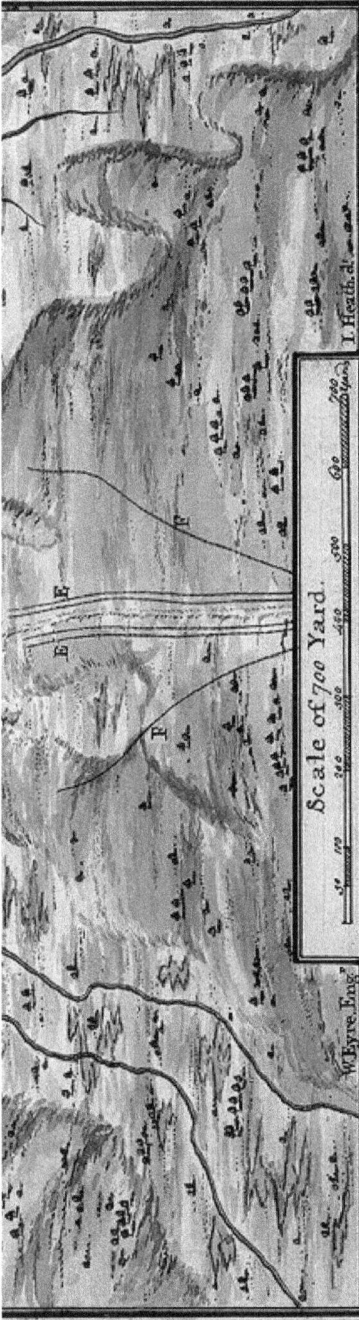

Scale of 700 Yard.

100   200   300   400   500   600   700

W. Eyre Eng.
I. Heath d.

This Fort is erected on a Plain, that is Natural, and which West of it, from 200 to 370 Yards, if any Enemy Ground at (A) it the most convenient for an Enemy to attack it from, but the Distance is more than the last mention'd from the Walls. The Ground that the Camp stands on, is not so high, but that the Barrier, except at (B & C), which is rather unsafe, to do any great Mischief, holds a week's Siege between these Rivers. The Lake sides, the Edges of Swamp, are pretty secure from any great Danger; & the Enemy will not find it an easy Matter to get Ground from (A) to do that that it is being suffered to Ground the Batteries from the Waters by the table, on the Edges of the Swamp; over to one of the Swamp by it's Width, without effectually some Inconvenience; being expos'd by being exposed to Cannon from A.

The Bastion here described is bound at the Wall and above it. Which the Water behind is about from the Walls who attach this Camp. The Encampment of (D) had a Breastwork mixed with Trees & Bushes (E, E). The Columns of regular French Troops, & Canadian who attach this Camp, 9th September 1756. — F.F. The Route the Indians took to fall upon the Flanks during the Engagement. — The Fort is large enough to contain a Garrison of 400, or 500. Men, with convenient Barracks; Two Magazines for Powder; Yard enough with a large Stockfish of several Strength, to Casemate for 200 Men, besides Storehouses for 2500 Barrels of Provisions. —

of Bengal and their inefficient French allies. Truly the time was out of joint, and it was Pitt's task to set it right. He was not long in formulating a new policy for the conduct of the war in America.

The campaign of 1758 was to be made on three main lines. In the first place, Fort Duquesne must be captured, and a hold obtained upon the Ohio Valley. For this operation Pitt selected Brigadier-General John Forbes, a man of more than sixty years, who had begun his career as a physician but now had been long in the military service of the country. He was given a strong regiment of Highlanders and about four thousand provincials with which to accomplish the purpose that had brought disaster to Braddock three years before.

Secondly, Lake George and Lake Champlain, the former the scene of the recent disaster at Fort William Henry, the latter strongly fortified by the French at Ticonderoga and Crown Point, must be cleared of the enemy. This would open one of the natural avenues to Canada, and relieve New York from the constant encroachments of Montcalm. Loudon, who had antagonized the colonists, besides showing himself to be woefully incapable in a military way, was recalled, and the chief command devolved upon Major-General James Abercromby. So far, the latter had done nothing to win distinction, favourable or unfavourable; but Horace Walpole, with his usual perspicacity, declared him to be "a commander whom a child might outwit, or terrify with a popgun," (*Letters of Horace Walpole*, iv.), a characterisation destined to be confirmed only too soon by disastrous facts.

Finally, the campaign of 1758 included an attack upon Louisburg, which, if successful, would be followed by an advance against Quebec by the way of the St. Lawrence. (Corbett's *England in the Seven Years' War*, i.) Of the three operations this was the most important, requiring both land and sea power. The military force assigned to it counted fourteen thousand regulars, supplemented by five hundred provincials, in command of which Pitt placed Colonel Jeffery Amherst, giving him the rank of Major-General in America, and assigning as his assistants three brigadiers, Whitmore, Lawrence, and his old friend Wolfe. Equally auspicious was the appointment that entrusted the naval part of the expedition to Admiral Edward Boscawen—"Old Dreadnought," as he was called by the British seamen, who had abundant confidence in his well-known fighting ability.

This was the plan of campaign for the war in America for 1758, and great credit has ever been given to Pitt for his judicious selection of officers for the Louisburg expedition. In these military appoint-

HIGHLAND REGIMENT UNIFORMS

ments, unlike that of Abercromby, claims of seniority were disregarded whenever they clashed with those of efficiency; preferment went neither by letter nor affection, nor "by old gradation, where each second stood heir to the first," but by merit and approved worth. This principle of selection which Pitt inaugurated fully justified itself within the year. But how did the War Minister, master of detail though he was, know where to put his finger upon the right man for every important command? How did he dare appoint to the leadership of an expedition of infinite importance, an obscure colonel who had obtained a regiment scarcely eighteen months before? The answer to this question is—Sir John Ligonier.

When the Duke of Cumberland, returning from an inglorious summer's work in Germany, resigned all his offices and appointments, Pitt seized the opportunity to complete his absolute control of the war. What he particularly needed was an able commander-in-chief, one who knew the personnel of the army and the merits or demerits of every officer. He believed Sir John Ligonier to be just such a man and eagerly pressed for his appointment, before the old king might relent and re-instate the Butcher of Culloden. George II proved tractable except upon one point. Whoever became chief of the army should not enjoy the title of Captain-General which the Duke of Cumberland had so recently borne. (Torrens' *History of Cabinets*, ii.)

It is difficult to understand precisely the grounds for the king's objection, but probably he regarded the headship of the army as one of the royal prerogatives, which had fast diminished in number since the accession of the Hanoverian dynasty. Of whatever else he might be robbed, George II, remembering his military prowess on the field of Dettingen, would never part with his nominal supremacy in the army. Charles II might grant the title to General Monk out of gratitude for the Restoration; William might confer the compliment upon the son of his favourite Lieutenant Schomberg; and Anne might donate such authority to Marlborough; but the soldier-king would have none but himself or one of his immediate family enjoy the dignity of being Captain-General.

With the resignation of Cumberland, the office passed out of existence forever. The Cabinet was united upon the advisability of having Ligonier the actual head of the army, with or without the title which the king so jealously withheld, and through the combined efforts of Newcastle, Hardwicke, and Pitt, the hero of the Battle of Laffeldt was made commander-in-chief of all His Majesty's forces in Great Britain.

For the War Minister the new appointment was of infinite importance. At last, he had as his right-hand man a brilliant soldier—and one who believed thoroughly in the new military policy. Sir John's first duty was to select the best officers; then he and Pitt would fit them into the scheme of war. Thus, it came about that Ligonier brought forward the name of Colonel Amherst, his favourite *aide-de-camp* in the previous war, who was then hiding his military talent in Germany as commissary to the Hessian soldiers in British pay. Pitt's confidence in the judgment of the commander-in-chief was unlimited. As far as we know, he had never heard of Jeffery Amherst; but, relying upon the assurances of Ligonier, he determined to put him in command of the expedition against Louisburg.

It was now the last week of December, 1757, and Pitt was anxious to see the preparations for the coming year under way. Although he was practically Prime Minister, and had complete control of the conduct of the war, the Great Commoner had learned by experience that it was never safe to take an important step without the consent and approval of his colleagues. The latter, although nonentities in themselves, controlled Parliament, and unless formally bound to Pitt's policy, might leave him high and dry at any time. Two things were necessary—the sanction of the Cabinet for the operations planned, and the king's consent to Colonel Amherst's sudden elevation. Both were accomplished before the end of the dying year.

A meeting of the Cabinet at Lord Holdernesse's was called for the evening of December 28, but the Duke of Newcastle was entertaining "the Bishop of Durham and some other company" at Claremont, and begged to be excused from attending. (*Additional MS.* No. 32876; British Museum). Pitt was annoyed and somewhat suspicious; he allowed the duke to remain out of town with his Christmas party, but took care to secure his written endorsement on the drafts which he intended to submit to the Cabinet.

On the evening of the 28th Pitt's plans for the North American campaign of 1758 were duly approved by the rest of the Cabinet, (*Ibid*), and only the king's sanction of Amherst was needed to complete the plan. To secure this there seems to have been no small amount of difficulty, presumably because of the obscurity of the officer in question.

The task was undertaken by Sir John Ligonier who was quite ready to stand sponsor for his one-time *aide-de-camp*. On December 30, he gained the king's ear and won the royal consent to Amherst's employment in America. (*Ibid.* Also Basil Williams' *Life of William Pitt*, i, which attributes the appointment to the entreaties of Lady Yarmouth.) Thus, the colonel's unlooked-for advancement was due first and last to the interest and friendship of his old chief, with whom he had seen service at Fontenoy. In writing to Newcastle concerning Ligonier's good offices in this connection, Pitt said:

> For this, and for how many right things done and fatal ones prevented, what do we owe in one place.

How well might Jeffery Amherst have spoken the same words of the same individual—but with a purely personal application!

On January 3, 1758, an order was signed by the Earl of Holdernesse requiring Amherst's immediate presence in England. A month later he was on his way home, awaiting transportation at Ritzbüttel, near the mouth of the Elbe, where Cuxhaven with its Hamburg-American establishments stands today, 1916. (*State Papers, Foreign Military Expeditions*, Vol. 27, in the Public Record Office.) Arriving in London, Amherst was subjected to a few direct questions about certain bills for the Hessians' forage, aggregating £200,000, which he was said to have contracted. The amount due was unexpectedly large, and, to make matters worse, Baron Munchausen, the Hanoverian minister in London, who rendered the account, had insisted that one half of it must be remitted by the next post.

The king summarily ordered the First Lord of the Treasury to provide the necessary funds, whereupon Newcastle showed the papers to Pitt, for he was cautious about paying bills presented by anyone other than the government's authorised agent, Colonel Amherst. The Hanoverian's name is suggestive of fiction and Pitt deemed his statement exaggerated to say the least. Newcastle made a partial payment by forwarding £60,000 to Amherst, but demanded an explanation. (*Additional MS. No. 32877.*) Consequently, the commissary had no sooner set foot on English soil than he was called to account by His Grace.

The contract, expensive as it was, proved to be genuine, and the agent declared it was advantageous to the government. Newcastle was embarrassed—the more so because the indignant War Minister obstinately refused to fulfil the demands of the contract, (*Additional MSS., Nos. 32878 and 32997*)—but before the matter was settled, Amherst was hurried off to Portsmouth where H. M. S. *Dublin*, 74, was waiting to convey him to America.

Delay had been the chief cause of defeat in the previous year and Pitt took care that the present attack on Louisburg should be begun as soon as the season permitted, not later than the twentieth of April. This would ensure a blockade of the port before the enemy's garrison and fleet could be revictualed or reinforced from France. With this in view, various convoys of troops destined for Cape Breton were got under way early in February.

On the 24th, Boscawen cleared the Channel and stood out to sea with a snug fighting force composed of ten large ships of the line and five or six frigates. The transports were well ahead of him, bound for the rendezvous at Halifax, where certain troops wintering in Boston, New York, and Philadelphia were to concentrate on April 12. To ensure still further the success of the expedition, Vice-Admiral Sir Charles Hardy, recently Governor of New York, was dispatched to Halifax in January to command the small squadron there, and to institute a preliminary blockade of Louisburg. (Corbett's *England in the Seven Years' War*, i.)

Major-General Amherst, as we must call him now, sailed from Portsmouth, March 16, 1758, on board the *Dublin*, a vessel with a record by no means enviable. In the previous summer she had been a part of the fleet told off for the attack on Rochefort, but a refractory rudder had kept the ship from active service. The rest of the season the *Dublin*, was a floating pest-house reeking with an epidemic fever. (Hannay's *Rodney*.) Her commander, Captain George Brydges Rodney, was destined to become the most famous of those English admirals who raised the navy to the level at which Nelson found it.

Twenty-four years later he sat in an armchair on the quarter-deck of the *Formidable* and won from the French off Dominica the greatest naval victory of the generation; but as yet Rodney had failed to achieve distinction. He was a man of about forty years, a little younger than Amherst, and if we may judge from his later habits of extravagance, he enjoyed good living. Since 1751, the captain of the *Dublin* had sat in the Commons as one of Newcastle's dependents, and he had been careful never to let his marine duties interfere with this comfortable sinecure. Whatever his shortcomings may have been, Rodney possessed abnormally good luck and no small amount of personal courage.

When the *Dublin* was four or five days out, and yet, owing to various kinds of wind and weather, found herself only twenty leagues off Brest, a sail was seen laying to. The wind blew a gale and the weather was thick, but as soon as Rodney was sure that it was an enemy-ship, he determined to capture it, storm or no storm. The vessel, which was armed with sixteen six-pounders, first hoisted the English colours, then the French. Thereupon the *Dublin* fired upon her. The sea was so rough that although twenty-five or thirty guns were discharged, not one took effect. After firing three guns and a few small arms in return the Frenchman struck.

It proved to be an East India ship laden with seven hundred thousand pounds of coffee and a rich cargo of rose-wood, a prize of no small value—whether Rodney was right in prolonging Amherst's journey on that account or not. The *Dublin* being alone, her captain was obliged to take his booty into the nearest port for safe keeping. Rather than return to Portsmouth, he turned his course to the Spanish port of Vigo, and waited there till he found a small cruiser to take charge of his prize. (Gertrude Selwyn Kimball's *Correspondence of William Pitt with Colonial Governors*, i.: Corbett's *England in the Seven Years' War*, i.) This episode retarded Amherst's already belated voyage by at least two weeks, and it was April 1 before the *Dublin* was again on her legitimate course.

Until the era of the American clipper-ship, westward transatlantic voyages were incredibly long. In the North Atlantic the west wind never owes the east wind anything, as the seamen express it, and a ship bound for America usually encounters headwinds almost the entire distance. Furthermore, the route from England to the New World was painfully circuitous. First the mariner steered south by west to the Canaries, then west by south until he guessed that he must be about five hundred leagues out from Ferro; it could be little more than a guess, for as yet there were no means of accurately determining one's longitude upon the high seas.

From this uncertain point the prow was turned toward the northwest with the hope of sighting the Bermudas before many days. Such was the course of the *Dublin*, as through calms and storms she made her tedious way across the ocean. (*Amherst to Pitt*, May 17, 1758, Colonial Office Papers, A. and W. I., vol. 53, in the Public Record Office.) April came and went, and yet no sign of land. On the 17th of May, almost nine weeks after her departure from Portsmouth, the man-of-war ran across a Virginia ship bound for England.

Amherst embraced the opportunity to send a letter by her to Pitt. He lamented the long delays and hoped to reach Halifax within a day or two. His expectations were not fulfilled, however, for contrary winds and the fogs which abound off that coast, especially during the spring, held him back for ten days more. Finally, on May 28, the long, low outline of Acadia came up over the horizon and was silhouetted against the western sky. (Kimball's *Pitt Correspondence*, i.)

As the vessel drew nearer to the shore, Amherst beheld a myriad of sails coming out of the harbour of Halifax. It proved to be Boscawen with the fleet and troops bound for Louisburg. The admiral had had no easy crossing; indeed, Wolfe, who was a notoriously poor sailor, maintained that "from Christopher Columbus' time to our days" there had never been "a more extraordinary voyage." (Willson's *Wolfe*.) The long passage, which was made by the same route pursued by Amherst, consumed almost three months, and Boscawen did not reach Halifax until the second week in May. There he waited for the troops from New York to appear. The latter arrived a few days later, but when at last everything was ready for the departure for Louisburg, contrary winds kept the flotilla in port another week.

Thus, it came about that when Boscawen, in order to prevent further loss of time, was starting for Cape Breton without the commander-in-chief, the *Dublin* met the expedition at the entrance to the harbour of Halifax. With business-like promptness Amherst immediately transferred himself and his belongings to the flagship *Namur*, and the fleet continued on its way to the Dunkirk of America.

CHAPTER 5

Louisburg

The town and fortress of Louisburg were situated on a tongue of land projecting from the coast of Cape Breton Island. This peninsula and a corresponding promontory to the northeast narrow the entrance to a well-sheltered harbour, which the French Government chose for a naval base soon after signing the Treaty of Utrecht. No expense was spared in fortifying the place, and in 1745 Louisburg was reckoned the second strongest citadel in North America. Nevertheless, in that year the town was captured by four thousand New Englanders commanded by a Kittery merchant, William Pepperrell. Few disasters in the eighteenth century so rankled in the hearts of Frenchmen as did this catastrophe, and hence the restoration of Louisburg was practically a *sine qua non* of the Treaty of Aix-la-Chapelle.

By that instrument the conquest of the provincials was undone. The island fortress was turned over to its founders and once more became a menace to the indignant colonists. All these events occurred while Amherst was an *aide-de-camp* to Ligonier, and later to the Duke of Cumberland, in the War of the Austrian Succession.

Since 1748, the stronghold on Cape Breton had assumed a much more formidable aspect. The town of Louisburg now contained about four thousand inhabitants. Its fortifications were more than a mile and a half in length, and these, supplemented by the Grand Battery opposite the mouth of the harbour, and by the Island Battery which commanded the entrance to the port, rendered the citadel the strongest in French or British America. The town itself was inconsequential, containing no public buildings except a convent, a hospital, the king's storehouses and the governor's quarters. There were perhaps a dozen private houses of stone in the place; the rest of the dwellings were the humble wooden abodes of fishermen.

The military establishment, however, was by no means so insignificant. The garrison consisted of more than three thousand well-disciplined troops, including two companies of artillery. In addition to these regular forces there was a body of armed inhabitants in the town and a band of Indians skulking outside. (Parkman.) Nor did Louisburg lack protection from an attack by sea, as it had in the siege of 1745. The harbour contained a fleet of five ships-of-the-line and seven frigates carrying about three thousand men. This meant a naval strength of more than five hundred guns.

Although vast sums had been expended upon strengthening the fortifications, they were not without their weaknesses. The masonry of the ramparts was so poor, probably owing to the bad quality of the mortar used, that in the cannonading of the next six weeks, it crumbled under the concussion of its own guns. (Fortescue.) In some places bundles of sticks were substituted for the original construction, but all in all Louisburg deserved to be called the Dunkirk of America. On two sides the triangular promontory was lapped by the water of the open sea, or of the harbour; across the third side extended the strongest front of the works, reinforced by four bastions, one of which formed a part of the citadel.

The greatest strength of Louisburg was its rock-bound coast stretching for miles in either direction, and only occasionally relenting sufficiently to afford a landing place for friend or foe. Drucour, the governor of the town, took precautions to have all these accessible points vigilantly guarded, and in this attitude of defence he awaited the coming of the enemy.

The English flotilla of more than one hundred and fifty ships, presenting a splendid spectacle as it departed from Halifax on the morning of May 28, 1758, soon separated into several small squadrons, with the men-of-war leading the procession towards Cape Breton Island. (*A Journal of the Siege and Surrender of Louisburg, etc.*) Fogs hid the ships at times, but they managed to keep near enough together to prevent many from being lost, and on the evening of the fifth day, June 1, General Amherst saw the entrance to Gabarus Bay, a deep bight bounded on the east by the promontory of Louisburg.

The next morning an impenetrable fog hung over the water until noon, and then suddenly rose, disclosing a view of the town and of the ships in the harbour. (Kimball's *Pitt Correspondence*, i.) By this time the British fleet had cast anchor in Gabarus Bay. While waiting for the transports to come up, for only one-third of them had arrived, Amherst with two of his brigadiers, Wolfe and Lawrence, reconnoitred the forbidding shore, and in the evening searched out possible landing places. If the troops arrived in time, an attempt to get a foothold on the island would be made in the morning. Three spots seemed practicable, although it was clear that the French had thrown up works and had placed batteries to command these vulnerable points.

On the morning of June 3, most of the missing transports came in, but in his plans for the day the general had not taken the weather into account. Landing on this rocky island was difficult under the best conditions, and now it was rendered almost impossible by "a very frightful surf," to use the words of one observer. The ships rolled prodigiously; and, to make matters worse, a dense fog settled down upon water and shore. Disappointed in their original plan, the men on the frigates amused themselves by returning the shots which the enemy, from their batteries, directed towards the fleet. By way of experiment a handful of soldiers landed under the fire of the frigates, and having succeeded in getting ashore, returned immediately to the ships. (*Journals of Captain John Montresor* in the New York Historical Society's *Collections* for 1881.)

The thing could be done, but Amherst and Boscawen deemed any serious attempt as yet unwise. The whole fleet lay at anchor in the bay, while the frigates now and then returned the insults of the enemy. From the British decks the men could see great numbers of Indians along the spray-drenched shore, then the town with its pretentious fortifications, and beyond the citadel, the ships in the harbour of Louisburg. One of the enemy's small magazines blew up and flared the news of its destruction through the fog; otherwise, the day passed uneventfully.

Every longshoreman of our northeast coast maintains that "a fog will always kick up a sea" and no other explanation is necessary to his *a posteriori* way of reasoning. The true cause of the phenomenon lies not in the fog, but in the dissipation of a well organised storm off the Banks, or to the southward. When such an area of low pressure fills up and becomes stationary, the neighbouring coast is apt to get, for days at a time, the roll which survived the dying storm, and the fog which hovered over its watery grave. Such seems to have been the meteorological conditions off Cape Breton Island in the first week of June, 1758.

Day after day the fog-swathed ships rolled and creaked at anchor in Gabarus Bay, while the roar of the breakers along the rocky shore was incessant. Once the weather gave promise of a change and Amherst hurried his men into the boats. Then the fog came in again and the swell increased until the admiral discouraged further prosecution of the attempt. In the meanwhile, the Frenchmen were busily reinforcing their works. Occasionally they cannonaded the ships, and any British boat that attempted to reconnoitre was sure of a smart fire from the enemy.

On the evening of the seventh there was every indication of better weather, and Amherst gave orders for a general landing to be made the next morning at dawn, the disembarkation to be accomplished in profound silence in order to surprise the enemy. When Amherst, Wolfe, and Lawrence had scrutinised the shore, almost a week before this time, they had pitched upon three points where attacks might be made with some hope of success. These accessible places were two little bays in Freshwater Cove, about four miles from Louisburg, and an inlet sheltered by White Point which was much nearer the fortifications of the town.

Amherst determined to divide the forces into three divisions and to threaten all three places at once. One of his brigadiers, Whitmore, was to proceed towards White Point, while Wolfe and Lawrence made the real attack and attempted to force a landing at Freshwater Cove. At two o'clock on the morning of June 8, the troops were in the boats. Some of the frigates edged in to attack the French entrenchments and to cover the landing of the soldiers, and after these had engaged the enemy for about a quarter of an hour, the boats put off for the shore.

Wolfe's division, which contained a corps of marksmen and the New England rangers, had the shortest course to land. The enemy acted wisely and reserved their fire until the invaders were almost inshore. Then from their entrenchments, artfully concealed by spruces and firs, came a deadly fire of cannon and musketry. The flag-staff of Wolfe's boat was snapped off by a swivel-shot, but to a man of his spirit this was only part of the fun. When things looked very black for the English, a boatload of light infantry spied a rocky inlet which was sheltered from the French artillery, and immediately changed their course and made for this spot. The officers leaped ashore and their men succeeded in doing likewise, but the next boat was caught by the breakers and crashed upon the rocks.

Major Scott, who commanded the light infantry, gained the land, however, and scrambled up the crags with ten followers. There he came face to face with about seventy Frenchmen and Indians. A des-

BRITISH INFANTRY SOLDIER

perate struggle for a foothold ensued, in which three bullets were shot through the gallant major's clothes, and five of his men were killed or wounded; but Scott stood his ground with a resolution worthy of Snowdon's knight. In the meantime, Wolfe signalled to the rest of the detachment to follow the light infantry and effect a landing in the rock-bound cove.

Many of the boats were staved upon the rocks, but the men leaped into surf up to their waists, and waded to the shore. Some poor wretches were caught by the undertow and were sucked back into the breakers, where they perished. Brigadier Wolfe was among the first to jump from his boat, and armed with only a cane was soon scaling the slippery rocks. Forming the soldiers who followed him in this spectacular landing, the dashing commander charged the nearest French battery and carried it with the bayonet. After that the British were secure in their position.

The other detachments, those under Lawrence and Whitmore, which were to make a feint at landing at other points along the coast, also succeeded in their design. By rowing along the shore, they diverted the attention of the enemy from any one place until Wolfe had made good his landing at Freshwater Cove. Then they turned westward and disembarked at a little beach, with very little opposition from the distracted French.

Now the enemy were attacked upon right and left and there was danger of their being cut off from the town. Amherst himself came ashore, while the boats plied busily between the ships and the land, unloading regiment after regiment upon the Island of Cape Breton. The French were thoroughly terrified. Abandoning their cannon, mortars, tools, stores, and ammunition, they at first retreated, and then fled, in the direction of Louisburg. Wolfe gave chase through the rough growth, which to Amherst's European eyes appeared to be the worst battle-ground he had ever seen. (Kimball's *Pitt Correspondence*, i.) The pursuit ended with a cannonade from the town, which was helpful rather than otherwise, as it gave the general a clue to the enemy's range, and thus determined to some extent the site for his camp.

The initial operations against Louisburg had been decidedly successful. In the process of landing and in the skirmish which followed, the British lost only about one hundred men, killed and wounded. Although some were drowned in the surf, the very size of the waves was a protection to the troops, for many a well-directed ball failed of its mark owing to the sudden rise or fall of the boats in the heavy swell. (Captain John Knox's *Historical Journal of the Campaigns in North America*, i.) The French lost several men killed, and seventy were taken prisoners. All things considered, the issue of the morning of June 8 was thoroughly satisfactory, and all had been accomplished before half-past eight o'clock.

The rest of the day would naturally have been devoted to landing tents and provisions, guns and stores, but the fickle weather turned against the English once more. The wind increased, the waves mounted higher than ever, and all communication with the fleet was cut off. Without tents, and enjoying a very short allowance of provisions, the soldiers were far from comfortable for several days and nights. Meanwhile, Amherst, establishing his camp just beyond range of the French cannon, commenced the actual siege of Louisburg.

With such a disparity of numbers as the French and British forces presented, there could be little doubt as to the ultimate outcome of the investment. Within the fortified town Drucour could count only about four thousand fighting men, while the besieging host numbered between eleven and twelve thousand, all except five hundred of whom were regulars. From the decks of the twelve French ships of war at anchor in the harbour, the officers could see the British armada of forty armed vessels of various descriptions, from the flagship *Namur*, of ninety guns, to the fireships *Ætna* and *Lightning*, carrying only eight guns each.

A few days after the landing of the English troops Sir Charles Hardy's squadron, which had hovered off Cape Breton since early spring, appeared in the bay and completed Boscawen's fleet. (Kimball's *Pitt Correspondence*, i.) One of the newcomer's ships, the *Captain*, is of particular interest to us because it was commanded by John Amherst, the general's brother. Louisburg was an old story to John, for his ship had been part of the ill-conducted expedition under Lord Loudon and Admiral Holburne in the previous autumn, when the fleet encountered a terrific storm in these very waters. (Robert Beatson's *Naval and Military Memoirs*, iii.)

In the spring of 1758, the *Captain* had again come hither—this time in Sir Charles Hardy's squadron, which was intended to prevent the revictualing or reinforcement of the island garrison, and which now united with the rest of the fleet to prosecute the siege of Louisburg.

So long as any part of the army was tentless, Amherst refused to proceed with his operations. On the eleventh of June communication with the fleet was easier and things began to straighten themselves out. That evening the glare of flames to the northeast blazed out the news of an event as important as it was unexpected: the enemy had abandoned the Grand Battery after setting fire to the buildings it contained, and to the huts and fish-houses fringing the water's edge. (Parkman's *Montcalm and Wolfe*, ii.)

This fortification stood on the north shore of the harbour opposite the entrance, where it could greet with a terrific front fire, any hostile squadron trying to force its way in. Formidable as it was to naval force, in case of land attack the post was helpless. This had been conclusively proved in 1745 when it was deserted at the first approach of the enterprising provincials, who, by the way, effected their landing on the island at almost the same spot where Wolfe and his companions were hurled ashore by the breaking waves thirteen years later.

In the first siege of Louisburg the abandonment of the Grand Battery had been the decisive event of the campaign, (Parkman's *Half-Century of Conflict*, ii), for thereby the New Englanders gained possession of what they most lacked—artillery, competent to do the work before them. To guard against a repetition of this blunder, Drucour took care to destroy the fort and to mutilate or carry away its equipment before Amherst forced his hand. Against such odds discretion was the better part of valour. The French governor called in his outposts, and Louisburg, tortoise-like, retired into its shell.

The destruction of the Grand Battery was Amherst's cue for an attack upon the fortified island in the mouth of the harbour. When this and the French fleet were disposed of, Boscawen might enter the landlocked haven with impunity and let loose his cannon upon the unprotected town. With this object in view, on the morning after the conflagration, Amherst detached Brigadier Wolfe with twelve hundred men, to skirt the water-front and seize Lighthouse Point opposite Louisburg. This promontory corresponded to that where the town stood and co-operated with it in sheltering the harbour from the sweep of the open sea.

From shore to shore the distance here was perhaps a mile, and in midstream lay the Island Battery. Amherst gave his brigadier additional instructions to attempt to destroy the enemy's ships which were riding at anchor in the port. While Wolfe circled the harbour by land, the general sent artillery and tools by sea, to await the brigadier at Lorambec, a fishing village on the way to his destination.

The enterprise was eminently successful. Wolfe reached Lighthouse Point that same day, and there took possession of a battery recently abandoned by the French. In the course of a week, he planted guns and mortars along the harbourside as well as on Lighthouse Hill, and on the night of the nineteenth of June the new posts opened fire on the French ships. This was a reversal of Amherst's plan, but the brigadier had determined that the destruction of the men-of-war should precede the suppression of the guns on the island. (Corbett's *England in the Seven Years' War*, i.) The enemy returned the compliment from the squadron, from the Island Battery, and even from the town.

Des Gouttes, who commanded the fleet, realised his danger at once and retired the ships as close as possible under the walls of the town. To guard against fire, the decks were piled with cordage and bales of tobacco, and Wolfe soon found that he could make no impression in that quarter. He then turned his attention to the rocky islet in the harbour's mouth and cannonaded it with a right good will. Day and night the bombardment continued until the evening of the twenty-fifth, when the British succeeded in silencing the shattered Island Battery. Then leaving a few men at the Point, with some ship-guns, to prevent the French from repairing their demolished works and batteries, Amherst's right-hand man rejoined the army in front of the town.

While these brilliant events were taking place to the eastward of Louisburg, General Amherst was primarily occupied with landing provisions, stores, and artillery, an undertaking of so great difficulty, owing to the boisterous waves, that over one hundred boats were lost in its accomplishment. On the eighteenth of June, in company with Colonel Bastide, the general reconnoitred the ground between the English camp and the town.

The terrain was by no means encouraging. Captain Knox, the soldier-historian of the war, described it as "a vile country, partly rough, but in general swampy." (Knox's *Historical Journal*, i.) The British troops were encamped about two miles from the fortress upon a wooded slope, down which flowed a stream supplying them with good water. Between this ground and the bastions of Louisburg there was a wide marsh, which terminated in *terra firma* with occasional hillocks, less than a half-mile from the ramparts.

Bastide, who was the chief engineer of the expedition, declared that the trenches should be opened on one of these knolls called Green Hill. Before this could be done, however, a road must be made across the swamp-land so that artillery and stores could be forwarded without danger or delay. Here, thirteen years before, Pepperrell's energetic rustics watched one of their cannon sink to the hubs of its wheels in the mud and moss, and finally drop completely out of sight. (Parkman's *Half-Century of Conflict*, ii.) A piece of Yankee ingenuity had saved the situation then, but Amherst with unlimited means at his disposal determined to construct a road protected by an epaulement, or lateral earthwork, which would shield the men from the raking fire of the *Arethuse*, a vexatious frigate in the upper harbour.

The road to Green Hill was begun at once and pushed on as fast as possible. On the first day four hundred men toiled at the construction from four in the morning until one in the afternoon, when they were relieved by a party of equal number who continued the work until ten o'clock at night. The long June days of this northern latitude were used to their best advantage by the resolute general. Now and then the enemy cannonaded the workmen and the camp itself, but the progress towards Green Hill went steadily and relentlessly on, until the evening of June 26 saw a British lodgement effected on the appointed hillock. (*Montresor's Journals*.)

Amherst's camp was not entirely free from misfortune, in spite of its commander's care and precaution. Among the provincials attached to the expedition was a band of New England carpenters, about one hundred in number, under the conduct of Colonel Messervé of New Hampshire. While this Yankee delegation was on its way to Louisburg "one Eliot of hallifax (who) came with us was taken with ye smalpox." (*Diary of Nathaniel Knap*, in the Society of Colonial Wars in Massachusetts *Publications*, No. 2.) As if this were not enough, their ship lost the rest of the armada in the fog, and when the weather cleared, they "saw none of ye fleet."

The next day the captain "spoke with a frigat and she said ye fleet had got in and we was 15 leags distance and dam'd us and then he left us." Contagion plus anathema made short work of the unfortunate carpenters. Within two weeks after their landing on the island, all but sixteen of the one hundred and eight men were stricken with smallpox. Among those who succumbed to the dread disease were the leader and his eldest son. Colonel Messervé, though a shipwright by profession, had acquired a handsome fortune and his death was a great loss to New Hampshire. (Jeremy Belknap's *History of New Hampshire*, ii.)

When Wolfe shattered the Island Battery, the French governor very naturally expected that Boscawen would follow up this advantage by a naval attack upon the men-of-war in the harbour. To prevent such a calamity Drucour resorted to heroic measures. On the evening of

LOUISBURG IN 1758

June 29, under cover of the darkness and fog, the enemy sank four of their ships in the mouth of the harbour. One of them was the *Apollon*, of fifty guns, while the others were less of a sacrifice. (Beatson's *Memoirs*, iii.) The haven was now considered safe from any design which the English admiral might have upon it, but as yet Boscawen entertained no idea of threading the treacherous channel in order to demolish his doomed opponent.

While Hardy's squadron patrolled the open sea about the entrance to the harbour and picked off the enemy's ships one by one, whenever they attempted to escape, "Old Wry-necked Dick," as Boscawen was occasionally referred to by the seamen, converted his sailors into marines, and lent Amherst several large guns from the fleet to be used in the batteries. He preferred to bombard the French ships from the shore, and he did so most successfully. The co-operation and harmony between the admiral and the major-general excited the admiration of all, including even the impatient and hypercritical Wolfe. (Willson's *Wolfe*.)

The siege progressed without any serious set-back. On the night of the ninth of July, the French rushed forth in a desperate sortie from the town, and surprised some of the British; but it availed them little in the end. The enemy's men were shamefully drunk and when once routed fired upon each other, an error whereby they lost more in killed and wounded than did the English. (*Montresor's Journals*: Knox's *Journal*, i.) Yet the hostilities were not without a gentler side. Drucour, for instance, wrote to Amherst that Louisburg contained a surgeon of great skill whom he would gladly lend to any English officer who might require his services.

On his side the Briton allowed wounded prisoners to send messages and letters through the lines to their beleaguered friends. Upon another occasion the general expressed his regret for the discomfort to which Madame Drucour was necessarily subjected by the vicissitudes of war, and accompanied his words with some pineapples from the West Indies. The lady reciprocated by sending him fifty bottles of wine. Amherst apparently approved of the exchange and it was not long before he sent another instalment of fruit to the governor's wife. This time Drucour gave the messenger two gold-pieces for conveying his acknowledgment to Amherst— but no wine, for he feared that his cellar would soon be empty if such courtesies continued. (Waddington's *Guerre de Sept Ans*, ii.)

More important were the tentative negotiations between the two commanders for the protection of the sick and wounded. Drucour requested that the French hospital be exempt from British fire. Amherst replied that in the case of so small a town he could scarcely guarantee that any part would be free from shot and shell; but if the French cared to remove their disabled to an island in the harbour's mouth, or to a ship, he would gladly permit them to do so. For some inscrutable reason the governor declined to avail himself of this privilege. Wolfe was quite right in declaring, "When the French are in a scrape, they are ready to cry out in behalf of the human species; when fortune favours them, none more bloody, more inhuman." (Willson's *Wolfe*.)

The British lines crept closer and closer to the doomed fortress and their fire became proportionally more deadly. At dusk on the sixteenth of July, Wolfe made a sudden dash forward and seized a bit of rising ground within three hundred yards of one of the bastions of Louisburg. In vain the guns of the town poured forth grape-shot upon the daring invaders. With pick and spade the dirt flew all night, and when morning came the English sappers were still burrowing on towards the rampart. The cannonading and firing of musketry grew hotter and hotter on both sides. Amherst was indefatigable. Visiting the outposts and the batteries every day, he was constantly reconnoitring to discover some new point from which to assail the enemy and accelerate the siege. (Knox's *Journal*, i.)

The twenty-first of July was an eventful day. In the afternoon one of Wolfe's shells dropped on the poop of the *Célèbre*. (*Montresor's Journals*.)

★★★★★★

Of this incident Knap's *Journal* gives an account, as vivid as it is illiterate. "General Wolfe hove a shell on board one of ye men of war and blew her up and ketcht on fire and she ketcht 2 more on fire and they were burnt down. By night there was but 2 ships left in ye harbour and there was 12 or 14 when we came in."

★★★★★★

With a deafening roar her magazine exploded, and soon the ship was in flames. The fire spread to the sails; ablaze she drifted from her moorings while the English concentrated their shot and shell upon the helpless man-of-war to prevent the boats and towns-people from going to her rescue. Soon two more ships were on fire, for the flames from the *Célèbre* spread to the canvas of her sisters the *Entreprenant* and the *Capricieux*. The cables of the menacing craft were speedily cut and the vessels drifted listlessly into the upper harbour. There the blazing trio ran aground and burned to the water's edge. Of the French squadron only two ships, the *Prudent* and the *Bienfaisant*, remained to bid defiance to the oncoming English.

The siege now rushed towards its inevitable conclusion. Event followed event in such close sequence that the besieged were frantic with apprehension. On the morning after the burning of the ships, the English dropped a shell into the citadel of Louisburg. Crashing through the roof, the missile plunged into a room full of soldiers, and exploded in their midst. At once that part of the building which was of wood burst into flames: the fire spread rapidly, consuming the chapel and all the northern part of the citadel. Soldiers and sailors hurried to the spot to put out the conflagration, but the British showered missiles relentlessly in that direction.

Sheets of flame and clouds of smoke swept towards a wooden barrier which shielded the casemates under the ramparts from exploding shells. If this took fire, the wounded soldiers and non-combatants who had taken refuge in the subterranean chambers would be in danger of suffocation. Those who had legs used them, and rushed forth into the chaos of flames and flying iron, the women and children shrieking with terror. (*Montresor's Journals.*) The enemy put up a gallant fight, nevertheless. They fired well from the town, throwing shells into the English works and dismounting at least two guns. (Kimball's *Pitt Correspondence*, i.) One of their shot went into the muzzle of a British twenty-four pounder and stuck there as if purposely rammed in.

Amherst's batteries were more destructive than those of the French, however, and once, while the enemy were firing "all sorts of old iron and any stuff they could pick up," the British hurled a shell filled with combustibles into a range of barracks in the town. The building was a flimsy affair and burned like tinder. Realising its nature, the French garrison had vacated it, and were now lying in the streets, or in any place which offered protection from the rain of bombs with which Wolfe pelted them. Their evacuation took place none too soon, for now night was turned into day by the glare of the crackling conflagration. Mortars roared, cannonballs screamed through the air, and the snapping of musketry from the ramparts was continuous.

At last, the enemy's fire grew daily weaker; and well it might, for almost one-fourth of the besieged were in the hospitals. The rest, wellnigh exhausted, continued the hopeless defence. On the twenty-fourth there were only four cannon in commission on the west wall of the town, and the French depended chiefly upon small arms which they used through the embrasures, while the English continued their bombardment without ceasing. The condition of Louisburg was pitiable. Each cannon-shot from the British batteries shook its ruinous walls and brought down great masses of the tottering structures. (*Journal of Chevalier de Johnstone.*)

Shot and shell poured in upon every part of the town, and whenever a few brave spirits endeavoured to return the fire from their remaining guns, they were beaten back by a deluge of bullets from the British musketry, which had now pressed close upon the ramparts. But one event remained to complete the downfall of the Dunkirk of America. This was the capture or destruction of the two surviving men-of-war which lay huddled together under the French batteries on the harbour side of the town.

Just before daybreak on July 26, Admiral Boscawen sent a flotilla manned by six hundred sailors to take or burn the *Prudent* and the *Bienfaisant*. The harbour was enshrouded in a dense fog, and as the boats pushed softly from shore, Amherst opened fire upon the works from every battery, in order to distract the attention of the enemy. The French men-of-war were completely surprised, and surrendered with scarcely a blow. The tide being low, the *Prudent* was aground. Allowing her crew to escape to the shore in boats, the boarders set the ship on fire.

While she burned at anchor, making the foggy night hideous with flaring light, Boscawen's men turned their attention to the *Bienfaisant*. This vessel was afloat and fell an easy prey to her bold assailants. The English towed their prize safely from her moorings to the northeast arm of the harbour, in spite of a concentrated fire directed upon them from all the available cannon and musketry of the enemy. It was a gallant action and cost the performers but seven men killed and nine wounded. (Kimball's *Pitt Correspondence*, i.)

The loss of the ships was the final blow to the spirit of resistance, for the water-front, protected by a mere wall, was now open to escalade or to a cannonade, if Boscawen saw fit to enter the harbour. The admiral had precisely that operation in mind, but upon going on shore to tell Amherst of his intentions, he found the general reading a letter from the governor of Louisburg. At ten o'clock that July morning a white flag had appeared over the breach in one of the bastions, and an officer came to the British camp with an offer to capitulate. Drucour demanded the same terms which the valiant Blakeney had received at Minorca two years before. This meant freedom and all the honours of war for the garrison.

Amherst's reply was short and to the point. The French troops must surrender as prisoners of war within an hour; otherwise, the place would be attacked by land and sea. Another officer emerged from the ruined town and pleaded for more lenient terms, but Amherst and Boscawen would not talk with him. To the governor they sent a repetition of their demands and requested a reply within thirty minutes. Drucour's second answer was a flat refusal; but the bearer of the note had scarcely got beyond the fortifications, when a third messenger overtook him and called him back.

One of the civil authorities of Louisburg, upon hearing of the governor's reply, had protested that such an attitude was eminently proper from a military point of view, but that Drucour could not have taken into consideration the sufferings of the four thousand inhabitants, and of the ten or twelve hundred sick in the hospitals, which further resistance must entail. This argument appealed to the gubernatorial mind, and in place of the note of refusal Drucour sent out three officers with instructions to accept the terms imposed by Amherst. One of these bearers of good tidings, afraid that the patience of the English would be exhausted before he reached their camp, ran out of the town, waving his arms about, and bawled out from afar, "We accept! We accept!"

At eleven o'clock that night the negotiators returned to Louisburg with the articles of capitulation, accompanied by a note from Amherst and Boscawen assuring their defeated opponent that they had no intention of distressing the unfortunate inhabitants of the town, but would do all in their power to aid them.

The terms of surrender were as follows: the garrison should be sent to England in English ships, as prisoners of war; all artillery, arms, ammunition, and provisions in Louisburg and the islands of Cape Breton and St. John (now, 1916, Prince Edward Island) should be given up intact; the gate called the Porte Dauphine should be surrendered to the British troops the next morning at eight o'clock, and the garrison should lay down their colours and arms on the esplanade at noon. (Beatson's *Memoirs*, iii.) One cannot help wondering whether Amherst, as he put down his pen, recalled that just one year ago that day the forces under the Duke of Cumberland went down to defeat before the French at the Battle of Hastenbeck.

The French governor signed the capitulation at midnight. Before noon of the twenty-seventh three companies of grenadiers marched through the west gate of the town. Soon the Union Jack was floating over the citadel and the vanquished garrison, drawn up on parade, laid

Surrender of Loiusburg to the British under General Jeffery Amherst

down their arms. Over fifty-five hundred officers, soldiers, and sailors were taken prisoners of war, while the amount of artillery, arms, ammunition, and stores which fell into the hands of the victors is astonishing. All that afternoon a long line of wagons streamed in and out of Louisburg, hauling away the guns and stores, over which sentries kept guard to see that nothing was carried elsewhere than to the king's depot. There were eighteen mortars and two hundred and twenty-one cannon, besides seventy-five hundred muskets with eighty thousand cartridges.

Louisburg had fallen and with it the islands of Cape Breton and St. John. The key to the St. Lawrence had been wrested from the enemy, and the conqueror hastened to send the glad news to England. As bearer of the tidings, he selected his younger brother, William, who had been with the army as Amherst's *aide-de-camp*, while Boscawen appointed one Captain Edgecomb to represent the navy in this happy mission. The elements which had conspired to delay the expedition coming out from England now did their best to speed the good word across the water. Captain Amherst and his naval companion sailed on the evening of July 30, (*Montresor's Journals*); in less than three weeks they set England on fire with the joyful tidings. (*Grenville Papers*, i.)

Congratulations poured in from all sides. Lady Yarmouth effusively hoped that the victory would bring about a glorious peace. Horace Walpole shared her sentiments. (*Horace Walpole to Sir Horace Mann*, Aug. 24, 1758.) The archbishop offered thanksgiving, while the more worldly Chesterfield declared that the country had been greatly in want of a cordial and here was one. (Torrens' *History of Cabinets*, ii.) Lord Temple, Pitt's brother-in-law, was intoxicated with joy.

In writing his "hundred thousand million of congratulations" to the War Minister "upon this great and glorious event," Temple addressed him "my dear brother Louisburg." (Von Ruville's *Pitt*, ii.) To understand the storm of enthusiasm which swept over England, one must realise that Amherst's feat was the first victory in a war that had been dragging on for two discouraging years.

George II, like his subjects, was carried away by the joyous news. He insisted upon giving each of the messengers a present of 500, and a further sum to be devoted to the purchase of a sword and a ring. (*Gentleman's Magazine*, xxviii, 448; Sept., 1758). It was not long before William Amherst, who was only twenty-six years old, was still further rewarded by being made deputy quarter-master-general of the forces in North America with the rank of lieutenant-colonel. (*Ibid.*, xxviii,

504; Oct., 1758).

The arrival of the French colours taken at Louisburg occasioned a great demonstration in the metropolis. First the trophies were carried to the palace at Kensington, whereupon the king ordered that they should be deposited in St. Paul's, which was done with great pomp and circumstance. A gorgeous procession of cavalry and foot escorted the eleven standards from Hyde Park to the west gate of the cathedral amidst the blare of trumpets and the roar of kettle-drums. While the guns at the Tower and in St. James's Park boomed over London, the dean and chapter, attended by the choir, received the Gallic emblems and hung them in a conspicuous place as a lasting memorial to the success of His Majesty's arms in the reduction of Louisburg. (*London Magazine*, Vol. xxvii, Oct, 1758).

The celebration of Amherst's victory was by no means confined to the Old World. To the American colonists, and to the men of New England in particular, the stronghold on Cape Breton Island had been doubly the Dunkirk of America, for the place was famous as a resort of privateers. (Parkman's *Half-Century of Conflict*, i.) Jean Bart and his followers never worried the English seamen of the Channel more than the marauders of Louisburg troubled our sea-going ancestors. When the good news arrived from the eastward, sermons of thanksgiving were preached in almost every New England meeting-house, while the seaport towns were still more demonstrative.

The jubilant Bostonians piled a great bonfire on the top of Fort Hill and let its light shine out over harbour and countryside to the glory of Amherst and his brave soldiers. Newport indulged in fire-works and a general illumination. The ringing of bells and the discharge of guns expressed Philadelphia's joy, while New York celebrated the occasion with a grand official dinner, where each toast was announced to the town by the cannon at Fort George. (Parkman's *Montcalm and Wolfe*, ii.) By the end of August, the good news had penetrated to the British camp at Lake George where timid Abercromby had settled down after one defeat at the hands of Montcalm. The dispirited army rose to the occasion with enthusiasm, and fired three rounds of artillery and small arms for the taking of Louisburg.

Nor did the rejoicing cease with bonfires and pyrotechnics, salutes and banquets. Some individuals more venturesome than the rest attempted to give vent to their exultation in verse. The results, as usual in such cases, were hardly subjects for congratulation, but one rhyme is perhaps less pitiful than the rest. This was written on board the *Oxford*, in Louisburg Harbor soon after the surrender. (Nevill's *The Reduction of Louisburg*. There is a copy of this "poem" in the John Carter Brown Library at Providence.) Its author, Valentine Nevill, is otherwise unknown to fame, but his characterisation and appreciation of Amherst may appropriately close this chapter of the general's career:

> *Calm and compos'd amid the hostile Scene,*
> *Judicious, steady, temp'rate, and serene,*
> *Prudently bold, considerate and good,*
> *Resolv'd, and yet not prodigal of Blood,*
> *Thy Virtues, Amherst, cannot be unsung,*
> *While Virtue's Praise employs the Poet's tongue.*

CHAPTER 6

Between Two Campaigns

According to Pitt's plan for the campaign of 1758 the capture of Louisburg was to be but the prelude to an attack upon Quebec itself. If the season were too far gone after the first stronghold fell, the commanders were to turn their hands to the destruction of the French settlements along the Canadian coast and in southern Louisiana. (Corbett's *England in the Seven Years' War*, i.) The Louisburg expedition arrived at the Island of Cape Breton seven weeks after schedule time; the siege consumed seven weeks; yet Amherst concluded his letter to Pitt, announcing his victory, with this sentence: "If I can go to Quebec, I will." (Kimball's *Pitt Correspondence*, i.) Four days later news arrived, so disturbing in its character that it was one of the strongest factors in the determination of plans for the rest of the summer. The unwelcome report came from Lake George, where a British Army of more than fifteen thousand men had gone down to defeat before Montcalm.

The irruption into Canada by the way of the lakes of northern New York was assigned to General Abercromby, the commander-in-chief of His Majesty's forces in North America. In July there were six thousand regulars and about nine thousand provincials under his orders at the southern end of Lake George. Although nominally the commander, Abercromby lacked the qualities of a leader, and Pitt, knowing this to be the case, appointed Brigadier Lord Howe to be second in command. The latter was beloved by every man in the army and was one of the few British officers to win the good-will of the colonial soldiers.

An engaging personality was not his only remarkable quality. The young nobleman, who was in his thirty-fourth year, possessed an exceptional amount of good sense, and was ever ready to break through the traditions of the service when wilderness conditions required tactics differing from those employed in European warfare. His men were equipped for efficiency rather than for show. They cut their hair close, and the tails of their gorgeous coats were amputated at the waist. Wolfe startles one with the statement that His Lordship "has taken away all the men's breeches," (Royal Commission on Historical Manuscripts' *Ninth Report*, Appendix iii), without explaining that he substituted leggings to protect their limbs from the briary undergrowth of the forest.

The musket-barrels were browned to render them inconspicuous, and every man carried in his knapsack thirty pounds of meal, which made him independent of supply-trains for a month. Before such numbers and such an efficiently equipped force, the French might well tremble for their posts, Ticonderoga and Crown Point, at the head of Lake Champlain. In fact, they did. Montcalm had only about thirty-five hundred men to pit against the invading host, but good luck, supplemented by admirable skill, triumphed over the disparity in numbers.

Early in July Abercromby embarked his forces upon Lake George and started on his way to attempt the capture of Ticonderoga. Landing at the northern end of the lake, where its spectacular shores converge until there is scarcely room for the rushing outlet which dances on its way to the water of Champlain, the army started through the forest primeval. The growth was dense from the first, and before long became almost impenetrable; but the troops struggled on until even the guides were at a loss where to turn.

One or two provincial regiments preceded the main parts of the army, and in their progress through the leafy wilderness must have got too far in advance before they realised it. The principal column was headed by Lord Howe with Major Israel Putnam and two hundred rangers. Bending aside saplings and climbing over fallen giants of the forest, the soldiers tramped towards the French fort at Ticonderoga. Suddenly in a dense thicket they heard a challenge: *Qui vive!* The cry was a desperate one, for it came from a party of three hundred and fifty Frenchmen who were caught between the advanced guard and the main body of the British Army. The enemy fired from the underbrush. Putnam and the rangers reciprocated in kind. A brisk skirmish ensued, and Lord Howe fell dead with a bullet in his breast.

The fighting continued until the small band of the enemy was destroyed almost to a man, but the outcome of the campaign had been practically determined when the brave and noble Howe dropped on the soft ground of the virgin forest. Upon his followers the effect of

R. ST. LAWRENCE

FT. FRONTENAC

CROWN POINT ◉
TICONDEROGA◉

L. GEORGE

FT. OSWEGO
FT. STANWIX
AFTERWARDS
FT. SCHUYLER

FT. WM. HENRY

FT. EDWARD

CHERRY VALLEY ◉

MOHAWK R.

ALBANY

MASSA-CHUSETTS

N E W   Y O R K

DELAWARE R.

CONNEC-TICUT

WYOMING ◉

HUDSON R.

NEW YORK

L. ISLAND

N I A

SUSQUEHANNA

PHILADELPHIA

N E W   J E R S E Y

A T L A N T I C   O C E A N

A N

TIMORE◉

his death was immeasurable. Well might Abercromby have said, "O what a fall was there, my countrymen! Then I, and you, and all of us fell down," for with the death of Howe the soul of the army expired. The hero's body was carried back to Albany, (*Boston Gazette*, July 17, 1758), where it rests under the vestibule of St. Peter's Church, although the visitor to Ticonderoga is usually led to believe that the nobleman's ashes are there.

Although the destructive party of Frenchmen were effectually disposed of, Abercromby shared the consternation of his troops and hastened to leave the spot where his gallant second had fallen. Retracing its steps, the dispirited army again came in sight of the shimmering surface of Lake George. In the meantime, Montcalm had retreated to Ticonderoga and awaited the approach of the British. About a half-mile from the enemy's forts an elevated ridge offered great natural advantages to the French position if the commander saw fit to avail himself of them.

Montcalm was ever awake to his opportunities and at the eleventh hour his men constructed along this axis a staunch wall of timber felled upon the spot. The logs were piled upon each other to a height of eight or nine feet, forming a complete shelter for the French soldiers. This protection was still further secured by a most ingenious abattis. The ground in front of the crude breastwork sloped away, and over that area, to the distance of a musket-shot, the enemy cut down trees in such manner that they lay with their tops towards the British, offering many a sharpened branch upon which a valiant soldier might be torn or impaled. As one Massachusetts officer said, it looked like a forest uprooted by a hurricane. (Parkman's *Montcalm and Wolfe*, ii.)

Montcalm had now done all he could, and he awaited developments in no easy frame of mind. If attacked in front he might hold his position, otherwise the danger would be extreme.

On the eighth of July Abercromby took his engineer's advice and attempted a front attack upon the cruel works of the enemy. This step was very unwise, the more so because it was undertaken without waiting for the artillery to come up. The result was a disaster second only to that in which Braddock had met his death just three years before. Whoever knows the joys of tramping across newly timbered land may appreciate to some extent the difficulty of advancing upon the enemy's works through an artificial barrier of felled trees. The English soldiers were ordered to carry the lines with the bayonet. They struggled across the abattis, now falling helpless, caught between the interlacing branches, now stumbling over logs, only to be swept at last by a killing fire of grape-shot and musket-balls.

The ranks were broken, but more by the obstructions which impeded their progress than by the fire of the French soldiers. The valour and impetuosity of the regulars and provincials, battling against an enemy whom they could neither reach nor see, were tragic. Within a few feet of the wooden wall, they were confronted with a more elaborate and deadly array of sharpened branches than that which they had succeeded in traversing. The French played upon them with a cross-fire here, and many a brave soldier, falling, was transfixed upon the jagged limbs.

Again, and again the attack was renewed that hot July afternoon, but all in vain. Once a gallant Scotch captain tore his way through the abattis and with a few of his men climbed the breastwork, only to be bayonetted by the enemy. Until sunset the fighting continued, but the last hour and a half of battle was merely an attempt on the part of the provincials to cover the disorderly retreat of the regulars and to protect their comrades who were collecting and removing the wounded. The dead were left where they had fallen, and the British forces hurriedly retreated to the head of Lake George. In the profitless slaughter the English had lost almost two thousand officers and men, while Montcalm's well-protected defenders of Ticonderoga were lessened by only about three hundred and twenty-five. This was the disheartening story which Abercromby related in his despatches to Amherst.

Upon the receipt of the bad news Amherst went immediately to Boscawen and discussed the situation. Should reinforcements be sent to Lake George at once? The admiral did not see how that could be done until the prisoners who had been taken at Louisburg were actually on shipboard, and on their way to England. The embarkation consumed a great deal of time because of frequent spells of foggy weather, but at last, on the fourteenth of August, the five thousand Frenchmen were all crowded into five men-of-war and ten transports. (Kimball's *Pitt Correspondence*, i.) Next morning the squadron of prison-ships, under the command of Captain Rodney, crept out of the harbour and started on its four weeks' voyage.

In the meantime, Wolfe had grown restless. Daily he besieged his chief with questions about the next operations. It was clear that he keenly desired to start at once for Quebec and had no doubt that such an attack would be successful. (Willson's *Wolfe*.) Amherst also wished to enter the St. Lawrence and make an attempt upon the capital of

New France, but Boscawen was less enthusiastic about the project. The fleet wanted provisions, and the ships had suffered so much damage from the waves in Gabarus Bay that he considered an expedition up the river impracticable. Still Amherst hoped to carry out the original plan.

Then came Abercromby's letter. The admiral and the general pondered the question for almost a week, and, on the sixth of August, came to the conclusion that the Quebec enterprise must be abandoned. (Kimball's *Pitt Correspondence*, i.) When Amherst broke this news to Wolfe, the latter showed his disappointment in a petulant reply, demanding that reinforcements be sent to Abercromby immediately. He would gladly have picked up four or five battalions and started at once for Boston or New York, but this being out of the question for the present, the disgruntled brigadier expended his energy in complaining that "This damned French garrison take up our time and attention which might be better bestowed upon the interesting affairs of the continent."

When the impracticability of attacking Quebec was certain, Amherst lost no time in putting into execution his alternative instructions—to destroy the French settlements along the Canadian coast. On the very next day Major Dalling was dispatched to Espagnolle, now Sydney, C. B., with orders to bring away all the French inhabitants able to carry arms; and ere long Colonel Rollo with five hundred men departed for Prince Edward Island, upon an equally grim mission. Towards the end of the month Amherst ordered another detachment under Colonel Monckton to proceed to the shores of the Bay of Fundy and the mouth of the St. John River "to destroy the vermin who are settled there."

Finally, a fourth expedition was organised and sent against the inhabitants of the western coast of the Gulf of St. Lawrence. This part of the program was assigned to Wolfe, who owned that he would be pleased "to see the Canadian vermin sacked and pillaged and justly repaid their unheard-of cruelty." (Willson's *Wolfe.*) All these operations, although seemingly unnecessary and cruel, were in fact entirely justifiable, for Quebec was chiefly supplied with provisions by these settlements. Prince Edward Island, or as we should more properly call it, lie St. Jean, abounded in corn and cattle and had no other market than the capital of New France. (Kimball's *Pitt Correspondence*, i.)

By destroying these supplies and removing the inhabitants who provided them, an important step towards the conquest of Quebec would be accomplished. England had experimented with French Canadian "neutrals" long enough to know that such phenomena could never exist; and, that being the case, these unfortunate beings must be removed from the field of military operations.

Lord Rollo found the governor of Prince Edward Island somewhat reluctant to consider himself bound by the capitulation of Louisburg, but a slight display of force quickly reduced him to submission. The British captured as many of the inhabitants as possible and sent them off to France. Few of the wretched exiles, however, were destined to see the shores of the Old World, for the vessels upon which they embarked proved unseaworthy, and hundreds of men and women were shipwrecked and drowned on the voyage. (Beatson's *Memoirs*, iii; Casgrain's *Une Seconde Acadie*.) If Lord Rollo had any misgivings about the justice of this deportation, his conscience was relieved by the discovery of several of his countrymen's scalps adorning the interior of the gubernatorial residence.

These ghastly trophies betokened the zeal of parties of fugitive Acadians who had eked out a living in their new surroundings by scalping Englishmen and carrying the results of their labours to the governor for a bounty. The removal of the inhabitants of Prince Edward Island, effected at this time, accounts for the comparative absence of French Canadians noticeable in that region today; for those who escaped the clutches of the British fled to Quebec, and the island became a wilderness once more.

The other ravaging expeditions were equally successful, although the conquerors were occasionally embarrassed by finding a number of Germans among their captives. These people had wandered from a colony founded in Acadia by the English five or ten years before, and Amherst decreed that they should be left unmolested, or else sent back to Lunenburg in Nova Scotia. (Kimball's *Pitt Correspondence*, i.)

Wolfe's excursion resulted in the temporary ruin of the enemy's fisheries on the west shore of the Gulf of St. Lawrence, upon which the Canadian and French troops were in a great measure dependent for subsistence. The quiet fisher-folk were not expecting the descent of the British with fire and sword and consequently there was no opposition. Gaspe, the first place attacked, was easily disposed of. The terrified habitants left their houses and rushed to the woods, while the invaders completely destroyed their settlement. A few of the miserable people escaped to Quebec, some were captured in the forest, while others were gradually driven from their hiding-places by starvation and gave themselves up.

At every wretched hamlet along that shore the same desolating operations were carried on. Houses and shallops, stages and nets, magazines and stores were burned. All the schooners and dried fish, and every bit of property, combustible or not, were consigned to the flames or were otherwise destroyed. Wolfe hustled the habitants on board the British ships; but some of those who commanded minor excursions were not so careful, and the ruined Canadians were left to face the approaching winter without food or shelter. It is a depressing picture; let us hope that Wolfe did not find so much pleasure in the deed as in its anticipation. These depredations occupied his restless spirit throughout September. Then returning to Louisburg, the brigadier carried out his intention of leaving America, supposedly forever, and sailed for England with Boscawen on the first day of October.

The future hero of the Plains of Abraham had acquitted himself well in the conquest of Louisburg, and Amherst must have appreciated how much he owed to the valour and inspiring leadership of his first brigadier; but on the other hand, the general's patience and good-nature had been put to a great test by this mercurial James Wolfe. Although the two men were never to meet again, it may be worth our while to study the personality and character of each as displayed in the recent campaign. Amherst, a mature soldier of forty-one years, was methodical almost to excess. Without an assuredly sufficient number of men and a well-established base, he would never make the slightest move.

When everything was arranged to his liking, he advanced, and never failed in carrying his plan into execution. He never hurried, and was so thorough that he never left dangling any loose ends of which the enemy might take advantage. Hence his operations were rarely spectacular, and never designedly so. To Amherst a campaign was to be played like a game of chess, and he never failed to checkmate his opponent. Nothing ruffled him, not even the officious suggestions and petulant outbursts of his right-hand man. His good nature was as remarkable as his deliberation.

In contrast to the serene general we have almost his antithesis in Wolfe. Every American is familiar with that strange and unmistakable profile. The tip of his long and slightly upturned nose was the apex of a triangle formed by a sloping forehead and a receding chin. His physique was no more prepossessing: his body was slender, his shoulders narrow, and his limbs long and thin. The caricature culminated in his red hair which he wore tied in a queue behind. The eye and the mouth alone were true indexes to his character. The one was bright and alert, the other beautiful and resolute.

Although a young man of thirty-one, Wolfe was almost an invalid, presumably a victim of tuberculosis aggravated by over-wrought nerves; but as a soldier, he was matchless for spirit or enterprise. No undertaking was too dangerous, no fire too hot. He enjoyed the battle for the battle's sake and never considered his own safety. What he could not endure was inaction. Yet inaction was sometimes imperative. When this was the case, Wolfe became restive, then critical, then officious. His superior found him invaluable when a position was to be seized or lines were to be carried; but in the tedious, yet necessary, interim he was a thorn in the flesh. He had no patience for the infinite amount of detail which, if neglected, might spell ruin for a campaign.

Wolfe wanted the dash, the charge, and the escalade—in any of which he was undeniably brilliant. Before Louisburg we have watched him leap into the breakers on the day of the landing, we have heard his guns from Lighthouse Point shattering the Island Battery, and when the French attempted a sortie, it was Wolfe who hurled them back into the town and incidentally gained an advanced position. But when not occupied with such enterprises the Brigadier's restless spirit relieved itself in criticism of his contemporaries, superiors as well as equals, and he never doubted the infallibility of his own opinion.

While the Louisburg expedition was waiting for a favourable wind to carry it out of the harbour of Halifax, Wolfe gave vent to his feelings to Lord George Sackville in a characteristic letter, beginning:

> The latter end of May and the fleet not sailed! What are they about? Why are they not landed at Louisburg?

He was sure that the enterprise would "cost a multitude of men," and lamented the sickly state of many of the regiments. (Willson's *Wolfe*.) As a matter of fact, the British losses before the island stronghold were only one hundred and seventy-two killed and about three hundred and fifty wounded out of an army of more than eleven thousand men. All went well until the siege was over. Then Wolfe broke out again. He seemed to consider Amherst incapable of dealing with the situation, and by writing to the general's brother he tried to make William the vehicle of his suggestions as to the proper conduct of affairs.

Then in letters to Sackville and to his father he indulged in personalities: his brother-brigadier, Whitmore, he called "a poor, old, sleepy man"; Abercromby, "a heavy man"; and Brigadier Provost, "the most detestable dog upon earth." (*Ibid.*) Amherst seems to have been singularly immune from the shrill chirp of the critic, but Wolfe pestered him daily by urging an attack upon Quebec.

Particularly unfortunate were the brigadier's remarks about the provincial soldiers. When Wolfe heard of Abercromby's defeat, he wrote to Amherst declaring that reinforcements should be sent at once to the camp at Lake George. "We all know how little the Americans are to be trusted; by this time, perhaps, our troops are left to defend themselves after losing the best of our officers." (*Ibid.*) Poor Wolfe! He little knew that in the very engagement to which he referred, it was those despised Americans who kept up a lingering fight until sunset, in order to protect the flight of the panic-stricken regulars—a flight so precipitate that forest and swamp were strewn with the arms, accoutrements, and even the shoes of the vanquished. In another letter his prejudiced pen did him even less credit:

> I am afraid that by this time Mr. Abercromby is left to defend himself with the remains of his regular troops. The Americans are in general the dirtiest, most contemptible cowardly dogs that you can conceive. There is no depending on them in action. They fall down dead in their own dirt and desert by battalions, officers and all. Such rascals as those are rather an encumbrance than any real strength to any army.

These sentiments were probably due to the author's failure to comprehend the frontier method of fighting, which taught every man to avail himself of the nearest protection, rather than to march towards the enemy in the pasteboard soldier fashion of the Europeans. Be that as it may, one cannot help regretting that the scornful Wolfe did not live to eat his words on the slope of Bunker Hill, or on the rocky sides of King's Mountain. But enough of the man's limitations. They were quite offset by his valour and his filial devotion; and long may James Wolfe stir the hearts of those who live in the land of the free and the home of the brave.

Towards the end of August Amherst saw his way to leave Louisburg and go to Abercromby's aid with reinforcements. The siege-trenches had been levelled, the battered walls patched up, and the Island Battery put in commission. The town resounded with the noisy hammers of the Yankee carpenters, who bent their restored energies to shingling houses and building barracks. The prisoners were on their way to

England, and at last there seemed to be nothing to keep the conqueror of Louisburg at the scene of his victory.

Abercromby had expressed a particular need of artillery officers and men along with whatever troops could be spared from the forces in the northeast, and Amherst responded by ordering five regiments to embark for Boston, while he himself went on board his brother's ship, the *Captain*, which Boscawen had assigned to convoy the transports to Massachusetts Bay. With a fair wind, on August 30, the little fleet sailed out of the harbour.

Amherst's voyages were no more expeditious than his campaigns. Almost two weeks passed before he came in sight of the wooded hills of Cape Ann. But worse trouble awaited him in Boston. The inhabitants of that Puritan town were still enthusiastic about the fall of Louisburg and intended to show their appreciation to the men who brought that glorious event to pass. The regiments encamped on the Common, and if the sacred Frog Pond itself had been filled with New England's traditional stimulant the feted soldiers could not have celebrated more unreservedly. For September fourteenth the general recorded that:

> It was impossible to hinder the people giving the soldiers rum in much too great quantities.

The next day's entry was veiled, but sententious:

> I halted to settle everything for the march.

When once more on his journey Amherst found thirteen men missing as the consequence of Boston hospitality, but confidently wrote:

> I believe I have quite got the better of the Rum, and that we shall have no more bad effects from that. (Kimball's *Pitt Correspondence*, i.)

The words were truly spoken, as we shall see in the next campaign.

Thomas Pownall, the energetic and business-like governor of Massachusetts, had provided ox-carts, camp necessaries and other supplies, and everything was in readiness to expedite the departure of the troops for the west. From Boston to Albany is about two hundred miles, a distance which Amherst and his men covered in nineteen days. When one considers that a part of the march was made through what the general termed "the greenwood" the time seems quite creditable.

Leaving appreciative Boston on September 16, the soldiers spent their first night on the banks of the Charles, at Watertown. Thence their route was through the happy autumn fields of Weston, Sudbury, and Marlborough.

At Worcester, Amherst encamped his four thousand men on a hill behind the court-house and halted a day. The general found quarters for himself at the house of Colonel Chandler, and delighted his host by taking an intelligent interest in his farm, over which he rambled to his heart's content. This military visitation added much to the usually colourless life of the inland town. The officers were very social, spending their evenings and taking their suppers with those of the inhabitants who aspired to be society-folk.

One of the regiments, composed of Scotch Highlanders, was particularly interesting to the provincial inhabitants who had never before beheld such an array of plaids and kilts, nor heard the shrilling of bagpipes. Among the spectators of the martial transit was a young graduate of Harvard College, who was studying law at this county-seat. His name was John Adams. The future president of the United States, was then, as ever, introspective and critical, but the excellent order and discipline of the troops extorted from him one of the few favourable comments to be found in his diary. John Adams' *Works*, ii.) It was fortunate that the puritanical young lawyer saw the regulars at Worcester and not at Boston.

The army resumed its march on the twenty-first and in three days' time arrived at Springfield, on the east bank of the Connecticut. Amherst's original plan was to travel only through the settled parts of the colony, but now he changed his mind and resolved to cut his way to Albany straight through the southern end of the forest-clad Berkshire Hills. Crossing the river, he did so; but he relished not this marching "through the greenwood," and lest the troops be surprised by the Indians or the French, they were ordered to sleep on their arms.

Emerging from the wilderness, the general found himself at Sheffield, in the Housatonic Valley, whence he lost no time in making his way to Albany in advance of the army. He soon got into communication with Abercromby, at whose request he hurried forward to the shores of Lake George, leaving instructions for the troops to halt at the Dutch town until further orders. (Kimball's *Pitt Correspondence*, i.)

On the fifth day of October, Jeffery Amherst arrived at Abercromby's headquarters. The commander-in-chief immediately held a council of war with the newcomer and Brigadier-General Gage, upon the advisability of a second attack upon the formidable French post at Ticonderoga. It is evident that the point was already settled in Abercromby's mind, and that all he desired was the moral support of Amherst's corroboration. He dwelt at length upon the increased strength of the enemy's works, upon his lack of artillery and engineers and finally upon the lateness of the season. Amherst acquiesced entirely in his superior's views, and active operations in the Lakes were postponed until the following year. (*Ibid.* i.)

In honour of the conqueror of Louisburg the whole army was drawn up at five o'clock the next afternoon, and the general viewed it in its splendid setting of mountains, gorgeous with autumnal colouring, reflected in the peaceful lake. At any season of the year Lake George compares favourably with the beautiful inland waters of England, but in October it easily eclipses its British rivals, for the picturesque shores of Windermere or Ullswater in all their glory are never arrayed in the flaming hues of maples and oaks. Although there is no expression of admiration for Nature in his letters, it seems as if Amherst must have been moved by the spectacular beauty of the New World.

The question of action or inaction in this region being settled for the present, Amherst departed for New York, where he arrived late on the night of October 12. Thence he returned to Halifax, his proper headquarters in North America, but on his way thither, the general stopped at Boston to confer with Governor Pownall about winter quarters for any overflow of troops or artillery which could not properly be accommodated in Nova Scotia. (Ibid., i.) The Massachusetts magistrate keenly desired to see a permanent garrison of regulars stationed in the vicinity of his capital, provided they were under his command, and doubtless fell in readily with Amherst's proposition.

The historic castle, now Fort Independence, where Andros was imprisoned at the time of the Glorious Revolution and to which the British troops were removed after the Boston Massacre in the early stages of a more glorious revolution, was the logical abiding-place for any military force charged with the defence of Boston. The fort crowns a small island in the harbour, about three miles from the heart of the town, and the general and Pownall spent part of one crisp October day in examining the post and in discussing its proper use.

★★★★★★

Ibid., i: Apparently Amherst and the popular governor of the Bay Colony were on the best of terms at this time. Certainly, the generous quota of provincial troops which the latter invariably persuaded the Assembly to furnish suggests hearty co-operation between the two men; but Thomas Hutchinson, who was then lieutenant-governor, and who knew both of them, gives an account of their relations, which, unless coloured by his dislike for Pownall, indicates anything but goodwill between Amherst and the chief magistrate.

> There had been an allowance of 4*d* per day per man, (when the Provincial troops were out on active service) made by the Assembly for provisions. He (Governor Pownall) took it into his head to advise some of the leading members of the House to reduce it to 3*d*, and desired Mr. Hutchinson to promote the measure, which he declined, as it would have a tendency to make a breach between the general and the province, and hurt the service. 'Oh, by ——,' says he, 'if I could not raise a party of the Civil, against the Military, whether it was Majority or Minority, I should not care a farthing, only let it be a party!'
>
> Whether Gen. Amherst ever heard of this or not, I do not know; but I have no doubt that the representations made by him to Ministry, caused the recall of Gov. Pownall. To let him down easily, he was nominated Governor of South Carolina; but upon Gen. Amherst hearing of this nomination, he said to Brigadier Ruggles, who was then in the army under the general, on the frontiers—'Depend upon it, Mr. Pownall will not go out a governor again to any of the American Colonies.' Another governor was soon after appointed to South Carolina. P. O. Hutchinson's *Diary and Letters of Thomas Hutchinson*, i.)
>
> ★★★★★★

Leaving Boston on October 30, Amherst continued on his way to Nova Scotia and landed at Halifax early in November. A few days later an express from New York arrived, bringing two missives from William Pitt. These were the first letters written after the news of Amherst's victory reached England. One contained formal, yet enthusiastic, expressions of the king's approbation and the Secretary's congratulations. The other disclosed two commissions, appointing Jeffery Amherst commander-in-chief of all the forces employed in North America. (Kimball's *Pitt Correspondence*, i.) Such were the first fruits of his splendid achievement on the rocky coast of Cape Breton. Besides the headship of the army the appointment carried with it the command of the 60th regiment as a sort of appanage.

This body of troops, known as the Royal Americans, was one of the most excellent in the service. Organised in 1756, it was recruited largely among the Germans in Pennsylvania, although its officers were from Europe. Among the latter Lord Howe had for a short time been prominent as colonel-*commandant*, (Maclachlan's *William Augustus, Duke of Cumberland.*) but the chief authority was always vested in the supreme military officer in British America, a distinction of which the regiment was duly proud. The new appointment changed Amherst's plans for the winter. Leaving the troops to hibernate at Halifax, while the artillery found quarters at Boston, the commander-in-chief left Nova Scotia for the Massachusetts capital, and travelled thence to New York where he arrived sometime before the middle of December.

At New York Amherst was greeted by more good news. This came from the third of the main operations planned for the year, the attack upon Fort Duquesne. (Kimball's *Pitt Correspondence*, i.) Brigadier-General Forbes commanded the forces assigned for this undertaking, and he was given about fifteen hundred regulars and five thousand provincials with which to accomplish the task that had brought death and disaster to Braddock. The American troops were drawn from Pennsylvania, Maryland, North Carolina, and Virginia, those of the last-named colony being commanded by Colonel George Washington. Forbes's tactics were not brilliant, but his operations do him credit, for, from beginning to end, he was racked with a painful disease which would have destroyed the resolution, as well as the disposition, of many a seasoned soldier.

In spite of his intense suffering, however, the faithful brigadier, swung in a litter between two horses, kept up with the army in its progress through the mountain wilderness. Very slowly the expedition crept westward. It was November before the British were within striking distance of Fort Duquesne and the tortured leader, discouraged by rains and snows, was on the point of giving up the business for that season, when he received authentic reports of the defenceless condition of the French post. The opportunity was too good to lose, and Forbes pressed forward until on November 25, he came in sight of the famous stronghold.

But the birds had flown. In place of an imposing fortress, bristling with cannon, the invaders beheld a heap of ruins, surrounded by the smouldering remains of barracks and storehouses. In despair the French garrison had blown up the fort on the previous night, and were now hastening up the Alleghany in the direction of Lake Erie. The success of the British was complete. Soon the vicinity of Fort Duquesne was dotted with soldiers' huts and traders' cabins, around which Forbes erected a stockade, and named the hamlet Pittsburgh in honour of his great chief, to whose genius so much of his own success was due.

Thus ended the campaign of 1758. France had held her own in the centre, while on the left, at Louisburg, and on the right, at Fort Duquesne, she had received telling blows. The tide of victory had turned, but the issue of the imperial clash was as yet by no means certain.

Amherst settled down for the winter at New York and the English-speaking world resounded with his praise. The Commons "resolved, *nemine contradicente*, that the thanks of this house be given to Major-General Amherst for the services he has done to his king and country; and that Mr. Speaker do signify the same to him." (*Journal of the House of Commons*.) Massachusetts was no less appreciative. When a precinct of one of her western towns petitioned to be made a separate entity, the Great and General Court enacted that it "be and hereby is erected into a separate and distinct district by the name of Amherst." (*Acts and Resolves of the Province of Massachusetts-Bay, 1758-59*, Chap. 12.)

The choice of an appellation for the new district rested with Governor Pownall; for, according to colonial custom, when a bill of this kind was passed by the legislature, a space was left for the name, the blank being filled in by the chief magistrate of the province. (Carpenter and Morehouse's *History of Amherst, Mass.*) Thus, it came about that one of the most beautiful of New England towns, lying among the hills of the Connecticut Valley, received the name of Amherst, a name which it was to share with an institution of learning founded there in the early years of the next century. New Hampshire was not far behind the Bay Colony in honouring the hero of the hour.

Less than a year after the christening of Amherst, Massachusetts, the northern province followed suit and conferred upon the township of Souhegan West, No. 3, the more euphonious name of the commander-in-chief. (D. F. Secomb's *History of Amherst*, N. H.) Before many months had passed away Virginia divided one of her counties into three parts and called one of them Amherst. (Hening's *Statutes of Virginia, I, Geo. III*, Ch. xx.) From these three sources the name has sped across the continent until today a dozen places in the United States bear the appellation of the conqueror of Louisburg.

The monotony of the winter at New York was broken by little except the report of marauding Indians in the vicinity of Fort Edward, at the bend of the Hudson. Much to Amherst's disgust "these scoundrels" got away unpunished, and the general's only satisfaction lay in characterizing as "a pack of lazy, rum-drinking people," those whom he gladly would have dispatched with his sword. The general was distinctly bored with the scene of his activities. In a letter to Lord George Sackville, one finds his impressions of America. It is evident that they were deeply tinged with homesickness, for in speaking of a friend's intended return to England Amherst expressed his sentiments in these words:

> 'Tis the place that everybody here thinks of going to. I do not, as long as the war lasts; when that is over—which I promise you, I will do all I can to finish in a right way—I will then rather hold a plough at Riverhead, than take here all that can be given to me. (*Stopford-Sackville Manuscripts*, vol. ii.)

The home-loving Englishman was obsessed with fear that one reward for the victories he fully expected to achieve might be the office of Governor of New York, which he "would rather not be obliged to refuse." With this in view he begged his aristocratic friend to do all in his power to prevent any such calamity from taking place. That his fears were not groundless we shall see, for in the ensuing year, the governorship of Virginia, (Torrens' *History of Cabinets*, ii), was given to Jeffery Amherst as a long-deferred reward for the conquest of Louisburg.

AREA OF FORT EDWARD

CHAPTER 7

Ticonderoga

His Majesty having nothing so much at heart as to improve the great and important advantages gained the last campaign, as well as to repair the disappointment at Ticonderoga, and by the most vigorous and decisive efforts, to establish, by the blessing of God on his arms, His Majesty's just and indubitable Rights, and to avert all future dangers to His Majesty's subjects in North America, I am now to acquaint you that the king has come to a resolution to allot an adequate proportion of his forces in North America amounting to 12,005 men, to make an attack upon Quebec, by the River St. Lawrence against which place they are to proceed from Louisburg, as early in the year, as on or about, the 7th of May, if the season shall happen to permit, under the direction of Brigadier-Genl. Wolfe, whom the king has appointed for the command of that operation, and who will have the rank of major-general, for that expedition only. (Kimball's *Pitt Correspondence*, i.)

This lengthy mandate, which Amherst received from William Pitt in March, 1759, practically sealed the fate of New France. When Wolfe returned to England in the autumn of 1758, with the hope of being employed in Germany in the next campaign, he discovered that Pitt had expected him to stay in the New World and to continue the good work begun there. The young brigadier smoothed the ruffled feathers of the minister with a declaration of his readiness to serve "in America, and particularly in the river St. Lawrence," (Willson's, *Wolfe*), and it was not long before he once more embarked upon the uncongenial sea with the ship's prow turned toward the rendezvous at Louisburg.

Although Amherst was commander-in-chief in America, the expedition against the capital of New France was so distinct in its field and so important in its bearing upon the conquest of Canada, that Wolfe was given a locally independent command analogous to that enjoyed by Nelson at the Nile. (William Wood's *Fight for Canada*.) In all other respects he was Amherst's subordinate. As the commander-in-chief remarked in a letter to Lord George Sackville:

> Quebec is everything, and I am not sure it is not the easiest, as well as the greatest plan to be pursued. (*Stopford-Sackville Manuscripts*, ii.)

And it sometimes seems as if Amherst were to play second fiddle to Wolfe in the operations of the coming year.

Such was hardly the case, however, the illusion being due to the fact that we look at the St. Lawrence expedition through the magnifying lens of the Plains of Abraham, whereas in the winter of 1758 and 1759 the menacing posts of the French at Crown Point and Ticonderoga loomed much larger than Quebec to the eyes of Englishmen on either side of the Atlantic. The capture of Quebec would be of great advantage to England and a feather in the cap of whatever commander accomplished it; but the more serious work of the campaign lay in expelling the enemy from northern New York and in relieving the strategic centre of the British colonies from the great pressure in that quarter. Time and again the English had attempted to break through this threatening Gallic barrier; but always in vain. Now the task fell to Amherst.

In the same letter in which Pitt announced his intention to give Wolfe an independent command, he outlined the operations "which, from their importance, difficulty and extent" must be undertaken by the commander-in-chief. First and foremost, Amherst was to make an irruption into Canada, either by the way of Crown Point, or by a western route with an attack upon the enemy's post at La Galette, where the many spires and smoking chimneys of Ogdensburg now picket the St. Lawrence. The objective of such an invasion was Montreal or Quebec, or both. Secondly, the port of Oswego, which had been destroyed by Montcalm two years before, must be re-established.

The third part of the program was left to Amherst's discretion, but Pitt expressed a hope that the general would find practicable an enterprise against the French fort at Niagara. These instructions make it clear that the war was no longer one of boundaries but one of conquest. At last England had adopted the principle, *Delenda est Canada,*

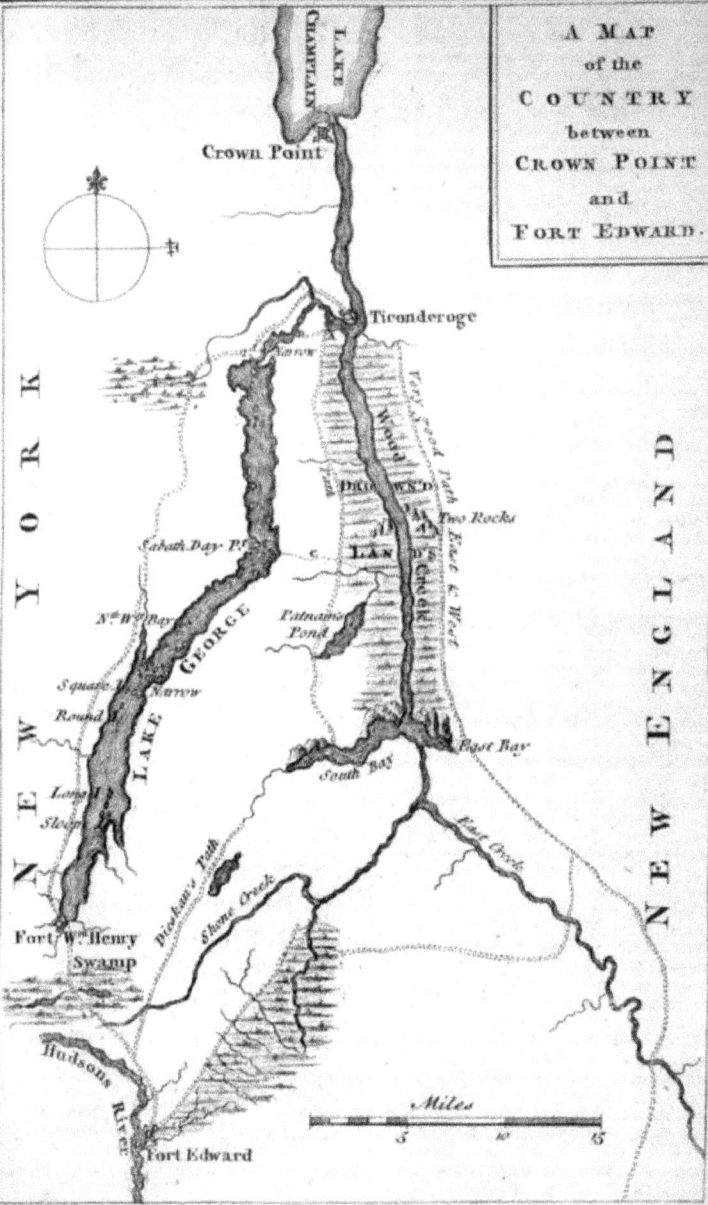

A MAP
of the
COUNTRY
between
CROWN POINT
and
FORT EDWARD.

LAKE CHAMPLAIN

Crown Point

Ticonderoge

Narrow

Very Great Path to Wood

DROWN'D LAN D'S Creek

Two Rocks

River & West

Sabath Day P.

Patnam's Pond

N.W Bay

LAKE GEORGE

Square I.

Narrow

Round I.

Long I.

Sleep

East Bay

South Bay

East Creek

Dieskau's Path

Stone Creek

Fort W. Henry

Swamp

Hudsons River

Fort Edward

NEW YORK

NEW ENGLAND

Miles

5   10   15

and she hoped to find a Scipio in Jeffery Amherst.

While Wolfe, intoxicated with the prospect of great victories over the French, strutted up and down, and alarmed Pitt for the future of the expedition which he had intrusted to such hands, (Mahon's *History of England*, ii), the commander-in-chief was busy with preparations for the year's work. Since the campaign in the lakes would require boats, and crews to man the oars, Amherst took Time by the forelock and advertised for "*batteau* men," even before the snow began to disappear. Equally important was the question of land-transportation, for which the general made provision by employing the winter months in the construction of carts and wagons; for he knew that the supply of vehicles among the country people was inadequate and unreliable. (Kimball's *Pitt Correspondence*, ii.)

The arms of the infantry were repaired and worn-out muskets were replaced by those captured at Louisburg. The latter were much needed, for, in Amherst's own words, the provincial troops "were far from being regular as they ought to have been" in turning in their arms at the end of the last campaign. In the previous year Pitt had inaugurated the policy of furnishing the colonial volunteers with everything except clothing and pay, which he left to the several provinces, (*Ibid.*, i.), and it is to be surmised that many a New England lad availed himself of His Majesty's generosity to carry home a musket as a useful souvenir of his summer's military service.

Towards the end of the winter a report came from Fort Edward telling of a skirmish between the French garrison at Ticonderoga and a handful of regulars, rangers, and Indians under the redoubtable Major Rogers. The excursion seems to have been undertaken merely as an outlet for the pent-up energies of the men stationed at the bend of the Hudson; but the leader brought back with him four scalps and half a dozen prisoners, besides a sketch of the intrenchments and fort, which he hoped might be useful to the commander-in-chief. A raid of this kind was hardly consonant with Amherst's notions of warfare, but it reduced the French by thirty men, more or less, while the marauders lost only three.

If Rogers and his adventurous companions found that the excitement recompensed them for the pains of frost-bite, he had no objection to their prowling about on snow-shoes and bagging what game they could. Parallel depredations of a more remunerative nature were carried on by New York privateers, who at one swoop captured half of a fleet of French merchant-men and brought in prizes to the value

AN INDIAN WEARING SNOW-SHOES

of over £100,000. With these occupations and diversions, the long winter passed, and gave way to a more active spring.

In a letter to the governors of the American colonies Pitt had urged them to provide twenty thousand provincial troops for the campaign of 1759, leaving to the discretion and zeal of each community the quota which it would furnish. In New England the response to the call was gratifying. The Massachusetts assembly agreed to send five thousand men, and a few weeks later Pownall, the popular governor of the Bay Colony, induced them to make provision for fifteen hundred more, although this required a bounty of more than 10 per man. (*Ibid.*, ii.)

Connecticut was not far behind with five thousand, while New York contributed about twenty-five hundred recruits. (*Calendar of Home Office Papers, 1760-1765.*) The other colonies north of the Carolinas complied with Pitt's requisition to a certain extent, with the exception of Pennsylvania and Maryland; these two provinces soon demanded Amherst's personal attention.

It was no mere coincidence that the two proprietary colonies were the two which declined to furnish troops for an attack upon the common enemy. In each case the cause lay in an irrepressible conflict between the proprietors and the inhabitants, and the principle at stake was one of taxation. In order to join forces with the neighbouring colonies in the campaign of 1759, the Pennsylvania assembly agreed to create £100,000 in bills of credit, based on a tax on all property, including that owned by the Penns. (Winfred T. Root's Relations of Pennsylvania with the British Government, 1696-1765.) This appears to us to be a just apportionment, but the proprietors entertained a different view. They were quite ready to pay taxes on lands from which they derived rent, but refused to have a penny levied upon their great tracts of ungranted domain. (Channing's *History of the United States*, ii.)

The governor, being under a bond of £5000 to the proprietors to obey their orders, could not give his assent to the supply bill in its original form; therefore, he amended it to exclude all their estates except the quit-rents and appropriated tracts. At such a proposition the House rose up in its wrath and declared that the governor had no power to change money bills. Whether the Assembly was right or not, Brigadier Stanwix, who was the chief army officer in the colony, took its protest as his cue, and asked Amherst to come to Philadelphia and break the deadlock; otherwise, there would be little prospect of a Pennsylvania contingent to the British forces in North America.

The commander-in-chief lost no time in starting for the scene of the political wrangle. He had contemplated a visit to the Delaware earlier in the season to discuss Indian affairs with the governors of the central colonies and Virginia, but the proposed congress of magistrates never actually met and the trip to Philadelphia had been given up. Now his presence was much needed in the Quaker capital, and on the morning of April 7, General Amherst, accompanied by his brother William, and a few other gentlemen, embarked upon a sloop and set out for the Jersey shore. They reached Elizabeth about noon, whence, after resting and refreshing themselves with "tea at West's" they continued on their way, arriving at New Brunswick before sundown.

From there the route lay through Trenton and Bristol. At noon of the third day Amherst got his first glimpse of the most populous town in the colonies, and soon took up his quarters at one "Mr. Griffith's, Quaker." (*Montresor's Journals*.) The next two days were full of business for the commander-in-chief. The supply bill must be passed, and Amherst took the matter seriously in hand. First, he talked to the Speaker of the Assembly and to some of the leading members, but all the arts of argumentation and persuasion were useless. The popular branch of the government cared more for the principle at stake than for the reputation of the province. Failing in this attack, the general resorted to a message, which he thought would stir the dormant patriotism of the legislators; "but that had not the consequence I designed." (Kimball's *Pitt Correspondence*, ii.)

The Assembly remained obdurate, and Amherst was forced to confess himself beaten. There remained but one way to cut the Gordian knot—the governor must disobey the proprietors' instructions and pass the supply bill with all its provisions. As long as his purposes could be accomplished in a legal way Amherst was careful to remain within the law; but in a case of emergency, he had no scruples against ignoring such sanctions, if they interfered with what he saw clearly to be the best course. This was true in 1780 when he suppressed the Gordon Riots with an iron hand, and his attitude was the same in 1759.

Governor Denny, like most provincial governors, was between the upper and the nether millstone. On the one hand he was under a bond of £5,000 to the Penns to obey their orders; on the other, he was dependent upon the Assembly for his salary and the expenses of government. It was the proverbial choice between the devil and the deep sea. Just which Denny would have chosen, if left to himself, it is difficult to say; but Amherst's influence tipped the scales in favour of the inhabitants of Pennsylvania. When the commander-in-chief left Philadelphia, he wrote to the governor asking him to waive his instructions and to give his assent to the supply bill as brought in by the Assembly. The exigent circumstances justified such action in the mind of the general and he promised to explain the situation to the ministry. (*Minutes of the Provincial Council of Pennsylvania*, better known as *Pennsylvania Colonial Records*, viii.)

Denny did as Amherst requested. Pennsylvania furnished over three thousand troops for the coming campaign, (*Calendar of Home Office Papers*, 1760-1765), and the governor was voted his stipend of £1,000. As far as Amherst was concerned, the incident was closed; but Denny's troubles had only begun. The proprietors looked upon his remuneration as a bribe and threatened to take action against the bond. This peril was averted by the decision of the Assembly to indemnify the governor in case the Penns went to such extremes, but Denny was dismissed from office. (Root's *Pennsylvania and Great Britain*, 1696-1765.) One cannot help thinking that the relations between Amherst and the fallen magistrate must have been considerably strained by the consequences of the general's request in the spring of 1759; but after all, it was only a request, and Denny had no one but himself to blame for the course of action pursued on that occasion.

★★★★★★

Maryland was even more refractory than Pennsylvania. Amherst wrote to Governor Sharpe every year, requiring Maryland's quota of provincial troops, but on each occasion the lower house granted it only under conditions which were not to be thought of by the upper house. The Maryland contingent was non-existent in this period. In 1762 the requisition was only 84 men, but even these were not forthcoming. *Maryland Archives*, vol. ix & xiv.

★★★★★★

While at Philadelphia Amherst conferred with another group of men. These were the deputies of the Iroquois and other Indian tribes, who desired specific information concerning a treaty entered into with the English in the previous year. Ever since Braddock's defeat the Delawares and Shawanoes had been in open hostility to the British and had displayed their animosity by frequent attacks upon the frontier settlements of Pennsylvania. The Iroquois, although nominally subjects of the King of Great Britain, wavered between the exhortations of their English champion, Sir William Johnson, and the cajoleries of the cunning Frenchmen. In each tribe there was an English party and one that favoured the enemy.

While pushing his tedious way towards Fort Duquesne in the summer of 1758, Brigadier Forbes brought about "a general convention of the Indians," which met at the town of Easton in October. The session lasted almost three weeks and terminated in a burial of the hatchet, "so deep that nobody can dig it up again." (Parkman's *Montcalm and Wolfe*, ii.) The pacification thus achieved extended also to the western Indians who were tributary to the Iroquois, and promised to remove one great annoyance to British arms in the present war. On her part England, or rather Pennsylvania, promised to make no more settlements west of the Alleghanies. (Clarence W. Alvord's *Genesis of the Proclamation of 1763*.)

During the winter the untutored mind seems to have been seized with an access of suspicion, and Indian deputies flocked to Philadelphia to ascertain the exact terms of the agreement. There Amherst received them and gave assurance that the English would live up to their obligations, (*Journals of the House of Burgesses of Virginia 1761-1765*), whereupon the red men, with restored confidence, grunted their satisfaction and departed for the wilderness, leaving the general to follow up his advantage by directing Sir William Johnson to engage as many Indians as possible for the year's operations. (Brodhead's *New York Documents*, vii.)

With at least one result to show for his southern excursion, Amherst turned his face once more towards New York, and left Philadelphia on April 11, a little before midday. The journey was broken by dinner at Burlington, whence the party went on to Crosswicks to spend the night. The next day carried them as far as Perth Amboy, where the general was entertained at dinner by Governor Bernard— the same gentleman who was soon to be transferred to Massachusetts and to earn a baronetcy by exasperating the people to the point of rebellion. Amherst reviewed a regiment quartered in the town, and at six o'clock in the evening took leave of his well-meaning host. Going on board his sloop, the general sailed across the bay and arrived at New York early the next morning. (*Montresors Journals.*)

Amherst's first care was to dispatch to Louisburg the troops destined for Wolfe's expedition against Quebec. When this was done, he turned his attention towards his own campaign. Pitt had appointed Albany as the rendezvous, and May 1 as the date for the assembling of the regular and provincial forces under Amherst's immediate command.

The general intended that he, at least, should be punctual. Leaving his headquarters on the afternoon of April 28, he went on board the official sloop, while the cannon at the Battery roared out a farewell salute of fifteen guns. (*Montresors Journals*.) Apparently, the winds did not favour a voyage up the Hudson, for the boats lay at anchor for more than twenty-four hours and prevented the commander-in-chief from making the early start which he so much desired. Before long, however, Amherst ascended the picturesque stream and arrived at Albany on the third day of May. Not a regiment of the provincial contingent had yet appeared at the rendezvous on the Hudson; but while he waited for the Americans to come in, the general made good use of his time by planning and organising an expedition against Fort Niagara, the French post between Lake Ontario and Lake Erie.

Pitt's instructions to Amherst had suggested "some enterprise" against Niagara, "the success of which would so greatly contribute to establish the uninterrupted dominion of that Lake, and, at the same time effectually cut off the communication between Canada and the French settlements to the South." The minister's idea was excellent, but he made his proposal before hearing of the outcome of Forbes' operations against Fort Duquesne. The latter undertaking was so slow and tedious that Pitt doubtless considered its success in that year to be dubious at best. Accordingly, he intended to cut the French line of communication through the Lakes at Niagara, and thus render the Ohio posts and those to the westward untenable if not useless.

In making this proposition, however, the Secretary of State left its adoption or rejection wholly to the discretion of Amherst. (Kimball's *Pitt Correspondence*, ii.) The general's decision to send five thousand men to capture a fortress which was in no sense a menace to the British, was an error in judgment scarcely justified even by the success of the enterprise. The troops thus drawn off from the main army might have been better employed by the commander-in-chief in pushing forward his "irruption into Canada" by the way of Lake Champlain, (Von Ruville's *William Pitt*, ii); 2 but with his mind made up to add the capture of Niagara to the growing list of victories, Amherst sent for Sir William Johnson, the manipulator of the Iroquois, to arrange for a goodly supply of Indian auxiliaries.

On the fourth of May the general and the frontier baronet met at Schenectady. Although the former would not confide his intentions to Sir William lest the secret leak out through him to his Indians, and thence to the enemy, Johnson was positive in his assertion that the *sachems* were "firm to the English" and that he was certain of eight hundred savages who would go with him.

Thus reassured, Amherst awaited the arrival of Brigadier-General Prideaux, whom he had selected to command the expedition. By the middle of the month the prospective leader was at Albany, and the commander-in-chief immediately gave him his instructions. Prideaux was to ascend the Mohawk and continue westward to Oswego: there he must leave about half of his force to build a fort, in accordance with Pitt's injunction, and with the rest of his men take Niagara. For this undertaking Amherst told off about five thousand regulars and provincials, of whom a slight majority were men from New York. These forces were to be increased at Oswego by as many Indians as Sir William Johnson could collect and retain. (*Amherst to Johnson, A. and W. I.,* Vol. 90, No. 63, in the Public Record Office.) On May 20 the Niagara expedition started on its way up the Mohawk.

Meanwhile Amherst patiently awaited the assembling of the colonial contingent of his army. The first troops to put in an appearance came from Rhode Island; then came the New Yorkers, who were closely followed by the men from Massachusetts. The month of May was exceptionally rainy, and the Hudson, rising "on a sudden," still further contributed to Amherst's difficulties. At first the general rejoiced in the high water because it promised to facilitate transportation up the rivers, but when the swelling of the stream was increased by a "very violent rain," some of the soldiers were given unlooked-for employment. Prideaux had collected a large number of boats at Schenectady for the use of his expedition. The unexpected inundation floated them off, and down the Mohawk sped the irresponsible craft, while the distressed brigadier sent to Amherst for help.

The commander-in-chief at once dispatched a body of men to the river with instructions to stop the runaway boats before they reached "the Great Falls." It was no easy task, but the feat was accomplished, fairly successfully, and only a few members of the unruly flotilla eluded their would-be captors and crashed to pieces in the seventy-foot plunge at Cohoes. While the wreckage of these *bateaux* swept by Albany on the turgid waters of the Hudson, Amherst, impatient of longer delay, took what troops he had and moved up the river. On the third of June he was at Half Moon. From there the army rowed up stream to Stillwater, Saratoga, and finally to Fort Edward, which stood at the sharp bend of the Hudson. Here Amherst called a halt, and gave the rain-drenched men, who, he declared, had "not a dry thread on them," an opportunity to recuperate from their hard tug against the rushing current.

From the outset of the campaign the general made a firm stand for two principles, temperance and humanity. We have seen that after the Boston episode Amherst was determined to prevent any repetition of that debauch. In the spring of 1759, he made this resolve an actuality by prohibiting the use of rum or other spirituous liquors in the forces under his command. (Bonney's *Legacy of Historical Gleanings*, i.)

This "prohibition" was a far greater denial to the army than the twentieth-century mind can easily comprehend, for our ancestors looked upon rum as a necessary of life. The farmer in the hay-field, the deacon at the church-raising, and the soldier on the march, each required his daily allowance of the cheap alcoholic stimulant, and regarded it as a preventive against the many ills which threatened his existence. Twenty years later the American soldiers in the Revolution refused to fight because their supply of rum was cut off; but Amherst succeeded in carrying out his temperance policy by substituting for the stronger liquor an interesting drink called spruce beer.

This beverage was brewed from the fresh green tips of spruce branches with a generous admixture of molasses, and was held to be efficacious as a cure for scurvy and other diseases which were likely to attack an army in the wilderness. Amherst was a confirmed believer in its medicinal virtue, for his men at Louisburg had fortified their constitutions with it—and had proved at least its innocuousness. (Knox's *Journal*, i.) In the present campaign spruce beer was brewed in great quantities and "served at cost," a half-penny per quart. (*Commissary Wilson's Orderly Book*; republished in *Narratives of the French and Indian War: 3*, Leonaur 2019.)

Later in the summer when the army became sickly, the general attributed the men's illness to their custom of "drinking water wherever they find it" and tried to overcome the trouble by his sovereign remedy. (Massachusetts Historical Society's *Proceedings*, viii.) The provincials, on the contrary, probably considered the prohibition of rum as the chief cause of their malady; and who shall say which attribution, if either, was correct?

The humanity of Jeffery Amherst displayed itself in his general orders of June 12, that no scouting parties or others in the army under his command should scalp any women or children belonging to the enemy. But if such deeds were perpetrated by the French upon the English, the general declared that they should be avenged by the death of two men of the enemy for every woman or child "murthered." The mathematics of this retribution attest the commander's detestation of the promiscuous butchering which had marked French and Indian raids upon the frontier settlements. One of these had just occurred in central New York and occasioned the expression of Amherst's sentiments in the general orders just mentioned. Lest there be any misunderstanding of his intentions, the general took pains to send an officer with a flag of truce to present a copy of his edict to the French officer in command at Ticonderoga.

Before dawn on the twenty-first of June the British camp at Fort Edward was the scene of great activity. Tents were struck at three o'clock; by four, the artillery and regiments began to embark upon the diminutive Hudson, whose course they were to follow as far as possible in the direction of Lake George. At ten o'clock Amherst left Fort Edward and followed the army in its progress through the wilderness. The advance-guard consisted of Rogers' Rangers and some light infantry, who kept flanking parties on either side to insure the forces against a surprise. The march was accomplished with such celerity that at sundown of that long June day the British emerged from the dark forest and encamped on the southern shores of the mountain lake.

Here occurred a discouragingly long delay of one month, much of the time being spent in building or repairing boats and rafts to carry the troops and artillery across the lake. At the end of his bungling campaign in these parts during the previous year Abercromby carefully sank the sloop-of-war which had patrolled those placid waters, and hid the whale boats in the woods lest they fall into the hands of the enemy. (Kimball's *Pitt Correspondence*, i.) It seems as if Amherst might have had these necessary means of transportation put in commission before the arrival of his army; but apparently little or nothing had been done, and while part of the troops were busy with this work, the general found occupation for the rest in the construction of a fort of no mean dimensions.

The latter undertaking was begun in earnest early in July, but only one bastion was ever finished, for the outcome of the campaign deprived a stronghold at this point of any *raison d'être*. Much blame has been heaped upon Amherst for building Fort George, as it was called, and his critics have lamented the time and energy wasted upon a needless post; but to do the general justice, it should be pointed out that Pitt had specifically directed him to build a fort "at Lake George," (Kimball's *Pitt Correspondence*, i), and that Amherst had promised to do so. In the light of what actually happened the construction of Fort George seems an unnecessary precaution, but Amherst, although confident, could not be sure of victory, where his predecessor had found defeat. If Fortune turned against the British arms, it would be well to have a fortified base nearer the scene of hostilities than Fort Edward.

As these shores had been the annual mustering place of armies for the past four years—and occasionally a battle-ground for the French and the English—it is not surprising that the soldiers were continually discovering pieces of old ammunition and discarded muskets. This led Amherst to issue the following amusing order:

> As shells and shot may have been left by the enemy or may be fired from the enemy during the campaign, which will be of use in firing back to them again, the following prices shall be allowed to those who shall pick them up and deliver them to the commanding officer at the artillery park: for a 13-inch shell, one dollar; an eight-inch shell, a quarter dollar; large shot, 2d each, smaller at 1d each. (*Wilson's Orderly Book.*)

Five shillings was the price "for every good repairable fire-lock." This quaint table of values makes one realise more vividly, perhaps, than any other one thing the difference between eighteenth-century warfare and that practised in our more efficient, if less economical, age.

Fort Ticonderoga stood upon a lonely promontory between the outlet of Lake George and the narrow southern end of Lake Champlain. On three sides the position was protected by rocky shores; on the fourth, by a swamp and by the deadly breastwork that Montcalm had erected to repel Abercromby. The fort itself was square, with four bastions, and the French, with their happy faculty for picturesque and appropriate names, called it *Carrillon*, which means a square piece of iron; so far it had justified its appellation. When Abercromby attempted its capture, the place was commanded by Montcalm; but now the gallant marquis was defending Quebec from the onslaught of the British under Wolfe and Saunders.

In his stead Bourlamaque, who had been dangerously wounded in the battle of the previous July, was in charge of Carrillon with instructions to hold the post if possible, but if overborne by numbers, to fall back to Isle aux Noix at the northern end of Lake Champlain. His forces were nearly equal to those at Montcalm's disposal in 1758, while Amherst's army was much smaller than that which Abercromby had hurled at the enemy's intrenchment in vain, and the prospect of smart fighting and a regular siege was before the English as they broke up their camp and prepared to embark upon Lake George.

On the morning of July 21, Amherst and his army of about eleven thousand men got into the boats and pushed out upon the mountain-rimmed lake. The departure was not without accidents. Many of the craft were so unseaworthy that no sooner were they loaded than they had to be relieved of their cargoes to prevent them from sinking One *bateau*, carrying a hundred barrels of gunpowder, went to the bottom in company with a raft overloaded with two heavy mortars. These mishaps provoked the general, but leaving the sunken vessels where they were, he went on board the *radeau Invincible*, which resembled both a raft and a boat, and gave the signal to advance. The flotilla presented a remarkable spectacle as it proceeded down the lake.

First came a flatbottomed affair mounting a three-pounder, then the vanguard of light infantry in forty whale-boats, followed by the main army, with the sloop *Halifax*, which had been reclaimed from the depths, bringing up the rear. The men used their blankets for sails whenever the fresh wind allowed them to do so, (Knox's Journal, i), and thus the long procession steered its way between the islands and across the broads. A little before dark Amherst made the signal to bring-to, and the army passed an uncomfortably windy night *en bateau*. At daybreak the boats pushed on until they reached the outlet of the lake, where the troops made an orderly landing at nearly the same spot chosen by Abercromby for his disembarkation the year before.

When all were on shore the general put the army in motion towards the dreaded fortress, and before long the advance-guard encountered a small band of French and Indians, who made only a feeble resistance. The British then found themselves on some heights, upon which they rested and waited for the artillery to come up, for Amherst had no intention of repeating the blunder of his predecessor. Bourlamaque, perceiving his opponent's plans, became uneasy: the intrenchments that had wrought destruction upon Abercromby's forces could not hold out for any length of time against regular approaches supported by artillery, and the Frenchman decided to retreat into the fort.

Amherst, advancing cautiously on the forenoon of July 23, found the famous lines abandoned, and at once encamped in front of them, where he was well sheltered from the cannon of Carrillon. So far Fortune had indeed smiled upon the general. But even better luck awaited him, for Bourlamaque, despairing of successful resistance, had already left Ticonderoga, and was hurrying toward Crown Point with all but

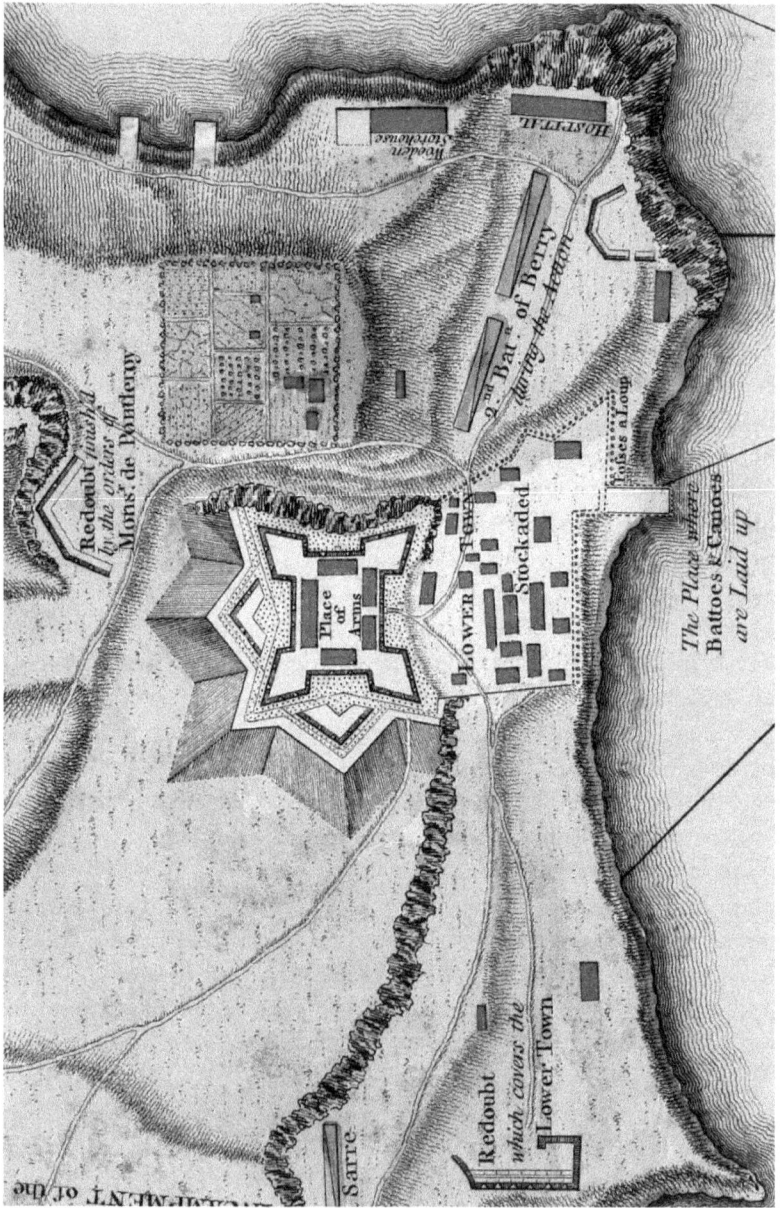

The Place where
Battoes & Canoes
are laid up

HOSPITAL

Wooden
Storehouse

2d. Batn. of Berry
during the Action

Loses a Loop

Stockaded

LOWER TOWN

Redoubt finish'd
by the orders of
Monsr. de Bontecqy

Place
of
Arms

Sarre

Redoubt
which covers the
Lower Town

MENT of the

four hundred of his troops. The enemy's conduct was inglorious, yet after the surrender of the lines this was doubtless their wisest course.

Meanwhile the detachment left at Carrillon fully occupied the attention of the British. The fort maintained a brisk fire, and in its dying gasp brought grief to the English Army. A cannon-shot, plunging over the reversed intrenchments, killed Colonel Roger Townshend. This officer has been called the Lord Howe of Amherst's army, and in many ways the metaphor is a good one. He was young and handsome, and came of a family that had belonged to the peerage ever since the Restoration. In 1758, Sir John Ligonier sent him to Louisburg as adjutant-general, in which capacity he acquitted himself so well that Amherst gave him the same duties for the present campaign. Had Roger Townshend not met sudden death at the lines of Ticonderoga, it is probable that he would have won a reputation comparable to that of either of his two elder brothers.

One of these succeeded to Wolfe's command and received the surrender of Quebec after the battle on the Plains of Abraham. The other was a dashing politician and a brilliant speaker, who is remembered chiefly for a scintillating speech, which justly gained its author the sobriquet of "Champagne" Townshend, and for certain revenue acts that were among the causes of the American Revolution. Although Roger Townshend failed to achieve the fame and notoriety of his brothers, he was "deservedly lamented by the general and the army," and his memory, like that of Lord Howe, is preserved by a monument in Westminster Abbey.

Amherst was aware of the flight of Bourlamaque but the good news by no means led him to precipitate action. He waited for his artillery to come up to the lines, planted batteries, and completed preparations for a regular siege. (Brodhead's *New York Documents*, vol. vii.) The evening of July 26, found everything arranged as the general would have it; at break of day, he intended to open fire. Suddenly at ten o'clock the silence of the forest night was broken by the roar of an explosion, and turning their eyes towards the French fortress, the English beheld a great conflagration rising above the treetops. Some deserters from the enemy reported that the garrison had abandoned the fort and were then hurrying down Lake Champlain in the direction of Crown Point. Amherst's first thought was to extinguish the fire and to capture Carrillon intact, but the French, before departing, had cleverly loaded all their guns and musketry to the muzzles and these, being automatically discharged by the flames, kept the British at a safe distance until the next day. The general, therefore, contented himself with harassing the rear of the retreating *bateaux* of the garrison, capturing a few prisoners and a goodly supply of powder.

It is possible that amid the crackle of the conflagration and the irregular explosions of the cannon, Jeffery Amherst thought of the extraordinary coincidence of events which had marked July 26 during the last two years of his life. The same month and day had witnessed in 1757 the Battle of Hastenbeck, in 1758 the surrender of Louisburg, and now in 1759 the downfall of Ticonderoga.

Early the next morning a sergeant of the regulars asked permission to venture into the smoking ruins in order to bring away a French flag which still waved over the abandoned fortress. Amherst readily gave his consent, and in a short time the bold volunteer returned with the Bourbon colours. At last, Carrillon, the destroyer of armies and the distressing thorn of the northern colonists, was no more.

Once again, the general's younger brother, Colonel William Amherst, sped across the seas to carry encouraging tidings to Old England, while America rejoiced and was exceeding glad. Amherst appointed the twenty-ninth of July as a day of thanksgiving in the camp, (Samuel Niles' *Summary Historical Narrative*, etc., printed in the Massachusetts Historical Society's, *Collections*, series iv, vol. v), and it is to be suspected that on that occasion the ban on stimulants was temporarily raised; for Colonel Montresor, who was at the head of Lake George, recorded in his journal under July 28:

> We celebrated the taking of Ticonderoga by making bonfires on the highest part of the camp and giving the workmen one gill of rum apiece.

After these demonstrations were over, the general turned the energies of his men to levelling the trenches and batteries, and to raising the boats, which the fleeing army had sunk in the lake, lest they fall into the hands of the English in good condition. When the fire in the fort was finally extinguished, Amherst discovered that only a small part of the whole structure had been ruined by the explosion and the flames, and he ordered it to be repaired by four provincial regiments under the superintendence of Colonel Schuyler.

Having seen these enterprises well under way, the deliberate commander-in-chief assembled the larger part of his forces and advanced down the Narrows of Lake Champlain. Fort Frederic, as the French called their long-established post at Crown Point, commanded these inland waters, and its massive stone tower, bristling with cannon, bade defiance to the rightful occupants of the region. Thither Bourlamaque had fled, and thither Amherst intended to follow and to conquer.

HIGHLANDERS AT TICONDEROGA

Lake Champlain

At noon on August 1, a scouting party came to the camp at Ticonderoga announcing that the enemy had abandoned Crown Point
and were headed northward' down the lake. The next day a heavy rain
prevented Amherst from confirming the report; but on the fourth the
British Army resumed its victorious journey, landed on the beautiful
promontory, and took possession of Fort Frederic, which was intact:
but undefended. The view from the new position was superb. On one
side the noble peaks of the Adirondacks, sweeping upward from the
western shores of Lake Champlain, demand the admiration of every
lover of Nature, while in the other direction meadows and gentle,
rolling country rise from the narrowing waters, and invite one to the
fertile fields of Vermont.

Enjoyment of the scenery, combined with elation over two easy
victories, must have made the soldiers feel that their progress through
the wilderness was a *fête champêtre* rather than a campaign, and the
illusion was increased by the advent of more good news. That very
evening a lieutenant arrived with a letter from Sir William Johnson
enclosing the capitulation of Niagara. Thus, at almost the same moment two gates to New France were thrown open, and there seemed
to be little doubt that the proposed "irruption into Canada" would
take place in the immediate future.

The enterprise against Niagara had been entrusted to Brigadier-
General Prideaux. According to his instructions he had proceeded
to Oswego, where he left nearly half his force under Colonel Haldimand to build a fort. With the remaining troops he went westward
to Niagara, and laid siege to the enemy's fortress, which was strong
and exceptionally well built. Its commander, Captain Pouchot, an excellent officer and a gallant fighter, had about six hundred men with

whom to defend the post, but his chief reliance was upon a motley band of bush-rangers and savages that had gathered on the southern side of Lake Erie with the intention of recovering Pittsburgh from the English.

These half-civilized forces were now called to the relief of Niagara, and Pouchot bent every energy to hold out until they arrived. Prideaux, who was joined by Sir William Johnson and about a thousand Indian warriors of the Five Nations, commenced a regular siege with great vigour. Unfortunately, the brigadier, while walking in the trenches one evening, was killed by the explosion of a British shell, which burst just as it left the mouth of a coehorn. In his pocket was found a written order for Sir William Johnson to take command of the expedition. (Niles' *History of the French and Indian Wars*.) Accordingly, the Baronet did so, continuing the same aggressive tactics which his ill-fated predecessor had employed until the garrison was wellnigh exhausted.

On the morning of July 24, Pouchot heard distant firing which told him of the approach of succour; but his hopes were dashed when from a bastion of the battered fortress he watched a short but desperate battle between the British and the party that had come to relieve Niagara. In an hour's time the French were cut to pieces, and those who were fortunate enough to escape hurried back to Lake Erie and thence to Detroit. Johnson's victory was complete. He followed the battle by a brisk cannonade of the fort and at four o'clock sent in a summons to surrender. The gallant Pouchot saw no rational alternative. On the following day, July 25, 1759, Niagara was surrendered to the English, and the French posts in the interior were still further isolated from the capital of New France.

Amherst was overjoyed with the recent victories which he termed "an happy presage of the entire reduction of Canada in this campaign;" (*Records of the Colony of Rhode Island*, vi), but, as usual, he proceeded with the utmost caution. In the first place, he considered it imperative to build at Crown Point a fort which should "secure entirely all His Majesty's dominions that are behind it from the inroads of the enemy and the scalping partys that have infested the whole country," and which should "give great peace and quiet to the king's subjects." The result of this unfortunate conviction was that for two months the British Army remained practically stationary upon the shores of Lake Champlain, while the French, at the opposite end of the lake, awaited its advance with fear and trembling.

The much talked-of "irruption into Canada" was not forthcoming. Granted that a strong fort on the frontier is of great advantage, nevertheless the most enthusiastic champion of Jeffery Amherst must find it difficult to justify this long delay in northern New York. Whatever his reasons may have been, the commander-in-chief refused to pursue the retreating enemy, and settling down at Crown Point, spent two valuable months in building a fort, in cutting a road through the Vermont wilderness, and in brewing spruce beer. The alleged cause of his inaction was that four armed vessels of the French made the advance of his flotilla impossible until the British had an equivalent naval force.

Accordingly, Amherst ordered the construction of a brigantine, a sloop, and a huge raft, eighty-four feet long and twenty feet broad. Ship-building in the forest was not easy at best, and in this case the work was hindered by frequent accidents at the one overworked sawmill. Almost ten weeks passed before the fresh water squadron was in commission. Ships cannot be built in a day, perhaps, but under the circumstances could not Amherst have employed his men better by turning their labour to the speedy creation of a navy instead of to the commencement of a prodigious fort?

It seems, however, that the underlying cause of the long delay was not so much the lack of naval power as it was the temperament of the commander. To a man of Amherst's cautious instincts and methodical habits any other course was impossible. To give chase to the French before his base was securely fortified was not to be thought of by a general as thorough and deliberate as he. Wolfe might rush in where strategists feared to tread, but Amherst always looked before he leaped, and also took care never to lose what had once been gained. If one takes into consideration this attitude of mind, the apparent apathy of the summer of 1759 is comprehensible, although historians will never cease to censure Amherst for the sacrifice of those two months after the occupation of Crown Point.

Be that as it may, what he attempted in that period he did with characteristic thoroughness. The fortifications were planned upon a stupendous scale. For eight weeks sixteen hundred men were kept at work upon the stronghold, (*Wilson's Orderly Book*); and this was but the beginning of a structure, the completion of which required three years of labour and three million pounds sterling. In form it was pentagonal, with walls of solid masonry twenty-five feet thick and twenty feet high. (*Vermont Historical Gazetteer, i.*) The plan also included stone

CROWN POINT AND LAKE CHAMPLAIN

barracks, a parade-ground, and other military accessories, all of which passed into the hands of the energetic Ethan Allen and his renowned Green Mountain Boys at the outbreak of the American Revolution, without a blow being struck on either side. (*Vide Ethan Allen at Ticonderoga During the American War of Independence*; Leonaur 2010.)

Another enterprise undertaken by Amherst while his miniature navy was being built was the construction of a road from the Vermont shore, opposite Crown Point, to Number Four, now Charlestown, New Hampshire, a frontier hamlet on the Connecticut River. The object was "to open a communication from the Massachusetts and New Hampshire governments to Crown Point," and the work was assigned to two hundred rangers under the command of Captain Stark, the future hero of Bennington. (Stark's *General John Stark*, vide also *John Stark of Rogers' Rangers: a Famous Ranger and His Associates During the French & Indian War* by Howard Parker Moore & Caleb Stark: Leonaur 2020)

As a result of these efforts the New Hampshire troops marching to Crown Point a year later, took the cross-country route from Number Four and found a good road all the way from Otter Creek, near Rutland, to the rendezvous. (Belknap's *History of New Hampshire*, i.) Number Four was one of the most exposed places on the frontier. In the previous war, the fort there had defended itself bravely and successfully against a band of French and Indians; now the new road linked it with the stronger post at Crown Point, besides opening up new country for settlement.

This enterprise was sound from a military standpoint and promised to be an aid to the expansion of New Hampshire; but from the point of view of the present campaign, Stark and his companions might have been occupied to better advantage in constructing rafts or rude ships, with which to attack the lake squadron of the enemy.

Amherst also amused himself by sending out exploring expeditions, one to discover the source of the Hudson, another to search out the course of Otter Creek, and still another to follow up the Sable River, not so much to view its famous chasm as to find out whether it afforded a short cut to the St. Lawrence near Ogdensburg. All of these interesting diversions consumed valuable time that might have been devoted to far more practical purposes.

In the meantime, the soldiers worked manfully at building the new fort, a task which, to the provincials at least, was quite as congenial as the more active form of warfare. Their lot was by no means an unenviable one. Behind the captured fort the men discovered three fields of peas, which recall the parable of the loaves and fishes, for if the report is to be trusted, they were "very grateful to the soldiers and served the whole army for three days." (Niles' *History of the French and Indian Wars*.) The long encampment also gives us an opportunity to study Amherst as a disciplinarian. Desertion and mutiny were invariably punished with death; at an early hour in the morning the culprit was shot in front of his regiment in the presence of the entire army.

Lesser offences were expiated with the cat-o'nine-tails, the usual sentence being five hundred or a thousand lashes. One black sheep, already pardoned for desertion on one occasion, had the misfortune to be captured soon after changing sides a second time. When caught by a scouting party the victim was wearing the enemy's uniform, and this time the general had no mercy, but ordered him "to be hanged in his French coat, with a libble on his breast, hanged for deserting to the French" The order goes on to specify that "he is to be hanging all day and at the retreat beating he is to be buried very deep under the gallos, and his French coat with him." (*Wilson's Orderly Book*.) No half-way measures these, and it is to be hoped that the execution *in terrorem* produced the desired effect upon any soldiers who contemplated going over to the enemy. On the other hand, Amherst occasionally tempered justice with mercy, as in the case of a soldier who was condemned to be hanged for thieving: upon the intercession of the man's captain, and a promise of no second offence, the commander-in-chief revoked the sentence and let the prisoner go. (*Ibid.*)

The summer of 1759 was exceptionally rainy, and often the general orders required that the tents of the army be struck at noon, in clear weather, so that the ground might be dried and aired. The sick were cared for even more solicitously. The men were "properly defended from the dampness by dried grass and brushwood," and every fair day witnessed a parade of the disabled, who "marched down to the lake to wash their hands and faces and cleaned themselves." After these required ablutions the men were "kept walking about for an hour," or such time as their strength permitted, while their tents were opened to the sun and air. Considering the abominable lack of hygiene and therapeutics that marked every age before the nineteenth century, we must acknowledge that the methods practiced in the camp at Crown Point were surprising and laudable.

There is a story of Jeffery Amherst which is worth repeating because it illustrates his tact in dealing with both provincials and regulars. While at Ticonderoga a boasting English major declared that no

116

American could lay him upon his back. The challenge was accepted by a young Lieutenant Rice from Connecticut, who, after a long-contested match, tripped his adversary and proved himself the better wrestler. Occasionally when an American wins an athletic victory over one of his British cousins there is a cry of foul play, and the rules of the game are amended to ensure English success in the future.

Such seems to have been the case at Ticonderoga. The vanquished major protested against the Yankee's method of wrestling, and declared that tripping was unfair and unmanly. Rice's answer was not calculated to turn away wrath. High words followed and before long the two men were ready to settle the affair by a duel. The time and place were already appointed, when reports of the quarrel reached the ears of the commander-in-chief. Amherst succeeded in appealing to his countryman's sense of military propriety, and substituted for the proposed exchange of shots a second wrestling-match, under rules agreeable to the Englishman. The arrangement was made over a glass of grog; and after the contest the athletes became firm friends, in spite of the fact that the second match, like the first, was won by the American. (B. J. Lossing's *Pictorial Field-Book of the Revolution*, i.)

While the army was occupied in these various pursuits in the vicinity of Lake Champlain, the news of Amherst's triple victory reached England. Pitt was greatly pleased at the progress of the campaign and embraced the opportunity to extort a reward from the reluctant George II. Ever since the capture of Louisburg the minister had urged that Amherst be given the governorship of Virginia as a token of the king's appreciation, but George had constantly withheld his consent. The reports from Ticonderoga, Niagara, and Crown Point, supplemented by Pitt's petulant threat to resign if his general were not rewarded, put a different aspect on the situation. (Torrens' *History of Cabinets*, ii.)

Therefore, on September 12, 1759, Jeffery Amherst was appointed Governor of Virginia to succeed Lord Loudon. (Acts of the Privy Council, Colonial Series, iv.) The new office sounds as if it were precisely what the general wished to avoid, but as a matter of fact it was a sinecure bringing in £1,500 a year. (*Grenville Correspondence*, iv.) In Virginia titular governors were appointed at different times. These fortunate individuals enjoyed the title and part of the emoluments of the position, while the actual conduct of the government was left to a resident lieutenant-governor. (E. B. Greene's *Provincial Governor*.) For Amherst an office which did not require his presence in America and yet contributed to his income was in every way agreeable, and he gladly accepted the appointment.

Another honour conferred upon him in this summer was promotion to the rank of major-general in the British Army, (Worthington C. Ford's *British Officers Serving in America, 1754-1774*), in contradistinction to his previous grade of colonel, "with the rank of major-general in America." Horace Walpole rarely let an event pass without note or comment of some sort, and his enthusiastic tribute, to Amherst on the occasion of the victory at Ticonderoga deserves quotation:

"We have taken more places and ships in a week than would have set up such pedant nations as Greece and Rome to all futurity. If we did but call Sir William Johnson 'Gulielmus Johnsonus Niagaricus' and Amherst 'Galfridus Amhersta Ticonderogicus' we should be quoted a thousand years hence as the patterns of valour, virtue, and disinterestedness." (*Horace Walpole to the Earl of Strafford*, Sept. 13, 1759.)

In the meantime, the crimson foliage of the tupelos fringing the rocky shores of Lake Champlain heralded the approach of autumn; yet Amherst and his ten thousand men advanced not. Wolfe, almost discouraged before Quebec, waited and hoped for help from his chief. Finally, he could delay operations no longer. The great difficulty in the St. Lawrence expedition had been to engage the French Army outside its defences, and Wolfe's one desperate chance lay in seizing the level heights above the town and thus forcing the hand of his wily adversary, the Marquis of Montcalm.

Early on the morning of September 13, the vanguard of the British forces scaled the almost impassable cliffs that formed the great protection of Quebec, and by the use of a convenient ravine the rest of the troops, with two small cannon, soon occupied the Plains of Abraham, within a mile and a half of the town. There the drill and discipline of the British regiments won the day for England: five days later Quebec and its garrison surrendered. The capital of New France fell, but not without costing England her most dashing soldier; for James Wolfe, like his adversary, Montcalm, was killed on the field of battle.

Even though one has difficulty in being reconciled to Amherst's two months of inaction at Crown Point, it is doubtful whether a more aggressive campaign on his part would have been of greater benefit to his colleague on the St. Lawrence. The mere presence of his army to the southward drew off from Quebec a considerable part of the French forces which otherwise would have made Wolfe's feat impossible. The nineteenth century, in its glorification of the hero of the Plains of Abraham, went so far as to cast aspersions upon Amherst and to lament his "wasted labours" on Lake Champlain; but his contemporaries took a more rational view and realised the value of his army-in-being, although its performances were hardly spectacular. Thomas Hutchinson, the last royal governor of Massachusetts under the charter, possessed the mind of a trained historian, and his judgment of Amherst's behaviour in the summer of 1759 is both enlightening and just:

"It is extremely probable, that, if a great part of the French forces had not been withdrawn from Quebec to attend the motions of General Amherst, the attempt made by General Wolfe must have failed." (Hutchinson's *History of Massachusetts-Bay*, ii.)

Not only was Bourlamaque with thirty-five hundred men kept on tenterhooks of uncertainty at the outlet of Lake Champlain, but Lévis, the second in command at Quebec, was sent up the St. Lawrence with eight hundred men to defend Montreal from an expected descent by the British from Niagara and Oswego. (Bancroft's *History of the United States*, ii; Parkman's *Montcalm and Wolfe*, ii.) Thus, Amherst's apparent failure to co-operate with Wolfe was in reality a great potential aid to the latter's brilliant conquest of the capital of New France.

On the very day when the fate of an empire was decided on the Plains of Abraham, General Amherst issued orders to Major Robert Rogers to set out with two hundred rangers to punish "the enemy's Indian scoundrels," particularly the Abenakis of St. Francis. The occasion of the general's wrath against this tribe was their seizure of two British officers bound for Quebec, who came to St. Francis with a flag of truce and a message of peace, which Amherst thought would be respected by the savages. The captives were sent to Montreal, and now the Indians were to suffer for their loyalty to the French. In his instructions to Rogers, Amherst wrote:

Take your revenge, but don't forget that though those villains have dastardly and promiscuously murdered the women and children of all ages, it is my orders that no women or children are killed or hurt.

For the business in hand the general made a judicious selection when he chose Major Robert Rogers for the leader. He was a New Hampshire man of thirty years or more, renowned for his self-reliance and boldness. Like many a lover of adventure he possessed a character less splendid than his physique, but ever since his appearance at Lake George, four years before this time, Rogers had been the terror of the French and of the Indians. Under his command was a battalion of

ABENAKI COUPLE

ABENAKI WARRIOR AND WOMAN

lynx-eyed rangers, who harried, the enemy at every season of the year and were sure to appear when least expected, on skates, on snowshoes, or in gliding birch-bark canoes. (Parkman's *Montcalm and Wolfe*, i.) The present task promised hardship and excitement in plenty, and Rogers lost no time in starting on his gory mission. (*Journals of Robert Rogers of the Rangers* by Robert Rogers; Leonaur 2005.)

The St. Francis Indians had been settled for about seventy-five years on the River St. Francis, a few miles above its confluence with the St. Lawrence. Of all the savage allies of the French no tribe had harassed and terrified the New England frontier as much as these bloodthirsty redskins: their unexpected excursions had been marked by burning farmhouses and murdered pioneers, men, women, and children; in six years' time they had killed, or carried into captivity, four hundred people from the border settlements.

Rogers and his men set out in whaleboats, and after successfully eluding the French vessels, landed the tenth day at Missisquoi Bay, at the north end of Lake Champlain. Concealing their boats on the shore, the expedition began to march towards St. Francis. For nine days they struggled through spruce bogs with the water up to their knees most of the time; finally, they came out upon better ground, and a few days more brought them within three miles of the Indian town which Rogers descried from a tree-top at sundown. There the party halted while the leader, with one or two companions, reconnoitred. They found the Indians yelling and singing "in a high frolic," and saw hundreds of English scalps dangling from poles over the doors of the houses.

At two o'clock in the morning Rogers returned to his party, and at three marched it towards St. Francis. Where pandemonium had reigned, all was quiet now. The men slipped off their packs and formed in a semi-circle. A half hour before sunrise the blow fell, and so suddenly that hardly a warrior escaped. Some were killed in their beds, others were pursued and shot down, while those who had thought to conceal themselves in the cellars and lofts of their houses were consumed in the wholesale conflagration that followed the slaughter.

So far, the expedition had been an unqualified success; but while the sky was still red with the flickering light of the holocaust, Nemesis appeared in the shape of a party of three hundred or more French and Indians, who had been sent to cut off the retreat of the intruders. Rogers knew that any attempt to regain the shores of Lake Champlain would be fatal: there was, however, one possible means of escape—to traverse the wilderness to the headwaters of the Connecticut and follow the course of that river southward to Number Four.

A council of war adopted the latter plan, and the rangers started on their two-hundred-mile flight. The rest of the story rivals the Ancient Mariner in horror. (*Journals of Robert Rogers.*) For a while the Frenchmen, following close upon their heels and picking off the stragglers one by one, caused them distress; but this enemy was as naught compared with the tortures of starvation that marked the last days of their journey. Some of the men dropped from exhaustion and perished where they fell; others kept themselves alive by subsisting on groundnut and lily bulbs, until at the end of many days the welcome sound of wood-cutting told them that at last they were nearing Number Four. There they were helped into the fort and nursed back to health and strength.

While Major Robert Rogers and his companions were paying dearly for the havoc they had wrought at St. Francis, the main body of the army at Crown Point finally bestirred itself. About the tenth of October the little navy came down from the yards at Ticonderoga: it consisted of a sloop, the *Boscawen*, a brigantine, the *Duke of Cumberland*, and a *radeau* which the provincials dubbed "the floating castle." (Niles' French and Indian Wars.) On the afternoon of October 11, this squadron, followed by the regulars in four columns of whaleboats, set out down the lake with fine weather and a fair breeze, while the provincials were left behind to work on the fort.

That night the troops spent on the water, and at daybreak some of the *bateaux*, having followed a misleading light, found themselves in the midst of the enemy's sloops. In the ensuing skirmish the French captured a boatload of men, and then sailed away at top speed. The rest of the regulars, preceded by the protecting *radeau*, continued on their way down the lake until afternoon when the wind began to blow hard from the northwest. One of the peculiarities of Lake Champlain is its susceptibility to wind. On that sheet of water, the waves raised by a breeze of no great force are quite out of proportion to the velocity of the air, a strange phenomenon which Amherst was soon to encounter.

Towards sundown it became evident that the boats must seek shelter or sink. On the western shore a well-protected bay promised a good haven and thither the general directed the men to row. There the windy night was passed in comparative comfort, but the following day found the lake noisy and angry with white caps racing by from the north; the pines on the shore of Ligonier Bay, as Amherst named the sheltering inlet, (now called Willsboro Bay), swished and roared in the autumnal gale, and all thought of going upon the water was abandoned. The high winds continued for five days, but during that time the brig and the sloop were busy on the lake.

First, they pursued the enemy's schooner until both British vessels ran aground. Recovering from this humiliating occurrence, they spied three French sloops and started after them at once. Up and down the lake the chase continued until the Frenchmen, refusing an action, were blockaded in a bay on the western shore, near the present town of Plattsburg. (Cumberland Bay.) Night came on while the British were at anchor off the entrance. In the morning they discovered that the enemy, in despair, had sunk two of their own vessels, while the third had been run aground, in order that the crews might escape through the woods to Isle aux Noix.

On the night of the fourteenth a rainstorm added to the gaiety of the elements. When that tempest cleared, a cold wave congealed the shivering army, causing Amherst to wonder if the season were not too far advanced for further operations. Midstream in the outlet at the northern end of the lake, Bourlamaque lay intrenched to the teeth, with thirty-five hundred men and one hundred cannon. On each side of Isle aux Noix, a *chevaux-de-frise* closed the Richelieu River to the British ships. Furthermore, the largest French vessel was still to be accounted for.

A gentle southerly breeze, however, restored the general's confidence temporarily, and ordering his men to re-embark, Amherst went down the lake to the place where the enemy's sloops were captured. There he received a letter from New York telling of the fall of Quebec. This news, combined with a north wind and "an appearance of winter," determined the course of operations. The conquest of Isle aux Noix must wait until another campaign. Turning their course southward, the men returned to Ligonier Bay, and thence to Crown Point, where the army reunited on the afternoon of October 21. Once again on familiar ground, Amherst found the new fort almost finished and Ticonderoga entirely restored. These were the monuments of his campaign.

"*When chill November's chilly blast made fields and forests bare,*" some of the provincials from Massachusetts and New Jersey decided that it was time they were disbanded and allowed to return to their homes. The result was a small mutiny on the first day of the month; but Amherst detailed a few regulars to restore discipline and the matter was soon settled. Towards the middle of November one American regiment after another was started on its homeward way, those from

New England following the new road to Number Four, which greatly lessened the distance and expense of their march.

The weather grew more and more severe, until the leaf-strewn ground was white with snow, and on the twenty-fifth the commander-in-chief broke camp. Leaving a garrison of six companies at Ticonderoga, the diminished army started on its march for New York. The first night was spent in the woods between Lake Champlain and Lake George, where the soldiers made good fires—and wisely so, for before morning several inches of snow had fallen. Another day or two brought them to the newly constructed Fort George, which Amherst inspected and declared satisfactory. (*Montresor's Journals.*)

Four companies were left to hold this post during the winter, while the rest of the troops continued their way south, seeking sheltered spots in the woods at night, and sleeping in clusters around the campfires, for it was not considered worthwhile to pitch tents for such short encampments.

At Albany, Amherst met Sir William Johnson, the recent hero of the Niagara expedition, and congratulated him upon his victory. During his three days' stay in town the Hudson froze over, which was annoying because the general had embarked his men upon vessels in the river, expecting them to go to New York by water. As the cold weather continued, however, he ordered the regiments off the ships and started them on the road for the metropolis. A day or two later, the fifth of December, Amherst left Brigadier Gage to command at Albany and crossed the Hudson on the ice. From there to New York he travelled on foot, making a very favourable impression upon the colonists and setting a good example for the soldiers. (Bonney's *Legacy of Historical Gleanings*, i.) After walking six days, the commander-in-chief arrived at his quarters on Manhattan Island and settled down for a well-earned winter's rest.

Among the indirect results of the campaign was a short-lived and comparatively unknown fourteenth colony, which came into being in the following manner. Major Philip Skene was one of the many British officers who were attracted by the remarkable fertility and beauty of the country around Crown Point. Like Amherst, he had fought at Fontenoy and Laffeldt in the previous war, and in the present conflict he had been with Lord Howe in the earlier campaign against Ticonderoga. (*Gentleman's Magazine,* lxxx.) During the recent summer of inaction on Lake Champlain, Skene's thoughts turned to the creation of a great estate in the wilderness, and early in November he asked Amherst for a grant which should lie "between South Bay, East Bay and the garrison-land of Fort Edward." This was no modest request, but Skene enjoyed the general's favour and through his influence might gain what he desired.

As the commander-in-chief had no direct authority to distribute land which properly belonged to the Crown or to the colonies, Skene was advised to present a petition to the Secretary of State. He did so, and, confident of success, settled "a number of poor families and some servants" on his intended domain. (Brodhead's *New York Colonial Documents*, vii.) Then from England came a temporary refusal of the application, which was due to the diffidence of the Lords of Trade about handling the matter until they were possessed of more definite knowledge concerning the location and jurisdiction of the proposed settlement.

Before the desired information was given and the terms of cultivation elucidated, duty called the major to the West Indies on the expeditions against Martinique and Havana. Returning from the South, he brought with him about two hundred and seventy prospective soldier-settlers, only to find that he had no land which he could legally assign to their use; indeed, that which he had already improved had been regranted over his head. This was discouraging, but Skene was determined to be a great landlord and crossed the ocean to present his case in person to the Lords of Trade.

In England Major Skene's arguments carried such conviction that in May, 1764, he was granted twenty thousand acres, about thirty square miles. (*Acts of the Privy Council; Colonial*, vol. iv.) As his regiment was one of those stationed in America after the war, the arrangement was a happy one, and the newly created proprietor entered enthusiastically into the development of his estate. In 1769 he retired from the army. The next year saw him established at Skenesborough, now Whitehall, New York, which is pleasantly situated at the head of the South Bay of Lake Champlain. There he set up forges for smelting iron, as well as a number of sawmills, and opened a road to Salem and Bennington to encourage the flow of colonization in his direction. (New York State Agricultural Society's *Transactions*, vol. viii.)

In the meantime, an interprovincial war was being waged between New Hampshire and New York, each claiming title to the land west of the Connecticut River. New Hampshire grants were superimposed upon those of New York, and *vice versa*, until it became evident that only might would make right. As Skene had almost lost his domain through the interference of the government of New York, he threw in his lot with the ultra-radical New Hampshire party, and for a time was hand in glove with the renowned Ethan Allen. ((*Vide Ethan Allen at Ticonderoga During the American War of Independence*; Leonaur 2010.)

In 1774, Skene, Allen, and a few other principal characters contrived a scheme to get rid of the jurisdiction of both contesting governments by having a new royal colony established. This should contain "the New Hampshire Grants" west of the Connecticut River, and also most of the present State of New York north of the Mohawk. If the influential major could induce the home government to solve the problem in this way, he might be appointed governor of the new province with his capital at Skenesborough. The idea appealed to Skene who once more sailed for England to solicit the accomplishment of the new project. (Ira Allen's *History of Vermont*, in the Vermont Historical Society's Collections, vol. i.) To a certain extent the enterprise succeeded.

Lord Dartmouth, Secretary of State for the Colonies, smiled upon the ingenious proposition and appointed Major Skene Lieutenant-Governor of Crown Point and Ticonderoga, for which favour the latter was duly grateful. (Historical Manuscripts Commission's *Fourteenth Report*, Appendix, Part 10.) But there the matter was brought to an abrupt close by the outbreak of the American Revolution, which temporarily placed in abeyance the intercolonial dispute and its possible solution. Precisely how far the British government would have gone or actually went in the prosecution of Skene's ambitious plan one cannot say. It is certain, however, that the Continental Congress considered him a dangerous partisan of the administration, and by providing for his imprisonment as soon as he arrived in America, (*Journals of the Continental Congress*, June 8 and June 27, 1775), put an end to the proposed colony that grew out of Amherst's campaign in northern New York in the summer of 1759.

CHAPTER 9

Montreal

As the spring of 1760 approached, the soldiers at New York began to speculate upon the plan of campaign for the coming season; none, however, could have been at a great loss to guess Amherst's objective, for Montreal still remained in the hands of the French, and thither the capital of New France had been transferred when Quebec surrendered to the English. Although Pitt had stipulated that this achievement was the "great and essential object remaining to complete the glory of His Majesty's arms in that part of the world," Amherst awaited specific instructions. He expected that these would arrive with his brother, the much-travelled William, who was returning from his second mission of bearing good news across the water. In the meantime, the general exhorted the colonial assemblies to co-operate with him in the conquest of Canada by providing as many provincial troops as in the previous year.

The governors did their best but the colonists, overjoyed at the victories of 1759, now regarded an early peace with France as a foregone conclusion. Indeed, there were rumours afloat that hostilities might cease at any time. Under the circumstances it is not surprising that, although the assemblies voted approximately the same number of troops, only four-fifths of the promised twenty thousand actually took the field, and these did so with such deliberation that Amherst's movements were much delayed. (George Louis Beer's *British Colonial Policy*.)

Pitt's instructions for the present campaign arrived unexpectedly at headquarters towards the end of February, eight weeks before William Amherst returned to the New World. The orders were flattering rather than specific. The object of the campaign was the capture of Montreal, but how this was to be accomplished was left entirely to the general's judgment. He might invade Canada in one body, or he might divide his forces into separate and distinct armies, whichever method he deemed the more expedient. The latter alternative appealed to Amherst in spite of its patent difficulties, and he decided to overwhelm Montreal with three expeditions acting simultaneously from east, south, and west.

While Murray, who was in command at Quebec, ascended the St. Lawrence, Colonel Haviland should carry the operations of the previous season to their logical conclusion by driving the enemy from the northern end of Lake Champlain. The third part of the program was to be conducted by the commander-in-chief who would lead the main army to Oswego, and thence eastward down Lake Ontario and the St. Lawrence to Montreal. The first would block the enemy's avenue of escape down the river; the second would dispose of the garrison at the Isle au Noix; while Amherst's circuitous route was calculated to prevent the French from retreating inland to Detroit and the western posts.

Obviously, the proposed arrangement was full of dangers. Each detachment would be isolated from the other two until the rendezvous was reached, and if separately attacked might be overpowered by the enemy. On the other hand, if all went well, the campaign would be one of the prettiest pieces of military co-operation imaginable. Amherst counted the cost and was confident of success. The old boats were repaired, new ones were built, and artillery and stores were brought around from Boston. On the second day of May the commander-in-chief set out for Albany, the accustomed assembling place of regulars and provincials.

As usual, the American troops were tardy in reaching the appointed ground, but Amherst made good use of the time by forwarding provisions and stores to Crown Point and Oswego, to facilitate the progress of the expeditions when once in motion. He also conferred with Sir William Johnson, who promised him a goodly supply of Indians, as in the previous year. By the middle of May, only a dozen companies of Massachusetts troops, a handful of men from Rhode Island, and a fraction of the New York quota had turned up at Albany, and Amherst was beginning to fume about "the sloth of the colonies," when disturbing news from Quebec gave him graver grounds for concern.

Brigadier Murray had been left in command of the erstwhile capital of New France, and his garrison had passed a comparatively comfortable winter, which they made more or less interesting by indulging in petty warfare with the bush-rangers and Indians of the surrounding country. Scurvy, fever, and dysentery, however, had reduced the original number of seven thousand by one-half, and in the following April there were scarcely more than three thousand British soldiers fit for duty in Quebec. Hundreds had been buried in the snow-drifts, which furnished temporary graves until the frozen ground should relax under the influence of a spring sun.

Meanwhile the French at Montreal—particularly Vaudreuil, the Governor of New France, kept a vigilant eye upon the state of affairs in the English garrison, and Lévis, who had succeeded Montcalm as military head of the colony, determined to fall upon the weakened enemy, and recover Quebec for Louis XV. Some faint-hearts scoffed at the enterprise, calling it "Lévis' folly"; but secret preparations went on apace until the commander had eight or nine thousand men ready to march down the river.

On the twentieth of April, the expedition of reconquest set out for the scene of action. The English abandoned their outpost at Old Lorette and fell back to Sainte-Foy, where their position was stronger. As soon as Murray realised the seriousness of the present attack, he called in his men from the various outlying districts and weighed the relative dangers of a siege and of a pitched battle. In view of the dubious condition of the town-walls, the latter choice seemed the more advisable, and a lively battle took place; but after two hours' fighting against double their number, the British were forced to retire within the fortifications of Quebec. Then indeed was there great danger of losing what Wolfe had so gallantly won. Every man worked to the utmost of his strength to put the place in a state of defence against its late owners, and it was at this critical juncture that Murray wrote to Amherst, imploring him to send relief to the besieged garrison on the St. Lawrence.

The commander-in-chief did so by ordering reinforcements up the river from Louisburg, (Kimball's *Pitt Correspondence*, ii), although there was little hope of their arriving at Quebec in time to rescue Murray and his fellow-sufferers. In the meantime, the English poured forth such a furious fire from the walls of the town that the month of May was well advanced before Lévis could plant his artillery and start an active siege. The enemy's great dependence was upon a ship which they had asked to have sent thither with munitions and heavy guns. The arrival of this vessel would seal the fate of the British, and Murray knew it; on the other hand, the appearance of an English ship-of-war would frustrate the attempted reconquest of Quebec.

Food became bad and scarce, and the men were worn out with

excessive labour. When, therefore, on the ninth of May a sail appeared far down the river, every eye was strained to discover its nationality. Finally, her colours were unfurled, and at the sight of the red cross of St. George the garrison went fairly mad with relief and joy. Lévis did not yet give up hope; but when the welcome *Lowestoffe* was followed by more representatives of the British navy, the game was up. The English ships passed the town and demoralised the enemy's squadron with little difficulty. The reconquest of Quebec was then out of the question, and the Frenchmen made all speed to return to their proper task, the defence of Montreal. (*Vide Commanders of the French & Indian War* by William Wood—contains *The Winning of Canada: a Chronicle of Wolfe & The Passing of New France: a Chronicle of Montcalm*; Leonaur 2012.)

At Albany, life was far less exciting. June was more than half gone before all the provincial troops had straggled into camp. Amherst divided their number between his own expedition and that which was to operate under Haviland, the general appropriating the men from Connecticut, New York and New Jersey, while the provincials from Rhode Island and Northern New England were sent to Crown Point. Having made this apportionment, he gave orders for the troops under his immediate command to proceed to Oswego as soon as possible, while he went on ahead to that secondary rendezvous. Oswego, it will be remembered, stood on the south-eastern shore of Lake Ontario, and having been extensively fortified by the British in 1759, was now one of the most defensible places in America. (*London Magazine*, vol. 28.)

Upon his arrival there, early in July, the commander-in-chief learned that two French vessels had been hovering off the settlement. As this performance was repeated, he reported their presence to the naval commander at Niagara, who responded by sending over two ships, the *Onondaga* and the *Mohawk*, which were immediately ordered to sail in quest of the enemy.

Towards the end of the month, Sir William Johnson, true to his word, appeared at Oswego, bringing with him the greatest number of Indians that had yet flocked to the English standard. Of the thirteen hundred redskins, however, only about one-half were warriors, and as Amherst was disgusted to be obliged to feed their women and children, (*Aspinwall Papers* in the Massachusetts Historical Society's *Collections*, Fourth Series, ix), the latter were soon encouraged to depart for their wilderness homes. Soon after the arrival of this savage host, the regular and provincial regiments, delayed no doubt by the "rainy, vile, and uncomfortable season," began to drift into camp, (*ibid*): by the ninth of the month all were present or accounted for.

At dawn of the following day, Amherst embarked with the regulars upon Lake Ontario, leaving Gage to bring up the provincials in the rear as soon as there were enough *bateaux*. Down the lake and into the St. Lawrence the whole flotilla steered its course. Before long they passed the two British ships, which the general had sent out to pursue the elusive French vessels, and came to rest at Ogdensburg.

This progress, remarkable for its celerity, was interrupted on the morning of August 17 by a spirited encounter with the enemy's one remaining vessel—the other having run aground. As the two British ships-of-war, the *Onondaga* and the *Mohawk*, had lost their way in the labyrinth of the Thousand Islands, the capture of the Frenchman devolved upon the infantry in the "row-galleys." Fortunately, there was little or no wind and the enemy's vessel tried in vain to slip by the English and to sail up the river to the lake. The attacking party fired over one hundred rounds to which the French ship replied with zest, but by seven o'clock in the morning her Bourbon colours came down. (*Aspinwall Papers.*) Amherst then took undisturbed possession of the southern shore of the St. Lawrence at the mouth of the Oswegatchie River, where there had been an Indian settlement, watched over by a French blockhouse, both of which were now abandoned.

About four or five miles farther down the river, upon an island in mid-stream, stood Fort Lévis, which was reported to be a strong post. Its commander was Pouchot, the same gallant Frenchman who, in the previous year, had held Niagara as long as there existed the slightest possibility of its relief. After the surrender of that fortress, he had been exchanged, and he now prepared to face a less hopeful siege. It would have been quite possible for Amherst to run by the batteries of Fort Lévis, without taking time to invest and capture it, but he had two reasons for not doing this. One was his characteristic thoroughness; the other, the possibility of finding in its garrison pilots to guide his boats through the dangerous rapids which lay between the English Army and Montreal.

After reconnoitring both shores and seizing the islands below Fort Lévis, Amherst invested the rocky islet on all sides so that none of its garrison might escape. In the meantime, Pouchot's resistance was by no means passive. While the British were circumnavigating the fort, they were treated to a smart cannonade, which sunk one of their boats, killed two men in another, and injured several. This ticklish operation consumed many hours, and it was eleven o'clock on the night of August 18 before the island was entirely surrounded. The next two days were spent in planting batteries and in bringing up the delinquent ships-of-war, whose strength was now supplemented by the *Ottawa*, the vessel recently captured from the enemy. On the twenty-third, Amherst opened fire from every side.

The fortress was raked fore and aft; its log walls were shivered and splintered by the furious cannonade, but Pouchot lived up to his well-deserved reputation for bravery. Although, one by one, the enemy's guns were dismounted the obstinate commander held out for three days. Finally, on the afternoon of August 25, the garrison beat a parley and Amherst received a letter from his adversary. The British general never wasted much time in haggling over terms of surrender: on this occasion he gave his victim only ten minutes in which to decide to give up his fort and all its appurtenances in their present condition, the garrison to be prisoners of war. Pouchot yielded at once, and soon the British Jack was hoisted over one more outpost of France in America.

Amherst's Indian allies had looked forward with eagerness and joy to the reduction of Fort Lévis, an event which they never doubted would be followed by a massacre of the garrison such as had marked the capture of Fort William Henry by the French three years before. In this expectation they were grievously disappointed, however, and when it became evident that the general would allow no violence of any kind against those who had fallen into his hands, three-quarters of his savages deserted from the army and returned home in rage and disgust.

Lingering in the vicinity of his most recent conquest, which was renamed Fort William Augustus in honour of the Duke of Cumberland, Amherst employed the men in repairing the fort, mending the *bateaux*, and overhauling the larger vessels. The prospect before him was not attractive. Between his present camp and Montreal, the St. Lawrence was torn with a series of dangerous rapids which might spell the ruin of the entire campaign. Pouchot took especial delight in painting them in their blackest colours to his conqueror's troubled fancy, and well-nigh succeeded in disturbing the Englishman's renowned equanimity. (Pouchot's *Memoirs*, ii.) However, the original plan must be executed or the tripartite concentration upon Montreal would lack its most important factor.

Already Murray with his forces from Quebec was within a few miles of the rendezvous, while Haviland, having driven the enemy from Isle aux Noix, was fast approaching the south bank of the St.

Lawrence. On the last day of August, Amherst again put the army in motion and soon had his first experience of shooting the rapids, which he found "more frightful than dangerous." While most of the men stayed in the boats in passing these precarious parts of the river, the general was careful to march covering parties along the shore lest the French or the Indians should add to the excitement of the occasion by attacking the flotilla. Fortunately, there was no resistance on the part of the enemy.

On the contrary, the inhabitants of the settlements traversed by the army were overcome by the sight of such a host and, abandoning their houses, rushed into the woods as fast as their legs could carry them. As Amherst had given strict orders that the Canadians were not to be plundered on pain of death, their panic-stricken evacuation was unnecessary. (*Woodbull's Journal* in the *Historical Magazine*, v.) Whenever it was possible, the general sent after them, while others came back of their own accord. They were disarmed, and after taking the oath of allegiance were repossessed of their habitations and lands, much to their surprise and happiness. (*Amherst to Governor Wentworth, Sept. 9, 1760: MS.* in the Boston Public Library.)

The first four rapids were passed with comparative ease, although a half-dozen men were drowned in the turbulent waters before Lake St. Francis afforded temporary relief and an opportunity to repair what little damage had been done. On the fourth of September, the boats pushed out into the stream once more, this time to battle with the most dangerous part of the river, the rapids known as the Cedars, the Buisson, and the Cascades. Here Amherst's worst fears were realised. His description of the river as being "full of broken waves," scarcely does justice to the tumultuous rush of the waters as they leap half-angrily, half-play fully in their mad dash over the rock-strewn shoals. Almost fifty boats were lost in the frightful torrent, several more were staved on the rocks, and eighty-four men were swept down to watery graves. At length when the last of the rapids was left behind, the general gave the army a day for rest, recuperation, and repairs before pressing on to Montreal.

The morning of September 6 was favourable for further progress down the river: the troops reembarked, and before long made a landing without opposition on the island of Montreal. Some flying parties of the enemy fired a few shots and then ran away, leaving Amherst to form his army as he saw fit on a plain before the town. At that very moment Brigadier Murray landed to the eastward of Montreal, and on the following morning, Colonel Haviland and his victorious forces, fresh from their seizure of Isle aux Noix, appeared on the south bank of the St. Lawrence.

Such a remarkable fruition of Amherst's well-laid plans demanded the admiration of both friend and foe. One Frenchman declared that neither more beautiful military combinations nor "so many troops reunited on the same point and in the same instant against a body already expiring" were ever seen. (Brodhead's *New York Colonial Documents*, x.) A careful historian has termed it "one of the most perfect and astonishing bits of work which the annals of British warfare can show." (Corbett's *England in the Seven Years' War*, ii.)

While the three British Armies were concentrating within sight of Montreal, the French governor called a council of war to determine what should be done to preserve the fast-fading glory of New France. Montreal in 1760 was a thin fringe of low houses, some of wood and some of stone, extending from east to west along the water-front, while here and there a church spire broke the even sky-line of the town. The whole area was enclosed by a moat and a slight wall of masonry, which might serve as a defence against Indian attacks but could avail nothing against a cannonade.

Amherst was already bringing up his artillery: when once the guns were in position the town was at his mercy. The enemy's military force numbered a scant twenty-five hundred with which to oppose the seventeen thousand English troops who practically surrounded them. Vaudreuil saw but one course to pursue—to surrender. His colleagues, including Lévis, who had so recently held Quebec in the hollow of his hand, agreed to the governor's proposition, and a lengthy capitulation, containing fifty-five articles, was drawn up. Early on the morning of September 7 news of these developments came to Amherst's ears, and at the same time he received a *naïve* proposal that hostilities be suspended for one month.

The general laughed at such an idea, but cheerfully agreed to a cessation of arms until noon. (Lévis' *Journal des Campagnes*.) About twelve o'clock the articles of surrender devised by the French authorities came in. Amherst read them through and wrote his comments in the margin of the document. Most of the terms he accepted, some he modified, and others he rejected. (Brodhead's *New York Colonial Documents*, x.) Among those which he flatly refused to grant was one stipulating that the troops should march out with arms, cannon, and the honours of war.

On the contrary, Amherst dictated that the whole garrison of Montreal and all the rest of the troops in Canada should lay down their arms and not serve again during the present war. He considered that the enemy deserved this disgrace because of "the infamous part the troops of France had acted in exciting the savages to perpetrate the most horrid and unheard-of barbarities in the whole progress of the war." (Knox's *Journal* ii.) When the draught was returned Amherst requested a speedy decision. Vaudreuil was ready to surrender upon these terms and at once, but the military pride of Lévis could not submit to such a humiliating capitulation.

When informed of Amherst's change in the articles, he wrote a high-sounding letter to Vaudreuil insisting that, weak and defenceless as Montreal was, it would be better to break off negotiations at once, and to make at least a show of resistance behind the walls of the town. If the governor should not see fit to act upon his suggestion, Lévis and his troops asked permission to withdraw to St. Helen's Island in the St. Lawrence, where they would maintain to the last the honour of Bourbon arms. When Vaudreuil declined to act upon this mock-heroic proposal, Lévis relieved his feelings by ordering his men to burn all their flags in order to lessen to that extent the victory of the English. (Lévis' *Journal des Campagnes.*)

In the meantime, Amherst's patience was tried by two or three emissaries who came out of Montreal to plead for more lenient terms. To each and all of them, the Englishman turned a deaf ear and insisted that the only words he would listen to were "Yes" or "No." (Brodhead's *New York Colonial Documents*, x.) When it became clear that the English general was resolute in maintaining his position, Vaudreuil was only too glad to sign the articles of capitulation.

At eight o'clock on the morning of September 8, 1760, Montreal was surrendered, and Canada became a part of the British Empire. By that strange identity of dates which is conspicuous throughout Amherst's military career, the day of this glorious event was the third anniversary of the Convention of Kloster Zeven, a capitulation, it will be remembered, whereby the Duke of Cumberland, forced back to the mouth of the Elbe by the French, was obliged to disband his forces.

The commander-in-chief sent Colonel Haldimand to take possession of the gates of the captured town. On the next day the French battalions laid down their arms; but when the British officer in charge demanded the enemy's flags, he was told that, although each regiment had brought its colours from France, they had found them troublesome in this woody country, and therefore had destroyed them. (Knox's *Journal* ii.) After both Vaudreuil and Lévis had affirmed this on their *parole d'honneur*, Amherst accepted their ingenious evasion of the truth; but we have the word of Lévis himself that the flags were burned in a moment of petty rage. (Lévis' *Journal des Campagnes*.)

Although the Gallic conception of honour is often incomprehensible to the Anglo-Saxon mind, the Frenchman certainly proved himself a poor loser on this occasion. Lévis would neither receive Amherst nor personally pay him the customary civilities, maintaining that it was his duty to show his resentment towards the relentless conqueror, and that the troops ought to have received more attention from Vaudreuil and more esteem from General Amherst. (Brodhead's *New York Colonial Documents*, x.) Two stands of British colours, captured by Montcalm at Oswego four years before, were restored to their original owners, but these were the only flags surrendered.

New France had fallen, and New England was jubilant with thanksgiving sermons and other forms of celebration. Boston indulged in a parade, followed by a dinner in Faneuil Hall; fireworks leaped skyward, and Castle William roared out a salute of sixty-three guns. (*Boston Post Boy and Advertiser*, Sept. 29, 1760.) The inland towns followed suit. On the evening of October 9, the people of Worcester illuminated their houses, and the windows of Sheriff Chandler's mansion, where Amherst had been a guest in the autumn of 1758, shone with a particular brilliance. (*Boston News Letter*, Oct. 16, 1760.)

Meanwhile the good news was on its way to England. Upon its receipt Pitt was unrestrained in his congratulations and expressions of approval, while the king gave each of the messengers five hundred pounds as a souvenir of their happy mission. Horace Walpole, coming up to London by accident one day in October, found the place alive with bonfires and squibs, and everybody drinking the health of General Amherst. So, the English-speaking world celebrated the final event which added New France to the British Empire and relieved the colonists forever of all fear of invasion from the north.

Amherst had proved himself "the greatest military administrator produced by England since the death of Marlborough, and he remained the greatest until the rise of Wellington" (Fortescue's *History of the British Army*, ii): he was hardly less remarkable as an organiser of the conquered province that lay at his feet. His labours in the second capacity were made difficult by three factors, the religion of the Canadians, the feudal system that had dominated New France, and the

French law, or *Coutume de Paris*, according to which the inhabitants were accustomed to settle their disputes. (For an exact analysis of the code of law under the old regime see Renton and Phillimore's *Colonial Laws and Courts*.)

By the terms of surrender, Amherst granted that "the free exercise of the Catholic, Apostolic, and Roman religion" should continue to flourish as it had under the old regime. (Article XXVII.) He also signed an article allowing the lords of manors to enjoy peaceable possession of their goods and other property; but their judicial authority was not mentioned in the document. (Article XXXVII.) This was a significant and all-important omission, for it inaugurated the breaking down of feudalism in Canada. Many an Englishman would have discarded at once the civil law, which had prevailed in New France since its foundation, and would have substituted for it the Common Law, with which he was more familiar.

Here again, however, the commander-in-chief displayed the tact and consideration that had characterised all his deeds in America. For administrative purposes he divided Canada into three military districts—Montreal, Three Rivers, and Quebec—coinciding with the old divisions under the French rule, and placed a governor over each of them. Local government was entrusted to Canadian militia captains, who, like the English justices of the peace at that time, belonged to the gentry. Each adjudicated the cases arising in his parish, and thus put an end to the judicial authority of the feudal seigniors. (Munro's *Seigniorial System in Canada*.)

In the settlement of civil differences between the inhabitants the *Coutume de Paris* obtained, while criminal offences were dealt with according to martial law. (Kingsford's *History of Canada*, iv.) This hybrid system of justice was calculated to afford the new subjects of the British Crown the greatest amount of satisfaction consistent with a strong government and a proper assertion of England's supremacy. From the decisions of these magistrates there was a right of appeal to the British officer commanding the regular troops in that part of the district, and ultimately to the governor.

This was the frame of government set up by Jeffery Amherst, and although it was modified in detail by his lieutenants to suit local conditions. (Garneau's *Histoire du Canada*, ii; Doutre et Lareau's *Le Droit Civil Canadien*; Shortt and Doughty's *Documents relating to the Constitutional History of Canada, 1759-1791*.) Its general principles were preserved and established a system far happier for all concerned than

CAPITULATION OF MONTREAL

that which succeeded it under the Royal Proclamation of 1763.

The commander-in-chief, as self-appointed Governor-General of Canada, named Brigadier Gage Governor of Montreal, and Colonel Burton, of Three Rivers, while Murray returned to Quebec to take charge of the government there. In order to remove any suspicions which, the Canadians might entertain, Amherst even went so far as to conduct his official correspondence with these deputies in French. (Royal Society of Canada's *Proceedings*, 1905, Appendix A, xliv.) All in all, the treatment of the vanquished people was thoroughly successful. The habitants settled down under their new masters with infinite content, and before many weeks had passed, the general reported to Pitt that the soldiers and the Canadians were fraternising on the best of terms. (Reuben Gold Thwaites' *France in America*.)

From a military standpoint all that remained to be done was to apply the finishing touches to the conquest of Canada; and with that end in view Major Rogers was ordered to Detroit to take possession of the western posts, which, although included in the capitulation of Montreal, still remained in French hands. Amherst then sent off the New England troops to spend the rest of the season in completing the forts under construction at Crown Point, at Oswego, and in central New York, while the soldiers from the Middle Colonies were given occupation in the St. Lawrence valley. The four thousand prisoners of war were shipped to sunny France, the Indians were given various trinkets as a reward for their good behaviour in the campaign, and finally the general found himself at liberty to go down the river to inspect the newly established governments of Three Rivers and Quebec.

Bidding goodbye to Montreal in the last days of September, Amherst went first to Three Rivers, where he spent two days. At St. Maurice he found an iron mine and some forges which had been worked by the Canadians for the benefit of the King of France. As the mine seemed to be profitable, Amherst kept the men at work for their new sovereign, and continued on his journey to Quebec. On the way he passed most of the transports bearing the French troops which had been stopped in the river by contrary winds. Finding everything satisfactory at Quebec, the commander-in-chief turned his steps towards Crown Point and New York.

At Isle aux Noix he viewed the fortress which had checked his advance in the previous year, and then ordered all the works there to be destroyed. As the maintenance of this post would be an unnecessary expense to the British and its abandonment intact might prove a danger, the measure was a wise one. Louisburg had already suffered the same ignominious fate. Early in 1760, Pitt had decreed that all its defences and fortifications should be completely demolished and its garrison transferred to Halifax. The work of annihilating the Dunkirk of America was no small task, but in December Amherst reported to his chief that the renowned Louisburg was no more. (Kimball's *Pitt Correspondence*, ii.)

After a week or two at Crown Point where the provincials still slaved at the construction of a prodigious fortress, the general proceeded leisurely on his way to New York by the way of Albany. His welcome to the cosmopolitan metropolis befitted the conqueror of New France. Early in the autumn, Amherst had been voted the freedom of the city, and Mr. Nicholas Roosevelt was directed to prepare a gold box in which to encase the document. When the general reached New York all was in readiness for his reception. On November 27, the mayor, aldermen, and assistants waited upon "His said Excellency" and presented him with the traditional gold box, the cover of which was beautifully engraved with a Latin inscription, eulogising in superlative terms the *Domitor Gallorum Canadensium*.

Besides the freedom of the city, the box contained an enthusiastic and not altogether unsuccessful bit of rhetoric, engrossed on parchment. This recited the virtues, as well as the military prowess, of the commander-in-chief, and in the following words assured him of immortality in the hearts of the American people.

> Minutely to describe the innumerable advantages resulting from so signal a conquest would be a vain attempt. Let millions yet unborn mark the distinguished blessings as they rise, and while they reap the happy fruits of your martial virtues, they will not cease to bless the name of Amherst.—New York Historical Society's *Collections* for 1885.

CHAPTER 10

Sir Jeffery Amherst, Kt.

When Canada fell, the American theatre of the Seven Years' War moved southward to the West Indies. Amherst had expected that the French forts and possessions on the Mobile and the Mississippi would be the next objective, but in January, 1761, Pitt informed him that attacks upon the islands of Dominica, Santa Lucia, and Martinique were to constitute this year's program, and that eight thousand of the regulars on the American continent would be required for that purpose. The selection of a commander for the expedition was left to Amherst.

In order to retain a secure hold upon England's conquests already accomplished in the New World, the colonies were asked to supply two-thirds as many troops as in the previous year. These provincials were to garrison the various Canadian and frontier posts and so release the regulars for active service in the West Indies. (Kimball's *Pitt Correspondence*, ii.) As the colonial axe was already ground and there was no longer any apprehension of an invasion from Canada, the assemblies made only a half-hearted response to the requisition: about ten thousand men were voted, but of this number less than nine thousand ever appeared on the muster-fields. (Beer's *British Colonial Policy*.)

Pitt probably foresaw this falling-off, and remembering the usual tardiness of the provincial troops at the rendezvous, felt sure that the expedition against Martinique could not be got under way before the hurricane season. As tropical storms were more to be feared than any French fleet, Amherst was instructed not to undertake that enterprise until the end of September or early in October. Meanwhile, lest Europe should think that England was resting on her laurels, the commander-in-chief was to send to Guadeloupe, the British base in the Caribbean, two thousand regulars to seize Dominica and Santa Lucia.

When these orders arrived at New York, Amherst speedily set

141

Perspective VIEW OF THE ATTACK OF Roseau in the Island of DOMINIQUE by His Majesty's Troops under y.e command of LORD ROLLO.

6 June 1761

about assembling the forces for the earlier expedition and summoned a number of ships to convoy them on their southward voyage. The command of the troops was entrusted to Colonel Lord Rollo, who had displayed efficiency when sent to receive the surrender of Prince Edward Island after the victory at Louisburg. The fleet sailed from New York in the last days of April. Six weeks later Dominica succumbed to the quick and determined assault of the British soldiers, (Kimball's *Pitt Correspondence*, ii), and foreshadowed the similar fate which befell its sister-island, Martinique, within eight months.

In the meantime, Amherst passed the spring and summer of 1761 in sending out provincial regiments to take the place of the regulars called in to prepare for the expedition against Martinique. For this purpose, the general moved his headquarters to Albany, while a camp for the returning regulars was established on Staten Island, just below New York. Sir William Johnson was sent to Detroit to settle affairs with the Indians in that part of the country, and to see that their trade was properly conducted. He carried with him about two hundred medals to distribute among the more faithful of the redskins who had accompanied the army down the St. Lawrence to Montreal in the previous year; and although Amherst did not, as yet, perceive the necessity of such rewards, he agreed that it would please the Indians much, and rejoiced, at any rate, that the expense was not great.

★★★★★★

Kimball's *Pitt Correspondence*, ii. A white marble replica of one of these badges, much enlarged, appears as a medallion over the door of the Amherst mansion, "Montreal," at Sevenoaks, Kent.

★★★★★★

Early in September the commander-in-chief went down the Hudson again and took up his quarters on Staten Island, where the troops under General Monckton awaited the arrival of transports to carry them to the West Indies. He found the camp healthy, the men in constant exercise, and every prospect of a strong expedition in both quality and quantity. Towards the end of October, the ships came in and anchored within Sandy Hook, but as they were in a "shattered condition" as the result of a hard voyage, repairs were necessary, and the fleet did not get to sea until four weeks later. In the interim the British camp was the scene of an unusual and interesting ceremony. On October 25, 1761, General Amherst was invested with the insignia of a Knight of the Bath.

When George II revived the "most honourable Order of the Bath" in 1725, he acted upon the advice of Sir Robert Walpole and intended that it should supply a fund of favours, in lieu of places, and prevent an excessive demand for the Garter. (Nicolas's *History of the Orders of Knighthood*, iii.) Among its early members was the Duke of Cumberland who was made "first and principal Companion," while at a later date Ligonier, by his gallant action at Dettingen, won a place upon the chosen list. In 1760 the old king died and was succeeded by his grandson, the young and independent George III, just at the time when the news of the fall of Montreal reached England. It was not long before the new monarch decided to decorate Jeffery Amherst with a red ribbon.

On the twenty-sixth of May in 1761, twelve knights-elect were installed in the royal chapel of Henry the Seventh in Westminster Abbey. After the procession had filed from the chapter-room to the chapel, the Dean administered the oath and admonished them to use their swords "for the glory of God, the defence of the gospel, the maintenance of their sovereign's right and honour, and of all equity and justice, to the utmost of their power." (*Gentleman's Magazine*, vol. 31.) To this injunction a further reminder of their duty was added by "the king's master-cook, who stood at the outside door of the Abbey with a linen apron on and a chopping-knife in his hand." To each newly created knight he addressed himself as follows:

> Sir, you know what great oath you have taken, which, if you keep it, will be great honour to you; but if you break it, I shall be compelled by my office to hack off your spurs from your heels.

As Amherst was in America at the time of the installation, he was spared this ordeal, his part being taken by a proxy, Sir Charles Cotter-el-Dormer, (Nicolas's *History of the Orders of Knighthood*, iii), but Pitt soon informed him of the honour conferred, and sending the insignia of the Order across the ocean, instructed the governor of New York to perform the ceremony of investiture "in the most honourable and distinguished manner the circumstances will allow of." At about the same time Major-General Robert Monckton, who had been Wolfe's second in command on the Plains of Abraham, was appointed chief executive of New York. It was Monckton, therefore, who, on almost the first day of his administration, invested Amherst with the gold collar and red ribbon of the Order of the Bath.

The ceremony took place in camp on Staten Island on October

25, in the presence of several officers of the army. General Monckton first read aloud Pitt's letter containing his instructions and then, making an apology for the informality of the occasion, put the ribbon over Sir Jeffery's shoulder. The new knight responded with a courteous acknowledgment of "this distinguishing mark of His Majesty's royal approbation," and the ceremony was completed. (*Universal Magazine,* vol. 29.) The general had received the first investiture ever performed in America, establishing a precedent in accordance with which, sixteen years later, General William Howe was decorated at New York by his brother, Viscount Howe, inappropriately soon after Washington's astonishing campaign in the Jerseys. (Nicolas's *History of the Orders of Knighthood*, iii.)

Late in November the fleet bound for the attack upon Martinique got away from Sandy Hook and bore off to the southward. The troops were under the command of Monckton, whose zeal for military glory was not to be hampered by his duties as governor of New York, while the naval force that supplemented the expedition was directed by Admiral Rodney, the same gentleman who had escorted Amherst to Louisburg in the spring of 1758. Together they silenced the guns of Fort Royal and frightened St. Pierre into submission. Early in February, 1762, Martinique was surrendered *in toto* to invincible Britain.

While his colleagues were increasing their reputations by active service in the West Indies, Sir Jeffery was occupied with civil and political concerns of various kinds. After the fall of Fort Lévis, and before the capitulation of Montreal, the general had written to the governor of New York recommending him to encourage settlement in the upper Mohawk Valley which was now freed from the raids of the French and Indians. (Brodhead's *New York Colonial Documents*, vii.) Colden, acting upon this suggestion, issued a proclamation inviting settlers to the newly opened territory. The response was immediate, and applications for grants of land poured in. (*Acts of the Privy Council—Colonial, Unbound Papers.*)

This development of the wilderness was highly desirable from every point of view, but Amherst's eagerness to increase the security of military posts in the interior got him into trouble with the people of New York, particularly with the merchants of Albany, whose prosperity depended to a great extent upon a lucrative trade with the Indians. As soon as the Lords of Trade learned of the new land grants made in the Mohawk Valley, they advised the Privy Council to put a stop to the expansion of New York at once, lest the Indians, cheated of their rightful domain, might start a serious disturbance on the frontier.

An order in council was issued enjoining many provincial governors, including Colden, to make no further grants, and reprimanding them and their councils for their past behaviour in this respect. (Brodhead's *New York Colonial Documents*, vii.) This edict was the forerunner of the Royal Proclamation of 1763, which put a definite stop to the territorial extension of the colonies until the home government decided upon an Indian policy, and its origin may be traced directly to Amherst's recommendation to Colden to colonise the upper Mohawk Valley in the summer of 1760.

Hardly had this disturbance blown over when the Lords of Trade received a dignified but determined petition from the merchants of Albany. They complained that Sir Jeffery had given ten thousand acres of Indian land near Niagara to a group of army officers. This land was part of a tract which had been guaranteed to the Iroquois for their use forever by the English government in 1726. The petitioners did not doubt that Amherst's generosity was due to ignorance of England's obligations, but if this encroachment upon the reservation were allowed, not only would the grantees enjoy a monopoly of the Indian trade, "and reduce thousands of His Majesty's American subjects to want," but they would also be likely to cause an outbreak on the part of the savages. (Brodhead's *New York Colonial Documents*, vii.)

The Albanians were distinctly in the right, however commercial their motives may have been, and when the Privy Council raked Amherst gently over the coals for overstepping his powers, the general cheerfully confessed his guilt, although he insisted that whatever grants he had made were understood to be only permits to occupy the land until the king's pleasure should be known. Now that the authorities had given him a definite answer, he ordered the territory to be vacated at once. (*Ibid.*)

Among the many people who "for want of being rightly informed" applied to Amherst for tracts of land on the frontier was one Eleazer Wheelock, a minister of the gospel at Lebanon, Connecticut, whose chief aim in life was the conversion and education of the Indians. Since 1754 he had been at the head of a "charity-school" in his home town where a handful of Indian youths endeavoured to acquire learning in company with some lads of English parentage.

After a few years Mr. Wheelock realised that the sort of education given to the aborigines at Moor's School, as it was called, would avail little so long as they were "ignorant of all the affairs of husbandry, and the use of tools," (Wheelock's *Narrative of the Indian Charity School at Lebanon, in Connecticut*), and from that moment he burned with a desire to establish an industrial school much like the modern institution at Carlisle, in which "well-instructed, sober, religious Indians" might be employed as teachers as well as the English.

In his own words the plan was:

> To have lands appropriated to the use of Indian schools, and prudent, skilful farmers, or tradesmen, to lead and instruct the boys, and mistresses to instruct the girls, in such manufactures as are proper for them, at certain hours, as a diversion from their school exercises, and the children, taken quite away from their parents and the pernicious influence of Indian examples, there may be some good prospect of great advantage by schools amongst them.

With this estimable purpose the broad-minded educator wrote to Sir Jeffery Amherst in the spring of 1763 and asked for a tract of land about fifteen or twenty miles square on the west side of the Susquehanna River, "or in some other place more convenient in the heart of the Indian country." (O'Callaghan's *Documentary History of New York*, iv.) There he would establish "an academy for all parts of useful learning" in the midst of a community "peopled with a chosen number of inhabitants of known honesty, integrity, and such as love, and will be kind to, and honest in their dealings with Indians."

To Mr. Wheelock's appeal Sir Jeffery could make but one reply, especially as the trouble about the Niagara grants was still fresh in his memory. With expressions of his high opinion of the minister's designs and aspirations, he reminded the gentleman that the disposal and settlement of all conquered lands must be determined by His Majesty, and wished him success in his application to the proper authority. (*Ibid.*, iv.)

A few years later Eleazer Wheelock's dream was realised in New Hampshire, on the eastern bank of the Connecticut River, where a few huts of green logs in the midst of a wilderness marked the beginnings of Dartmouth College.

As the institution took its name from its benefactor, the Earl of Dartmouth, one cannot help wondering what name the proposed school on the Susquehanna would have borne, had Amherst been able to oblige the zealous educator with a grant of land. Whatever it might have been, the general's name was destined to be adopted a half-century later by another college situated in the same beautiful valley and equally well known in the world of letters.

A matter of great concern to Amherst was the illicit trade which the colonists carried on with the enemy throughout the war. The inhabitants of the French sugar islands in the West Indies depended almost entirely upon the produce of the British colonies on the continent for food. Thus, for fifty years or more a highly profitable trade had flourished between the foreign islands and the bread colonies of the north. If the food supply of the former were cut off, as would naturally happen in time of war between England and France, starvation would stare the islanders in the face, and their conquest would be a simple matter.

With this in view England forbade all commercial intercourse with the French colonies in June, 1756, and sent instructions to that effect to America. (Beer's British Colonial Policy, 1754-1765.) This prohibition was reinforced in the following year by an act of Parliament making it illegal to export any food-stuffs (except fish and rice) from the American colonies. It is not strange that the provincial traders were not at all favourably impressed with such legislation. Commerce with the French West Indies, which had been thoroughly remunerative in time of peace, now promised to be abnormally profitable.

The enemy's provisions were scarce and supplies would bring high prices, while the islanders' difficulty in marketing their chief products, sugar and molasses, would permit the New Englanders to purchase them almost on their own terms. France could no longer send food to the West Indies, nor could the sugar-planters, on the other hand, be at all sure that their cargoes would reach Europe in safety. The temptation to indulge in the forbidden trade was indeed great, and the British colonists did not long resist it.

Such intercourse with the enemy was dangerous, for although the French governors were quite ready to supply the ships with licenses exempting them from capture by Bourbon cruisers or privateers, to escape the eye of British officials was a different matter. At first this was accomplished by false certificates and mendacious bills-of-lading, a practice which soon gave way to a safer and more elaborate means of evasion known as a "flag of truce." (Channing's *History of the United States,* ii.) This was a pass from the government authorizing the ship to go to the French islands, ostensibly to exchange prisoners of war, but actually to share in the enormous profits which trade with the enemy under these conditions assured.

The exportation of foodstuffs, particularly flour, was as great a hindrance to England's military movements in America as it was a benefit to the French islanders. Amherst seems to have been surprisingly cognizant of this illegal trade, and although in 1759 he complained to the governor of New York that as a result of it his operations against Canada were seriously handicapped by a lack of flour, there is no evidence that he informed Pitt of the questionable state of affairs. Other authorities, however, did not hesitate to call the attention of the home government to "these dangerous and traiterous proceedings." Among the first to enlighten Pitt were Commodore Moore and General Crump, who were stationed in the West Indies; but more effective was the exposure of Pennsylvania by its over-zealous proprietary, Thomas Penn. (Beer's *Colonial Policy*.)

Although this son of the founder had renounced America for England as a place of residence long before the present war, he had kept in touch with the province, and thus was able to give accurate information about conditions existing on the Delaware. In 1759 relations were strained between the colonists and the proprietaries, and it may have been a desire to cause trouble for the Pennsylvanians that led Thomas Penn to present a few facts to Pitt's attention. His text was the illicit trade carried on between the bread colonies and the foreign West Indies, and his description of the Philadelphia wharves swarming "with shallops unloading these illegal cargoes, brought at their return, and cheating the king of his duties besides carrying provisions and ready money to the enemy," was both graphic and alarming.

William Pitt acted in the matter with his accustomed promptness and vigour. Letters were sent to all the governors in North America and the West Indies, informing them of the recent reports and ordering them to make inquiries "into the state of this dangerous and ignominious trade," to discover all persons in any way concerned in it, and to bring "such heinous offenders to the most exemplary and condign punishment." (Kimball's *Pitt Correspondence*, ii.) The results of the ensuing investigations were astounding. New York pleaded guilty, but insisted that Philadelphia was a greater offender.

Pennsylvania's governor lamented the grievous state of affairs under his predecessor, the unfortunate Denny—who, "as it were, opened a shop" where flags of truce might be bought by all comers—but assured the home government that the days of such iniquity were over. Governor Stephen Hopkins of Rhode Island boldly justified the game which the merchants of his colony had been playing, while

Virginia's chief magistrate gave an illuminating account of the way the trade was carried on from his colony. Few investigations in history have been more gratifying to the muck-raker. Governor Bernard's seizure of a vessel and crew in Boston Harbor yielded the intelligence that the Cherokee Indians, who were then ravaging the frontier of South Carolina, had been indirectly supplied with ammunition by the English trading at New Orleans. (*Sparks MSS.*, "Bernard Official Correspondence," Vol. ii) Yet commerce with the enemy apparently went on as before.

In the Spring of 1762, Amherst became aware that the evil, under a different guise, still continued. On the fifteenth of April he sent a circular letter to the governors asking them to put a stop to "such infamous practices" at once, and to prohibit the exportation of any kind of provisions from their ports. The latter measure he hoped would be effectual: otherwise, an embargo on all shipping must be resorted to. (Beer's *Colonial Policy; Colonial Records of Rhode Island*, vi.) A few days later the "papers and effects of several gentlemen subjects of the King of France," seized by the sheriff in New York, added more fuel to the fire. (New York Historical Society's *Collections* for 1876.)

From these it appeared that French agents had come to America with the express purpose of promoting the illegal West Indian trade, not only to furnish the enemy's settlements with provisions but also to supply their fleets and armies, if any should be stationed in the Antilles. There was every indication that the Frenchmen placed their chief reliance upon Rhode Island, and that several merchants of Newport were implicated in the business. (*Rhode Island Colonial Records*, vi.)

As the commander-in-chief needed every barrel of flour he could lay his hands on, to victual the four thousand men about to join the expedition against Havana, he wrote at once to the governor of Rhode Island and asked him to decree a general embargo on all shipping. The same fate was shared by other colonies. The embargo was laid and enforced; but as soon as Amherst had assurance that a quantity of provisions for the army was on its way out from England, he hastened to free the ports from restriction, much to the gratification of the merchants, just and unjust. (*Ibid.*, vi.)

In January, 1762, England declared war against Spain. The latter power had been preparing to join forces with France against Britain for a long time, and yet England had persistently refused to listen to Pitt's predictions to that effect. At last, when the truth of his prophecy was realised and it became obvious that His Catholic Majesty was merely waiting for a favourable occasion to open hostilities, George III took the initiative and declared war. The far-seeing Pitt had laid the foundations for a successful descent upon the Spanish West Indies when the expedition against Martinique was sent out: now the great minister had resigned, but the impetus of his genius still carried England on to victory.

The first blow was aimed at Havana, the key to Spain's insular possessions. Early in March, 1762, Lord Albemarle sailed from England with four regiments under convoy of Admiral Sir George Pocock, and toward the end of April they arrived at Martinique. There Monckton's forces, "much reduced by sickness," were added to the fresh troops, giving Albemarle in all a force of twelve thousand men with which to attack Havana.

Early in the winter orders had been sent to Amherst to provide four thousand men, some of whom were to be provincials, and to send them to Cape St. Nicholas, the north-western tip of Haiti, to join the rest of the expedition. If the attack on Cuba proved successful, these troops were to be returned to the commander-in-chief immediately after the conquest, and he should then undertake a similar enterprise against the Spanish settlements along the north coast of the Gulf of Mexico. Amherst organised his contingent as early in the season as the deliberation of the colonial assemblies allowed; but it was the end of June before all the troops had left New York. (Corbett's *England in the Seven Years' War*, ii.) Albemarle and Pocock decided not to wait for them. Passing through the dangerous Old Bahama Channel, the fleet came in sight of Matanzas, and on the sixth of June approached the island capital. The Spaniards, although previously warned, were completely surprised.

The chief fortification of Havana was Morro Castle, which stood on a rocky point at the harbour's mouth, bidding defiance to attack by land or by sea. Strangely enough, this bulwark of strength lacked a garrison versed in the use of artillery, and to remedy that deficiency its defence was assigned to Don Luis de Velasco, the captain of a ship-of-war. Velasco manned the fortress with gunners from the navy and prepared to discharge his important trust. The British Army landed almost unresisted about six miles to the eastward of the city. After a few minor engagements the main attack was concentrated on Morro Castle, while the enemy, with the Spanish faculty of doing the wrong thing at the right time, bottled up their own fleet by sinking three ships in the narrow entrance to the harbour.

This achievement removed all possibility of a naval engagement which might have frustrated the whole expedition. If the English fleet had been disabled the city might have been saved, but now the fall of Havana must mean the capture of the fleet. (Captain Stockton's *Military and Naval Operations against Cuba and Puerto Rico*, in Military Historical Society of Massachusetts' *Papers*, vol. xi.) The soil in front of the castle was so thin and rocky that earthworks were almost out of the question. Bundles of faggots were employed instead, and when these, scorched to tinder by the frightful June sun, caught fire, Albemarle used cotton bales to form the approaches and batteries—an expedient resorted to by Andrew Jackson in the defence of New Orleans some forty years later.

As at Louisburg and at Martinique, the sailors turned artillerymen, and in spite of the torrid heat of a Cuban summer, did splendid work on shore. The siege, however, was far from enjoyable. Bad food and lack of water played havoc with the English, until five thousand soldiers and three thousand seamen were disabled with wounds or fever. But though the sea was scattered over with floating corpses, and though the camp was a pest-house, the British sappers and miners continued their relentless approach to the walls of Morro Castle.

Men looked out to sea in the hope of descrying the belated ships from New York bringing the American contingent, but July was almost gone before their sails came up over the horizon. Even then the forces that arrived were but a fraction of those that were expected, for part had been intercepted and captured by a French fleet hovering about the Caicos Passage, and part had been wrecked in the perilous Old Bahama Channel. (Corbett's *England in the Seven Years' War*, ii.) Nevertheless, the moral effect: of the reinforcements was great.

On the thirtieth day of July a breach was made in the wall of the castle and an assault followed. Don Luis de Velasco, although seriously hurt, rushed to the ramparts to help beat back the onslaught of the British grenadiers: but all in vain. The brave Spaniard was shot in the breast, and when he had fallen, mortally wounded, Morro Castle followed the example of Louisburg, Quebec, and Montreal.

★★★★★

When the news of Velasco's gallant defines and dramatic death reached Madrid the King of Spain ordered that there should always be a ship in the Spanish Navy named *Velasco*. The last man-of-war to bear that appellation was captured by the fleet under Commodore Dewey in Manila Bay on the first of May,

1898. (Stockton's *Military and Naval Operations.*)

★★★★★★

The second instalment of American reinforcements arrived off Havana on the second day of August. The surrender of the city was then inevitable, and on the tenth Albemarle sent in his summons. Out of bravado the Spaniards refused it, but the next day's bombardment produced a myriad of white flags all over the town. On the thirteenth of August, 1762, Havana capitulated, and great was the fall thereof. At one blow Spain lost nearly one-fifth of her entire navy, while the amount of prize-money acquired by the army and navy recalled the days of Sir Francis Drake. Three million pounds sterling fell into England's lap. Much of this was divided among the soldiers and sailors, although the lion's share went to the Earl of Albemarle and Admiral Sir George Pocock, each of whom received over one hundred thousand pounds.

Before the good news from Cuba reached New York an unexpected development to the north-eastward diverted Amherst's thoughts. By the concentration in the West Indies the British garrisons in North America were reduced to a minimum, and the French ministry availed itself of the opportunity to give England a saucy slap by attacking Newfoundland. In May the Chevalier de Ternay slipped out of Brest with two ships of the line, two frigates, and about fifteen hundred troops under the Comte de Haussonville, and on one of the longest days in the year the squadron came in sight of St. John's, Newfoundland. The English garrison of one hundred men quickly surrendered the place, after which the Frenchmen amused themselves by destroying the fisheries, shipping, and whatever property the island afforded.

The governor of Newfoundland, Captain Graves, who later became a well-known admiral, was absent from St. John's at the time, and so escaped capture. To his appeal for aid Amherst made as quick a response as circumstances would permit. The situation was difficult, for no troops were available except those at Nova Scotia. Nevertheless, Sir Jeffery collected fifteen hundred men in the course of a month and entrusted them to his brother William, who had never before enjoyed an independent command.

The expedition sailed from Louisburg on September 5. About a week later it was joined by Lord Colville with his flag-ship and a frigate, a few leagues to the southward of St. John's. Finding a very good beach at Torbay, which was not far from his objective, Colonel Amherst landed his troops early on the morning of the thirteenth. From that point a rough path led through the woods to the open country around the town. The British soon drove the enemy out of the woods and back to "two very high and steep hills" which seemed to control the harbour and all the ground between the attacking party and St. John's.

One smart engagement snatched the first hill from the French; the second they vacated voluntarily and withdrew into the town. (*Gentleman's Magazine*, vol. 32.) While Colonel Amherst was landing his artillery and stores and planting his batteries on the night of the sixteenth, the enemy's fleet took advantage of a dense fog and stole out of the harbour. Colville and Graves were on the watch for just such a move, but the sly Ternay towed out his ships with boats, and when the fog lifted, the hostile squadron was far beyond pursuit. St. John's was doomed and Ternay knew it. His object was merely to save what he could.

On September 18, 1762, the anniversary of the surrender of Quebec, the Comte de Haussonville asked for Amherst's terms. With an insistence upon a speedy decision which would have done justice to his brother, the British colonel demanded that the garrison of St. John's surrender as prisoners of war. The Frenchman readily agreed to the conditions imposed, and Newfoundland was restored to its traditional sovereign. As Amherst's losses did not exceed fifty men killed and wounded and the surrendered garrison numbered over six hundred, it is difficult to see what the French had gained by their summer excursion to the coast of Newfoundland.

CHAPTER 11

Pontiac's War

From the time Jeffery Amherst's ship cast anchor off Louisburg until the general left New York for England five years later, the bane of his military existence was the American Indian. In 1758 savages skulked in the woods of Cape Breton Island and fell upon any unwary English regular who separated himself from his fellows; in the following year the seizure of two messengers whom the Commander-in-Chief had despatched to Quebec with important communications for Wolfe was the occasion of Major Rogers' expedition against the St. Francis Indians.

As doubtful allies of the English in the descent upon Montreal in 1760, the redskins became disgusted with Amherst's prohibition of inhumanity, and the majority of them returned to their wilderness homes in a rage. Then came a dangerous uprising of the Cherokees on the Carolina frontier. This had hardly been suppressed with fire and sword when an Indian outbreak, the most serious and widespread of all, broke out at Detroit in May, 1763. The last disturbance bears the name of its chief organiser and promoter and is known as the Conspiracy of Pontiac. Two Indian grievances of the first magnitude were the causes of the war that came as the aftermath of the conquest of Canada.

The first of these was the constant encroachment of the white man upon the forest domain of the savages in spite of all promises and treaties to the contrary. As early as 1760 Amherst had sent a written message to the Iroquois in the vicinity of Fort Pitt, assuring them that they would be compensated for any ground taken for military posts, (*Journals of the House of Burgesses of Virginia, 1761-1765.*) but that engagement had never been fulfilled, and the Indians began to suspect that this was the first step towards their enslavement and the invasion of their domain. (Brodhead's *New York Colonial Documents*, vii.) More disturbing than the military occupation of strategic points was the fact that "a number of vagabonds," under pretence of hunting, had over-run their lands and were making settlements in many parts of them. (*Report on Canadian Archives for 1889.*)

This usurpation shook what little faith the Indians had in their white neighbours, for, by the Treaty of Easton, Pennsylvania had ret-roceded to them all the country west of the Alleghany Mountains for their hunting-ground. (*Ibid*; O'Callaghan's *Documentary History of New York*, ii.) Although the Privy Council accepted this self-denying ordinance as the solution of frontier troubles and, in 1761, extended its provisions to apply to Virginia, (*Acts of the Privy Council—Colonial,* iv), the aborigines continued to make "grievous and repeated com-plaints" that the treaty was not lived up to. There was abundant room for misinterpretation of the phrase "westward of the great ridge." Did it mean beyond the foothills, or beyond the watershed? The Indians construed it in one way, the colonists in another. The uncertainty was not cleared up until the Royal Proclamation of 1763 set the limit of the expanding colonies at "the heads or sources of any of the rivers which fall into the Atlantic Ocean from the west or northwest": in the meantime, the Indians took it upon themselves to enforce the terms of the treaty as they understood them.

The second great cause of discontent was the scarcity of supplies felt by the Indians as soon as New France fell into the hands of the English. Hardly had Major Rogers taken possession of the western posts in the name of the King of Great Britain, when it became ap-parent that the new masters of the country were neither so generous as the French nor so pleasant to deal with in business relations. The Frenchmen had taken pains to secure the good will of the Indians who came to the forts. They gave the redmen guns, ammunition, and cloth-ing, until the latter became entirely dependent upon the devices of the Europeans and forgot the use of their primitive weapons and garments. The English had always neglected the Indians, enemy or ally. Now they saw no reason for continuing the crafty *largesse* of their Bourbon en-emies. Supplies ceased to flow from the wilderness posts, and want and suffering among the Indians followed, as a matter of course.

At first Amherst acted upon the advice of Sir William Johnson, the superintendent of Indian affairs for the northern tribes, and sent pork and flour to the baronet's house "for the use of the most necessitous Indians during the winter," (*Amherst to Bradstreet*, Nov. 8, 1760, *Myers Collection of MSS.*, in the New York Public Library), but when it appeared that this charity was likely to become a permanent institution, the commander-in-chief very naturally felt that affairs were being managed on a wrong basis. He decided that Johnson's policy of treating the Indians like children, pleasing their vanity, and buying their friendship with little presents and favours, was not sound. It was not consistent with the dignity of England, nor was it calculated to secure the Indians' friendship and respect for any length of time.

Furthermore, it was uneconomic, and Amherst begrudged every penny that went from his military chest as a *douceur* to a people whom he despised. His first move was to cut off their supply of arms and ammunition, "lest they should increase their stock from our bounty." (*Amherst to Sir William Johnson*, August 18, 1761, *Emmet MS.* 8814, New York Public Library.) When Johnson asked for £1,000 to purchase the usual presents for the meeting of the Six Nations, Sir Jeffery granted the sum, but charged the recipient "to be as sparing in these presents as possible." (*Miscellaneous MSS.*, New York Public Library.)

In like vein Amherst wrote to Colonel Henry Bouquet, who was commanding in Pennsylvania; he insisted upon economy in the matter of presents to the Indians in that quarter, and increased the resentment of the redskins by making it difficult for them to get rum. Bouquet remonstrated, declaring that a lack of presents was the chief cause of the discontent among the Indians; but Amherst could not see the matter in that light. His reply to Bouquet's representations makes clear the Indian policy of the commander-in-chief:

> As to appropriating a particular sum to be laid out yearly to the warriors in presents, etc., that I can by no means agree to; nor can I think it necessary to give them any presents by way of *bribes*, for if they do not behave properly, they are to be punished. (Parkman's *Conspiracy of Pontiac*, i)

Sir Jeffery acted according to his convictions, which were based upon a military man's point of view, but in the end his policy, or lack of policy, proved to be penny-wise and pound-foolish.

An entirely different attitude toward the Indian question was that of Sir William Johnson, a man who had been singularly successful in his dealings with the redmen. For almost thirty years this adventurous Irishman had lived on the frontier of New York, and by a prosperous traffic with the natives had accumulated a small fortune. His two mansions in the Mohawk Valley, Johnson Castle and Johnson Hall, were gathering-places for the Indians, who came in crowds to visit their good-natured host. Johnson's first wife was a Dutch woman. After her death his affections centred upon Molly Brant, the sister of the Mohawk war-chief, and thus the *entente cordiale* between the frontier plutocrat and his savage neighbours was consummated into an enduring friendship.

Johnson's military career in the French and Indian War brought him recognition in England. After the unsatisfactory but hard-fought Battle of Lake George he was made a baronet, and was still further rewarded by a gift of five thousand pounds from the king. More important for England was his appointment as superintendent of Indian affairs for the northern tribes, which was made about this time. It was Johnson, too, who captured Niagara in the same season which saw Ticonderoga and Crown Point fall into Amherst's hands.

Whatever estimate one may form of Sir William's career as a whole, one must admit that his faculty for dealing with the Indians was little short of genius. His policy was diametrically opposed to that of the commander-in-chief, but since their jurisdictions conflicted, and military measures became entangled with Indian affairs, even Sir William Johnson could not roll back the tide of discontent which was sweeping eastward from the northwest. He saw the danger, but without Amherst's support his soothing influence could not be really efficacious. In vain the Iroquois brought their troubles to his sympathetic ear, for Amherst refused to continue the French practice of flattering them and of making them presents.

As Johnson rightly declared, the customary gifts, however expensive and bountifully bestowed, were "infinitely cheaper and much more effectual than the keeping of a large body of regular troops in their several countries." (Parkman's *Conspiracy of Pontiac*, i.) Where Indian hostility was concerned, he believed that an ounce of prevention was worth a pound of cure, a conviction which events were to justify only too soon. To Johnson's warnings and suggestions Sir Jeffery, thoroughly irritated by the unrest of the western Indians, finally retorted that unless the savages became loyal subjects of George III:

> They must not only expect the severest retaliation, but an entire destruction of all their nations, for I am firmly resolved, whenever they give me an occasion, to extirpate them root and branch. (*Amherst to Johnson, Emmet MS. 8814.*)

But when the occasion was given, the general found his proposed extermination more easily threatened than accomplished.

LA RIVIERE DU DETROIT
Depuis le Lac Sainte Claire
jusqu'au Lac Erié
Echelle de Deux Lieuës Communes

PLAN DU FORT DU DETROIT
Echelle de Soixante Toises

A. Logement du Commandant
B. Corps de Garde
C. L'Eglise
D. Magasin à Poudre
E. Magasin du Commissaire

Marché du Roy

For the first two years after the surrender of New France all that the Indian discontent lacked was a leader. In the winter of 1762-63 the deficiency was supplied by the appearance of an Indian of extraordinary powers. This man was Pontiac, the principal chief of the Ottawas. Proud in spirit and keen in perception, Pontiac realised the crisis that confronted his race and determined to overthrow the existing order of things. A return to the days of French ascendancy seemed to him the surest way of putting an end to the evils that oppressed his brethren. In this belief he was encouraged by "French missionaries and others" who assured him that though the King of France had been asleep in recent years he was now awake, and that his armies were advancing up the Mississippi and the St. Lawrence to rescue his red children from the encroaching English. (*Parkman's Conspiracy of Pontiac,* i.)

Now was the time to strike. Towards the end of the year 1762, Pontiac sent ambassadors to many different nations, urging them to rise simultaneously at a certain time in May and fall upon every English fort in the wilderness. When these were destroyed, the whole pack would assail the frontier. The exhortation was received with enthusiasm throughout the Ohio Valley and the district of the Great Lakes; even one member of the Iroquois confederacy, the Senecas, who were geographically the most remote from Sir William Johnson, joined the insurgent league. In the early spring of 1763 rumours of a general uprising floated into the British forts, but the dissimulation of the savages was so successful that no one suspected how formidable a blow was in preparation.

On the evening of May 6, 1763, an Ottawa Indian who had only half-heartedly acquiesced in Pontiac's designs came to the gate of the fort at Detroit and asked to speak to the commander. It was evident that he had an important secret to impart. The gates were opened to him and in a few minutes, he found himself in the presence of Major Gladwin and his second in command, Captain Campbell. To them the Indian divulged the plot which his chief had contrived for the destruction of all the English at Detroit. The plan was this: Pontiac, at the head of sixty picked warriors with weapons concealed under their blankets, was to come to the fort to ask the *commandant* for a great council.

After this delegation the rest of the village should follow, as unconcernedly as possible; but all were to be armed with hidden tomahawks and knives. The women of the Ottawas, too, should straggle in with the others, carrying guns cut short enough to be hidden under their blan-

kets. These squaws should take position in the back street of the fortified village and await the war-cry of the great chief. At the given signal
all would hurl themselves upon the English and destroy them, but care
would be taken not to hurt any Frenchman. This was part of the conspiracy of Pontiac, and its execution was set for the very next day.

The truth of the communication was apparent to Major Gladwin.
He recalled rumours that many Indians had recently visited the black-
smith's shop to borrow files and saws for some mysterious purpose.
When these suspicious acts were described to the *commandant*, with
friendly suggestions to be on his guard, he had given little heed to the
news; but now the events assumed serious significance. The desired
tools were to be used in amputating the muzzles of the guns, in preparation for the surprise of the garrison.

The major thanked his informant and wished to reward him with
presents; but the savage shook his head, asking only that the Englishmen would never reveal his identity to the conspirators. Gladwin
and Campbell relieved his mind on that point, and without disclosing
what startling words had been poured into their ears, the commanders
quietly doubled the guards and closed all entrances, except the main
gates. At each of the latter two sentinels were posted, while the officers
were ordered to inspect the arms of the troops under their command
and to notify their men to be ready for duty at a moment's notice.

All these precautions were taken, and with so little disturbance
that neither the French dwelling within the fortified town, called the
Fort, nor the watchful Indians beyond the palisade had any occasion
to suspect that the plot was discovered. (*The Pontiac Manuscript*, printed
in the Michigan Pioneer and Historical Society's *Collections*, Vol. viii.)

On the morning following, May 7, Pontiac ordered all his people
to chant the war-song in their village, to paint their faces, and to put
on their feather bonnets in preparation for the attack. Eagerly his followers obeyed his instructions, making themselves frightful with the
paraphernalia of savage warfare. Under their blankets or hidden within
their crude garments, the Indians carried whatever weapons they could
best conceal and yet use to advantage when the appointed moment
came. Thus equipped, the chief and his motley rabble appeared before
the fort at about ten o'clock. Pontiac demanded a council with the
English officers. There was nothing extraordinary in the request, for
the redmen were frequently moved to wait upon the military commanders and ask for a hearing of their grievances, real or imaginary.

Indeed, on the first day of May Pontiac, with malice aforethought, had been to the fort and had told Gladwin that he intended to pay him a formal visit before long. (*Parkman's Conspiracy of Pontiac,* i.) Now the time had come. His wish was granted, and soon the crafty Indian with his sixty trusted warriors crowded into the house of Captain Campbell. There Major Gladwin, accompanied by a party of officers who were warned of the impending danger, received them: other officers were busy about the town, stationing the troops where they would be of the most service when the outbreak occurred. The council was opened, and while it was in progress the rest of the Indians flocked through the gates, settled down wherever their chief had ordained that they should place themselves, and awaited the war-cry.

When Pontiac calculated that the trap was ready to be sprung, he stepped outside the council-house and looked about the enclosure to make sure that all was as it should be. To his great surprise, instead of seeing groups of idle soldiers lounging about the fort, he found the drill-ground alive with armed troops going through their exercises. At once the scheming redskin realised that his designs were discovered. His only thought then was to get his people safely out of the fort. When this was accomplished, he might deceive the English commander into believing that there was no plot. After that he would take other measures and crown a second attempt with complete success.

Disappointed and disconcerted, the proud Ottawa turned back to the house where his conspirators impatiently awaited the signal for attack. But one look at his face, full of vexation and wrath, dampened their ardour. There was to be no massacre that day. Pontiac, however, took care that no action on his part should justify Gladwin's suspicions or jeopardise the safe departure of the Indians. He killed time by making a meaningless speech, which the major answered calmly without intimating any knowledge of the hostile intentions of his uncouth guests.

The art of dissimulation was practised with remarkable *finesse* on both sides, but perhaps the height of diplomacy was reached when Gladwin presented the departing Indians with numerous trifles which he knew would please them. The discomfited conspirators, however, were too furious to remember what few manners they possessed. They "went out without saying goodbye or anything else," and passing through the gate returned to their camp. The first attempt to destroy the English at Detroit had been frustrated, but this failure was only the beginning of the end.

Two days later, on the ninth of May, the common outside the

stockade was again alive with a greasy horde of Indians. From their midst out strode the haughty Pontiac. He approached the gate of the fort, but it was barred against him. He called to the sentinels and asked why he, the chief of the Ottawas, was refused admittance. The commander replied sententiously that Pontiac might enter, but that most of his friends must remain outside the palisade.

The Indian protested that all his people wished to smell the smoke of the peace-pipe, that would bind their interests with those of the English; but Gladwin, disgusted with the transparency of the savage's designs, answered him with a flat refusal, which ended the conversation. Furious at the failure of his second stratagem, Pontiac turned on his heel and went back to the Ottawa village. Seizing a tomahawk, he chanted the war-song and cried that "since he could not slay the English at the fort, he would slay those outside of it." Thenceforth no British subject in the region, man, woman or child, was safe except within the stockade of Detroit.

Foiled in his attempts to capture the fort by treachery, Pontiac now made an open attack. For six hours on May 10 the Indians assailed the palisades with furious persistency; but their efforts were in vain. In spite of this hostile demonstration, Major Gladwin continued to believe that the outbreak was merely a passing mood, and now that the savages had given vent to their feelings, he felt that a reconciliation would be easily effected. As the town was in great need of provisions and there was no prospect of supplies, peace, or at least a truce, would be highly advantageous to the Englishmen.

Captain Campbell and a junior officer were sent to the enemy's camp to negotiate with the wily Pontiac, who pretended to show a strong desire for amity; but Gladwin's hopes were soon dashed. Campbell and his companion were immediately made captives, and before many days the older man was murdered by the savages, while his more fortunate fellow-prisoner succeeded in making his escape. (*Parkman's Conspiracy of Pontiac,* i.) It became clear that Detroit was to be blockaded in earnest, and the harassed garrison resigned themselves to a long and vigilant defence.

The tactics by which Pontiac had failed to surprise and destroy the Englishmen at Detroit were employed by his allies and followers with almost universal success in compassing the downfall of the other British posts in the Lake Region. Less than ten days after the fiasco in Gladwin's council-room, the unsuspecting garrison at Fort Sandusky were pounced upon by a band of Indian visitors. The parade-ground was soon strewn with the bodies of butchered soldiers and the fort was put to the torch. A week later a friendly talk between the British *commandant* at St. Joseph's and a group of Indian chiefs suddenly changed into a massacre of the garrison. Lower Lake Michigan was thus purged of the English. Then in quick succession came the loss of Fort Miami on the Maumee River, the capture of Ouatanon on the Wabash, and the bloody slaughter at Fort Michilimackinac, which gave Lakes Michigan and Huron into the complete control of the savages.

Towards the east fortune favoured Pontiac's schemes with equal success. The little garrison at Presqu' isle on Lake Erie had long mistrusted that an Indian attack upon their fort was impending, and on the fifteenth of June their expectations were realised. At early dawn the yelling of a large number of redmen announced the opening of a hot fight. The blockhouse was supposedly impregnable, but its shingled roof was showered with fire-arrows and frequently burst into flames. The defence was gallant and exciting. For two days and two nights Ensign Christie and his twenty-seven men held the enemy at bay, and the soldiers, in spite of their weariness, were resolved to hold the post until the end—although it was clear that sooner or later a conflagration must terminate the conflict.

The Indians proposed that the garrison surrender the fort and retire unmolested to the nearest post. The terms were dismally reminiscent of the capitulation of Fort William Henry in 1757, but the *commandant* chose them rather than to face the certain death which must come with the burning of the blockhouse. The place was surrendered, and, as might be expected, its recent defenders, instead of being allowed to go to Fort Le Boeuf or Niagara, were carried prisoners to Pontiac's camp at Detroit. (*Parkman's Conspiracy of Pontiac*, i.)

When Presqu' isle fell, it was inevitable that the wilderness posts linking it with Fort Pitt would be swept away by the tide of Indian victory which was rolling eastward towards the Alleghany Mountains. Such indeed proved to be the gruesome fact. The handful of men to whom the security of Fort Le Boeuf was entrusted stood their ground until the fort became a burning prison, from which the gallant defenders made good their escape into the dark night, eventually reaching the stout walls of Fort Pitt. Less fortunate were the occupants of Venango. There a pretence of friendship on the part of the savages opened the gates to a band of Senecas, who treacherously fell upon the garrison and killed them all, except the *commandant*, Lieutenant Gordon. A worse fate awaited this unfortunate officer. For several nights in succession, he was roasted over a slow fire, until at length death put an end to his tortures. (*Parkman's Conspiracy of Pontiac*, ii.)

In the first two months of the war the savages had been astoundingly victorious. West of Niagara, but two forts, Detroit and Fort Pitt, remained in the hands of the English. Around these two storm-centres the fury of the redmen now whirled with increasing energy.

At about the time the last of these tragedies occurred, Amherst received his first intimation that there was trouble in the Lake Region. Early in the spring he had sent a strong detachment up the inland waterway with a supply of provisions for Detroit and the other western posts. The convoy consisted of several boats manned and guarded by about a hundred men under Lieutenant Cuyler. Leaving Fort Niagara in the middle of May, they cruised along the northern shore of Lake Erie on their way to Detroit. On the twenty-eighth of the month the expedition landed at Point Pelee, not far from the mouth of the Detroit River.

There they were attacked by a ferocious band of Wyandots, who captured almost the entire party and their equipment. Cuyler with a few others escaped, and returning to Niagara, sent a report of the disaster to the commander-in-chief. His unhappy comrades were not so fortunate. Made captive by their savage foes, the soldiers were forced to man the oars and to propel the flotilla on its way to expectant Detroit, where the sight of the approaching vessels was hailed with delight until proximity disclosed the horrid reality of the situation. Worse than the disappointment of the besieged, who now were confronted by the prospect of starvation, was another sequel to the capture of Cuyler's expedition.

For several succeeding days the smiling surface of the river was hideous with bloody corpses and half-roasted human bodies floating downstream from Pontiac's camp. Every conceivable form of torture had been practised upon the wretched Englishmen, only a few of whom were saved for adoption and slavery. (*Pontiac Manuscript.*) With such sickening suggestions of their probable fate, Gladwin and his garrison continued their endeavours to save the post for England.

The first relief came to Detroit towards the end of June. A schooner which Gladwin had sent towards Niagara to hasten the progress of Cuyler's supply ships, now returned, bringing the leader of that ill-starred expedition, a few of the survivors, and such reinforcements as could be spared from the fort near the great waterfall. The blockade was successfully run after a hot skirmish with the Indians, and the vessel safely discharged its precious cargo of men, provisions, and ammunition under the guns of the fort. Upon this the enemy, by land and water, redoubled their efforts to reduce Detroit.

When the news of the siege reached Amherst, the general found himself in an embarrassing situation. The military establishment in North America was reduced to almost nothing by the expeditions recently sent against the French and Spanish West Indies. The troops returning from Havana were worn out by the hardships of that frightful campaign and formed but remnants of the valiant regiments that had stormed the Morro. The provincial contingent, too, was only a fraction of what it had been, and was chiefly employed in garrison duty in Canada and on the frontier; hence the mobile force ready for use in this emergency was appallingly meagre. For Amherst it was not a question of what he would do, but rather of what he could do, to suppress the Indian uprising.

Under the circumstances he acted admirably. His first move was to send to the front his *aide-de-camp*, Captain Dalyell, for whom he had both military esteem and personal affection. Sir Jeffery ordered him to go to Niagara with all the reinforcements he could possibly collect, and if developments justified a campaign, to proceed thence to Detroit. Dalyell gathered together two hundred and eighty men and several small cannon; with these and a fresh supply of provisions and ammunition, he sailed from Niagara to relieve the western fort. Though small in quantity, the troops under his command were rare in quality, for they included the incomparable Major Robert Rogers and a score of his rangers.

The expedition reached Detroit in safety on the twenty-ninth of July and did much to restore the spirits of the long-suffering soldiers there. But Dalyell was not content with strengthening the defence. He was a soldier of the type of James Wolfe, and was bitten with a desire to inflict an immediate and decisive defeat upon the savages. In a conference with Gladwin on the day of his arrival, he urged the latter to allow him to lead an attack against the Indian camp at the earliest possible date. The *commandant* was reluctant to grant the request, but remembering, perhaps, that his friend was by no means a novice in Indian warfare, as he had been the companion of Israel Putnam on more than one adventurous occasion, Gladwin finally yielded to his entreaty.

Long before dawn on the thirty-first of July two hundred and fifty British troops passed out of the gates of the fort, while two large *bateaux* paralleled their movements on the river. A mile and a half from the stockade the road crossed a small creek by a wooden bridge—known ever since that fatal morning as Bloody Bridge—and there the Indians, forewarned by some tell-tale Canadians, awaited their on-coming assailants. When the advance-guard of the British were half-way across the stream, the savages fell upon them unmercifully. The night was intensely dark, and the Indians seemed to be on all sides.

It was the same old story. The savages shot down the British by scores, while the Englishmen could not guess where the enemy were, except by the flash of their deadly muskets. When it became evident that his men were entirely surrounded, Dalyell ordered an instant re-treat. The return to Detroit would have been a flight had not the commander, twice wounded though he was, enforced order upon his terror-stricken soldiers. As the men hurried along in the grey light of daybreak, their leader caught sight of a sergeant who had fallen helplessly wounded and who must soon feel the blow of a savage tomahawk.

With quick sympathy Dalyell turned back to rescue the subaltern. A third shot struck him and he fell dead, while his detachment con-tinued on their frenzied way towards the shelter of the fort. At last, the nightmare was over and four-fifths of the men, with the aid of the resourceful Rogers, were once more within the walls of Detroit.

Far from achieving the purpose which its advocate had intended, the fight at Bloody Bridge elated the besieging Indians, giving to the tedious monotony of the blockade just that excitement which was necessary to revive the flagging interest of the restless savages. Dalyell's body was recovered by the English and brought into the fort, but not until the Indians had torn out the gallant soldier's heart and smeared its blood upon the faces of their prisoners.

The other centre of Indian activity in the summer of 1763 was Fort Pitt. Since the last week in May, pioneers and settlers in its vi-cinity had been menaced by the savages, and on June 22 an unsuc-cessful attack upon the fort itself inaugurated a blockade. (Parkman's *Conspiracy of Pontiac*, ii.) Thenceforth that strategic post was practically isolated from the rest of the military establishments of the English. Fortunately Fort Pitt was commanded by an officer of remarkable intelligence and fortitude. Captain Ecuyer was a lively Swiss who en-joyed fighting for fighting's sake, and if his post had not been burdened with refugees, many of whom were women and children, he would have looked upon the siege as a most entertaining game. His garrison numbered more than three hundred, provisions were plenty and the fort was in an excellent posture of defence.

The *commandant's* only anxiety arose from the fact that smallpox had broken out in his camp; this danger, however, did not assume alarming proportions. Throughout July Fort Pitt was closely hemmed in by the savages, but their assaults were only half-hearted until the morning of the twenty-seventh. Then the red-skinned warriors opened a general fire which continued for several days. Ecuyer was in his element, and his soldiers were not far behind him in their enjoyment of the fray. Many wished to make a sortie and drive the Indians from their hiding-places, but this was wisely forbidden. Though the *commandant* was wounded in the leg by a swift arrow, he merely made sport of the accident, and day after day the same martial program went on. Suddenly, on the first of August, the savages decamped, leaving the tired garrison to speculate upon the cause of their unexpected departure.

The redskins had good reason for abandoning the attack upon Fort Pitt. An army of British regulars was approaching the forks of the Ohio, and this expedition could be better disposed of in the depths of the wilderness than before the walls of the obstinate fortress. Early in June, before the news of Cuyler's mishap or of the blockade of Detroit reached Amherst's ears, the commander-in-chief had heard reports of trouble with the Indians along the frontier of Pennsylvania. At first, he was not greatly disturbed by the alarm; but when bad tidings were constantly followed by worse, Sir Jeffery's apparent indifference changed to grave concern, particularly when the developments in the Lake Region made it clear that this was no ordinary uprising of the Indians. Collecting and organising what troops he could, Amherst sent them off to Philadelphia to be used as Colonel Bouquet, his right-hand man in the Quaker province, should see fit.

Colonel Henry Bouquet was one of those rare spirits who relieve the monotony of military annals. Like the gallant Ecuyer, he was a Swiss, and had been a soldier from boyhood. His first appearance in America was as a lieutenant-colonel of the Royal Americans, the crack regiment of which Amherst was colonel *ex officio*. In 1763 Bouquet was in command of the first battalion, and ready for service at a moment's notice. For the business in hand, he was one man in a thousand. His hatred of the Indians, whom he termed "the vilest of brutes," was equalled only by his chief's regard for that "execrable race." As he sped on his way to the relief of Fort Pitt, the colonel exchanged interesting suggestions with the general as to the most efficient manner of getting rid of the redskins.

Amherst had just heard of two particularly atrocious murders per-petrated by the savages and his blood was up. His first orders to Bou-quet were that he wished "to hear of no prisoners should any of the villains be met with in arms," but this injunction was mild in com-parison with subsequent ideas which occurred to Sir Jeffery. (Park-man's *Conspiracy of Pontiac*, ii.) Learning that smallpox had broken out at Fort Pitt, the commander-in-chief wondered whether the disease could not be spread to good advantage among the hostile Indians. He expressed this thought in a postscript to Bouquet. The resourceful Swiss seized upon the idea and developed it. In his reply to Amherst, he wrote:

I will try to inoculate the ——— with some blankets that may fall in their hands, and take care not to get the disease myself. As it is a pity to expose good men against them, I wish we could make use of the Spanish method, to hunt them with English dogs, supported by rangers and some light horse, who would, I think, effectually extirpate or remove that vermin.

Sir Jeffery's rejoinder approved the smallpox method of extermina-tion and expressed his regret that the remoteness of merry England made the suggestion of canine aid impracticable. (Parkman's *Conspiracy of Pontiac*, ii.) Whether the blanket treatment was practised or not must remain a question, but the credulous may draw their own conclusions from the fact that a few months later smallpox broke out with unusual severity among the Indians of the Ohio Valley.

Colonel Bouquet lost no time in getting to the front. From Car-lisle, which was filled with terror-stricken refugees, he pushed west-ward with about five hundred men, the best of whom were High-landers of the Forty-Second Regiment. All along the way there were depressing evidences of Indian ravages. The whole countryside was deserted by its erstwhile inhabitants, and here and there the charred timbers of a settler's cabin told a tragic story of frontier life. At Bedford the troops rested three days before setting out upon the most difficult part of their route, the crossing of the Alleghany Mountains and the traversing of the rough wilderness beyond the ridge.

Here Bouquet was happily reinforced by a band of thirty back-woodsmen, whose familiarity with forest conditions made them in-valuable adjuncts in the van and in the rear. The road followed by Bouquet and his little army was that rugged trail hacked out by Forbes's axe-men on their way to the conquest of Fort Duquesne in the summer and autumn of 1758. It was indeed a difficult track. Up precipitous mountain-sides and through dangerous defiles the sweating soldiers and struggling wagon trains pressed on to the relief of Fort Pitt. After a few days of such exertion the commander decided to leave behind the more cumbrous part of his convoy and let the troops advance with greater speed.

The change was made, but hardly had the unhampered expedition resumed its march when war-whoops and the rattle of musketry informed the soldiers that they were in the presence of an enemy more to be feared than the mountain fastnesses which they had scaled, and more treacherous than the quagmires that had occasionally arrested their wearisome progress.

It was shortly after noon on August 5th when the advance-guard was thus suddenly attacked in the woods of Edge Hill by an invisible band of Indians. Two companies immediately came to its support, succeeded in driving the enemy from their ambuscade, "and pursued them a good way." The savages, however, returned to the attack with vigour; their fire which was obstinate in front soon extended along the flanks of the British. The position became serious. Bouquet ordered a general charge, hoping to drive the enemy from the heights they occupied; and although to all immediate appearances the troops accomplished that object, no real advantage was gained.

The enemy, in true Indian fashion, gave way—only to reappear upon all sides soon afterwards. The light convoy, consisting of three hundred and fifty horses loaded with flour, had been left in the rear in supposed safety, but now it was mercilessly assailed by the savages. The troops fell back to protect the horses and provisions, and the action became general and deadly. All that afternoon the fighting continued. At night the battle subsided, giving the English an opportunity to count their losses. More than sixty men out of a scant five hundred lay dead or wounded on the forest battleground.

Such a diminution of his effectives could not be easily afforded by Colonel Bouquet. With gloomy forebodings he looked forward to the next day's encounter, which would doubtless begin with the earliest light of dawn. In the meantime, the men improvised out of bags of flour a shelter for the wounded, and about this central stronghold they arranged themselves in a defensive circle. (*Bouquet to Amherst*, August 5, 1763.) Then the tired soldiers lay upon their arms and snatched what sleep they could.

True to Bouquet's expectations, the battle began at daybreak before the British troops had had much opportunity to recover from their fatigue of the preceding day. The soldiers' chief lack was water, of which not a drop was to be had. A small stream called Bushy Run, from which this desperate struggle afterwards ironically took its name, lay only a half-mile distant, but between the thirst-maddened troops and its refreshing waters the forest bristled with a host of redskins. As on the previous afternoon, the Indians shouted and yelled in a terrifying manner; their efforts to reach the stronghold, however, were unsuccessful. The Englishmen fought splendidly. Again, and again they apparently routed the enemy only to see them reappear when least expected. This sort of fighting was too exasperating and too dangerous for Colonel Henry Bouquet.

With ingenuity worthy of Pontiac himself, the Swiss commander devised a ruse whereby the Indians, deceived into thinking that the British were retreating, rushed into a trap and were practically surrounded by those whom they thought to have conquered. Then indeed were the tables turned. The English poured deadly volleys upon the front and right flank of the astonished savages. At first the Indians returned the fire, but the shock of the surprise and the fury of this unlooked-for onslaught soon gave them but one thought—to fly. The rout of the enemy was complete, and the British pursued them until "they were totally dispersed." When the chase was over and the woods seemed quite cleared of lurking savages, the victorious little army "marched without molestation" to the banks of Bushy Run. (*Bouquet to Amherst*, August 6, 1763.) Four days later Colonel Bouquet and his men relieved Fort Pitt. The right arm of Pontiac's rebellion was broken.

Amherst was well pleased with the success of Bouquet's expedition and particularly with that "very wisely concerted and as happily executed" stratagem at Edge Hill, which had spelled defeat for the Indians. (*Amherst to Bouquet*, August 31, 1763.) While the general rejoiced in the ebbing tide of Pontiac's victories in the upper Ohio Valley, Indian impatience was doing much to relieve the precarious state of affairs at Detroit. The savages had not anticipated such a prolonged and uninteresting siege as that which had lasted from late spring until early autumn, with only occasional encouraging and enlivening episodes. Their ardour waned with the summer solstice, the more so when rumours came to them that a strong British force was on its way up the lakes.

Three of the four tribes, until now under Pontiac's leadership, decided to sue for peace. Gladwin, only too glad to see the turn affairs were taking, feigned reluctance to grant an absolute pacification, but consented to a truce. The Ottawas alone continued in open war against the English. The thirty-first of October, however, saw the final blow fall upon Pontiac's pet project. On that day a letter arrived from M. Neyon, who commanded the principal French post in the Illinois country, informing the Ottawa leader that any expectation of assistance from the French was futile. England and France were at peace and the Indians had better abandon their hopeless hostilities. (Parkman's *Conspiracy of Pontiac*, ii.)

This was virtually the end of the Conspiracy of Pontiac. Had the defeated chieftain known the history of the persuasive letter, he would have been even less happy than he was—for its existence was due entirely to the efforts of an astute Englishman. That Englishman was none other than Sir Jeffery Amherst. Realising how powerful an influence the French still wielded among the Indians, and knowing, too, that much of the present trouble was due to the savages' delusion that a Bourbon Army was coming to their aid, he had demanded that M. Neyon write a circular letter to all the nations of the Ohio Valley and of the Lake Region, putting an end to their false hopes and advising them to bury the hatchet.

The Frenchman reluctantly complied with this requisition, and thus the rebellion received its death blow. The Indian troubles of 1763 have often been regarded as a blight upon the otherwise flawless laurels Amherst won in America. But is such an estimate just? Granted that Sir Jeffery's short-sighted economy in part occasioned the uprising of the savages, when the storm broke did he not handle the crisis exceptionally well? The war was not of the kind to produce brilliant exploits, but its conduct demanded both energy and sagacity. With almost no military resources, the commander-in-chief faced the situation resolutely and made a wise disposition of such troops as he could muster.

His selection of Colonel Bouquet as the leader of the expedition to Fort Pitt was a stroke of genius, which demonstrated itself on the battle-ground of Edge Hill. Few conflicts have so hinged upon the strategy and resourcefulness of one man. In the far West it was Amherst's sagacity that put an end to the machinations of Pontiac. After the fight at Bloody Bridge there was no immediate prospect of sending further military aid to the beleaguered garrison at Detroit. In this predicament the general suppressed the uprising by an expedient, more humane than infected blankets, more economical than arms, and more effectual than either or both.

(See *Bouquet & the Ohio Indian War* which contains two accounts of the campaigns of 1763-1764; *Bouquet's Campaigns* by Cyrus Cort and *The History of Bouquet's Expeditions* by William Smith: Leonaur 2009.)

The Neyon letter both dispelled the enemy's hopes of success and shook their faith in their deceptive friends, the French. On this occasion, as on many others in history, the pen proved mightier than the sword; but seldom has it been the soldier's lot to wield the conquering quill. Within six months of its outbreak, the most formidable and extensive Indian war in our history was brought to a successful conclusion by the energy and sagacity of a general who had almost no available soldiers. Few of Amherst's achievements display his skill and wisdom so forcibly as the crushing of Pontiac's rebellion, yet few of his deeds have been so unjustly appraised.

CHAPTER 12

Favour and Disfavour

More than five years had now passed since Jeffery Amherst came to America, but prolonged residence in the New World had not diminished his longing for England. In June, 1760, he had been careful to ask Pitt's permission to go home as soon as peace should be declared. (Kimball's *Pitt Correspondence*, ii.) Montreal surrendered in that year, but the worldwide conflict of nations continued until the signing of the Treaty of Paris in February, 1763. Not till then was Sir Jeffery granted his long-deferred leave—and then only on condition that Indian disturbances no longer required his presence in the colonies. (Brodhead's *New York Colonial Documents*, vii.)

Hardly had the welcome furlough arrived, when Pontiac's uprising still further delayed the general's departure; but in the autumn of 1763 he decided that conditions justified his return to England. His task was done, and done well. Leaving the chief command to Major-General Gage, Amherst took passage on the sloop-of-war *Weasel*, and setting sail from New York about the middle of November, looked for the last time upon the continent of his many victories. (*Calendar of the Sir William Johnson Manuscripts.*)

The general had not been in England many days before he was presented at court, and was knighted in person by his youthful Majesty George III. (Nicolas's History of Knighthood, iii.) The newly crowned king had succeeded to the throne during Amherst's absence; he was twenty-five years old at that time, and though by no means a fool, one would hardly describe him as "young in years, but in sage counsel old." His whole ambition was to break down the coalition of great Whig families which had ruled England during the reign of his "wise and unlovely" grandfather.

His chief assets in this attempt were determination of the kind

174

that is likely to be mistaken for obstinacy, and a willingness to corrupt Parliament in order to achieve his purpose. Sir Jeffery's relations with the misguided despot were various in the course of the next decade, but at this time he was especially smiled upon. At a levee at St. James', in the last week of January, it was noticeable that the king took the late commander-in-chief aside and had a long conference with him, an attention which must have been disconcerting, to say the least, to one so unused to royalty. (*Gentleman's Magazine,* January, 1764.)

Although Amherst basked in royal sunshine during the first few weeks after his arrival in England, he was not without enemies. Among the latter the most prominent and most dangerous was Major Charles Lee, who later won a bad name for himself in the American Revolution. It was not many years since this soldier of fortune had been generous in his praise of the general under whom he served, (New York Historical Society's *Collections,* 1871), but loyalty was not Lee's long suit, particularly when anything could be gained by a change of front. Now he bent every effort to stir up a hornet's nest for the returning conqueror.

Just what Lee's grievance was it is difficult to determine. It may have been that Amherst's advice upon Indian affairs had led to the injunction in the Royal Proclamation of October 7, 1763, forbidding the further purchase of land from the Indians, a measure which seriously interfered with the Major's Utopian scheme for creating a military colony of New Englanders, Germans, and Swiss in the Ohio Valley. This possible ground for attack, however, is hardly consistent with Sir Jeffery's attitude towards western colonisation, for at an earlier date he had recommended Detroit as a proper seat for a new government. (Historical Manuscripts Commission's *Report V,* Appendix.) Whatever his complaint, Lee plied his mephitic pen to the best of his ability in decrying Amherst's conduct during his command in America. (Morgan's *Documentary History of New York,* ii.)

Some of these criticisms appeared in print, and the late commander-in-chief was advised by his friends to publish his instructions and orders from the ministry. Then Lee turned his hand to less open warfare. Knowing well the difference of opinion which existed between Amherst and Sir William Johnson, the aggrieved major wrote to the latter lamenting the colonial policy of the Administration and declaring his conviction that Sir Jeffery Amherst contributed "all in his power to continue them in their errors by his most wicked misrepresentations." (*Lee Papers,* i, in the New York Historical Society's Collections, 1871.) Like all detractors of public personages, Lee was not without a party, but the upshot of all his efforts was little more than a temporary bad odour, which clung quite as much to himself as to the object of his wrath.

About the time of Amherst's return from America, his elder brother, Sackville, died. The latter was unmarried, and as Jeffery was the second son, this event brought the general into unexpected possession of the family estate at Riverhead, in the parish of Sevenoaks. Although his income was not large, probably not much over £3,000, it was adequate to the maintenance of a more pretentious establishment than that which had suited his brother's comparatively obscure life.

******

Amherst's income as computed in 1768 was:

Government in Virginia	£1,500
15th regiment	600
60th regiment	200
Paternal estate	800
Total	£3,100

Woodfall's *Letters of Junius*, iii; *Grenville Papers*, iv.

******

The old seat, which had been known as "Brook's Place," was torn down and at a small distance from it, Amherst erected his new house, "Montreal." A contemporary account speaks of the building as "an elegant stone mansion," (*Universal Magazine*, vol. 63), but Major Kemble, an American, who visited the place with his brother-in-law, General Gage, in 1774, was content with calling it "a very clever convenient small house." Whatever estimate they formed of the edifice, all visitors agreed that it was beautifully situated. Mrs. Boscawen has left us perhaps the best description of the countryside, as she saw it from a neighbouring window:

> I see at this moment such an amphitheatre spread all around, first gently descending, then as gently rising, field above field, and church beyond church, that it is like the map of an estate laid down before me. I see Knowl, Seven Oak and its various buildings; and Lord Amherst's new house and pillar are very conspicuous.

Such was, is, and, let us hope, always will be the aspect of that charming part of Kent where Sir Jeffery established himself in the middle of the eighteenth century. (*Autobiography and Correspondence of*

Mary Granville, etc. v.)

The "pillar" mentioned by the enthusiastic Mrs. Boscawen deserves further notice, for, to quote its own inscription, it commemorated "the providential and happy meeting of three brothers, on this their paternal ground, on the 25th of January 1764, after a six years' glorious war, in which the three were successfully engaged in various climes, seasons, and services." The monument, which resembles an obelisk rather than a pillar, was appropriately dedicated to William Pitt, and bore upon two of its faces lists of the battles leading to the conquest of Canada in which Sir Jeffery figured. It is about thirty-five feet high, and still stands upon a pleasant eminence near the house, a lasting memorial, as was intended, to the close fraternal friendship of Jeffery, John, and William Amherst.

★★★★★★

For the text of the inscription on the monument and for many interesting details concerning the house and grounds, I am indebted to Earl Amherst, the present owner (1916), of "Montreal," whose friendly interest in this book has contributed much to the pleasure of my work.

★★★★★★

Although the general had not wished to make America his permanent home, his five years' residence in that country had introduced him to much that afforded enjoyment. Both Jeffery and William Amherst had a decided interest in botany, and the American trees and shrubs seem to have particularly attracted them by their variety and beauty. During their campaigns the two soldiers collected seeds and roots of many kinds to plant near the garden at Riverhead; the exotics took kindly to their new home, and the part of the grounds in which they flourished is still called the American wood.

These trees and shrubs were not the only New World products to find favour in the Englishmen's eyes. Apparently, William had acquired a taste for Indian corn, and a consignment of it was shipped to him by a friend in America in the autumn of 1765. It is doubtful, however, whether that great staple of the continental colonies prospered in the less genial climate of England. American apples, too, were sent across the Atlantic, and even game-birds, when cooked, bore the long journey without spoiling. (*Aspinwall Papers,* Massachusetts Historical Society's *Collections,* Fourth Series, x.)

While Amherst was erecting a mansion worthy of his social and military standing, another indication of his rise in the world appeared.

He decided that it was high time his portrait was painted. Accordingly, Joshua Reynolds, already the leading artist in England, was engaged to make the counterfeit presentment. The work, begun in May, 1765, now (1916) hangs in the home of the present Lord Amherst and is indeed an amazing bit of fine art. General Amherst, clad in the armour and regalia of a Knight of the Bath, regards the landscape with great composure, in spite of the fact that in the background the rapids of the St. Lawrence, which the painter seems to have confused with Niagara Falls, play havoc with the troops on their way to Montreal.

Under the circumstances the general's serenity is surprising, but to make matters worse his untroubled expression is accentuated by a pose of the body and hand which would be far more appropriate for a poet than for a military man of energy and force. (See frontispiece.) If, however, one blots out the ridiculous background, the mediaeval helmet, and indeed everything except Amherst's head, he will find that the face itself is strong and satisfactory. Its chief attribute is the quiet self-control that characterised Sir Jeffery throughout his career in America. Reynolds painted, in all, three likenesses, and sketched a fourth. Gainsborough, too, tried his hand at portraying the general's features; the somewhat characterless result of his labours hangs in the National Portrait Gallery.

Still another picture "of the king, Lord Amherst, and Lord (blank) at a distance on horseback" was undertaken by the American artist, Benjamin West, but the writer has not been able to locate it today, (1916.) In July, 1779, it was in West's studio in an unfinished condition. (P. O. Hutchinson's *Diary of Thomas Hutchinson*, ii.) Last, but not least, the ingenious Wedgwood immortalised Sir Jeffery's countenance in a medallion which is preserved in the National Gallery at Edinburgh.

The services that Amherst rendered his country in the Seven Years' War practically guaranteed his steady promotion in military rank for the rest of his life. In the spring of 1765, he was made a lieutenant-general, (*London Magazine*, May 1765), and not long afterwards his friends in the government offered him the post of master-general of the ordnance in Ireland. The latter proposition did not appeal to the general at all, in spite the fact that George Grenville, then on his last legs as Premier, insisted that he was "the properest person" for the office, (Grenville Papers, iii): Sir Jeffery was apparently as averse to Ireland as a place of residence as to America, for even Pitt tried in vain to get him to take command of the army there in the summer of 1764. (Anson's *Grafton.*) The wise general knew when he was well off and would not be enticed from his hard-earned enjoyment of Sevenoaks by the mere promise of empty honours away from home.

Hardly twelve months after Amherst's return to England, his wife, who was also his cousin, died, leaving the general without heirs. Two years later, in March, 1767, Sir Jeffery married again. This time his bride was Miss Elizabeth Gary, a daughter of General George Gary and a niece of Viscount Falkland. She brought with her a dowry of £10,000. (*Grenville Papers*, iv.) From the fact that Lady Amherst lived until 1830, one may assume that the general's second wife was decidedly young at the time of her marriage. In later years, Horace Walpole dubbed her "White Pussy," but whether because she was a pretty blonde, or for some reason best known to himself and his correspondent, Miss Berry, the writer cannot say. (Horace Walpole to Miss Berry, March 27, 1791.)

Two or three years after the Peace of Paris gave England undisputed right to the Ohio Valley, Governor Franklin of New Jersey and Sir William Johnson planned to establish a colony in the Illinois country. As the Proclamation of 1763 had prohibited all settlement beyond the Appalachians without His Majesty's "special leave and license for that purpose first obtained," the two promoters made their wishes known to the Ministry, Sir William writing directly to the king's advisers and William Franklin enlisting the services of his influential father, who was then in London as agent for the province of Pennsylvania. General Gage and a number of Philadelphia merchants also joined the enterprise, which soon interested Lord Shelburne and seemed in a fair way to succeed.

The petitioners asked for a modest tract of 63,000,000 acres, comprising almost all the territory between the Wabash, the Mississippi, and the Great Lakes, an area occupied today (1916) by the state of Illinois, the northern part of Indiana, and the southern portions of Michigan and Wisconsin. (Winsor's *The Colonies and the Republic West of the Alleghanies 1763*-1798.) The project: could not have had a better advocate than Benjamin Franklin, who gave it his hearty support. Shelburne was easily persuaded that the proposed colony would strengthen the English Government in those regions where the French were still unenthusiastic about their new masters, and might prevent a revolt on the part of the inhabitants. Furthermore, it would be a growing market for British goods and a reassuring barrier against the Indians.

These arguments were fortified by letters from Amherst, who, the Secretary declared, was one of "the best authorities for anything that

THE OBELISK

related to America." (*Benjamin Franklin to William Franklin*, Nov. 25, 1767.) The general recommended the establishment of further new governments on the Mississippi, the Ohio, and at Detroit, and his opinion doubtless had considerable weight with those ministers who were not yet committed to either side. With such support the measure was presented to the King in Council, by whom it was adopted, subject to the approval of the Board of Trade, in the autumn of 1767. (George Henry Alden's *New Governments West of the Alleghanies before 1780*.)

The Lords of Trade, however, proved averse to the plan. Their attitude was probably due to the narrow-minded counsels of the President of the Board, Wills Hill, Earl of Hillsborough, who, it was said, opposed the scheme for fear of "dispeopling Ireland." (Sparks' *Franklin*, iv.) Of Hillsborough, George III once remarked he did "not know any man of less judgment," an observation which decidedly increases one's respect for that monarch as a judge of character. At all events, the combined forces of Franklin's shrewdness, Shelburne's enthusiasm, and Amherst's advice failed to achieve what had been almost a foregone conclusion, the creation of a new colony in the Northwest, and the Ohio Valley continued to be a wilderness, broken only here and there by British military posts and the settlements of happy-go-lucky Frenchmen.

The year of our Lord 1768 was one of those periods in the course of human events when the social atmosphere is surcharged with a spirit of unrest. Throughout the English-speaking world a wave of discontent and disorder dominated society. In England economic conditions led to riotous actions on the part of various kinds of laborers. The year was hardly begun before the weavers in Spitalfields disturbed the peace, and their example was soon followed by sailors and hatters, who clamoured for an increase in wages. A large body of sawyers tore down a mill that had been recently erected, while even the coalheavers made a demonstration which threatened to become dangerous.

In politics the same spirit of lawlessness prevailed. John Wilkes, an undesirable citizen if there ever was one, returned from his retirement on the Continent and stood for election to Parliament in Middlesex. A few years before this time he had been expelled from the House of Commons for libel, and outlawed by the courts for failing to answer the indictments against him. Pitt had called him the "blasphemer of his God and the libeller of his King," but the public continued to regard him as a persecuted man who should be upheld. His reappearance in 1768 occurred at the psychological moment; it was all that was needed to pour oil upon the smouldering fires of discontent. At once Wilkes became the idol of the opposition to the existing order of things, and his election to the Commons in March was tumultuous and enthusiastic.

The turbulent state of the popular mind became more apparent when the adventurer was arrested and sent to prison for outlawry. His trip to the prison resembled a disorderly triumphal progress, and on the day of the meeting of Parliament the metropolis was turned upside down by a riotous mob. In America economic and political grievances combined to overthrow the rule of law and order. The seizure of John Hancock's sloop *Liberty*, in June, was followed by a riot in Boston so alarming in its proportions that the Commissioners of the Customs made the fatal mistake of sending for British troops to overawe the lawless citizens of Massachusetts Bay. Such was the psychological atmosphere of 1768, and perhaps to that intangible cause, rather than to any other, may be attributed the extraordinary behaviour of Sir Jeffery Amherst during the summer of that restless year.

On July 27, 1768, the anniversary of the surrender of Louisburg and of the capture of Ticonderoga, the Earl of Hillsborough, who had been recently appointed Secretary of State for the Colonies, indited the following epistle to the unsuspecting sinecure Governor of Virginia, (Woodfall's *Junius*, vol. iii):

Sir: I am commanded by the king to acquaint you that His Majesty, upon a consideration of the dispatches lately received from Virginia, thinks it necessary for his service that his governor of that colony should immediately repair to his government; and at the same time to express to you the high opinion His Majesty has of your ability to serve him in that situation. But it is not the king's intention to press you to go upon that service unless it shall be perfectly agreeable to your inclination as well as entirely convenient to you.

His Majesty does not forget that the Government of Virginia was conferred upon you as a mark of royal favour, and as a reward for the very great services you have done for the public, so much to your own honour, and so much to the advantage of this kingdom, and therefore His Majesty is very solicitous that you should not mistake his gracious intention on this occasion.

If you choose to go immediately to your government it will be extremely satisfactory to His Majesty; if you do not, His Majesty wishes to appoint a new governor, and to continue to you in some other shape that emolument which was, as I have said before, intended as a mark of the royal sense of your meritorious services; it is a particular pleasure to me to have the honour of expressing to you these very favourable sentiments of our royal master. To add anything from myself would be a degree of presumption; I will therefore only request the favour of your answer as soon as may be convenient, and the liberty to assure you that I am, (etc.)

Hillsborough.

When the Secretary penned this letter, Sir Jeffery was on his way up to London from Yorkshire. Arriving in town unexpectedly on Thursday, the general was informed that a communication from Lord Hillsborough, left the previous day, had been forwarded to Riverhead. As there was disturbing news from America about town, Amherst went at once to wait upon Hillsborough and learn the contents of the letter in question. Upon showing him a copy of the document, the Secretary did not have long to wait for an answer. Sir Jeffery declared that he could not possibly go to Virginia, because Gage, who had served under him, was the commander-in-chief in the continental colonies.

Hillsborough thought that such a reason was hardly valid for "a governor was always the superior person in his own province, and that his office, being a civil one, had no relation to the command of the king's troops." (*Political Register*, September, 1768.) However, as he was not to urge Sir Jeffery to go, he would not pursue the matter, but he wished that Amherst would tell him how much the emoluments of that office were so that the king might make him an annuity for that amount.

The general, turning the situation over in his mind and speaking aloud, said:

Annuity! An annuity is a pension; the word pension is grating to my ears. If, my Lord, the King would bestow upon me some mark of honour, or something in the military line, I should be happy in the distinction, but a pension, my Lord, is grating to my ears. (*Grenville Papers,* iv.)

In vain Hillsborough sought to soothe the irate soldier, who had flared up so unexpectedly. He reminded him that Lord Chatham's pension was given to him for his magnificent direction of the Seven Years' War, and that Sir Edward Hawke was rewarded in a like manner for saving Ireland. Why should not Amherst have a pension for adding

Canada to the British Empire? What was the difference to him between a pension out of the revenue of Virginia, and one derived from the four and a half *per cent* duty upon sugar, or the duty upon tobacco? But the more His Lordship talked, the less amiable Amherst became. He merely repeated that he should dislike a pension, and bowed himself off. (*Ibid.*, iv; *Political Register*, September, 1768.)

The next day, Friday, Colonel William Amherst heard at Court that Norborne Berkeley, Lord Botetourt, a member of the House of Peers, had been appointed governor of Virginia. With fraternal interest he forwarded the news post-haste to Riverhead, knowing well enough that this sudden development was not likely to smooth the general's ruffled feathers. His expectations were indeed realised. Such a speedy filling of the office, from which he felt that he had been forced to retire, convinced Amherst that the whole business was pre-arranged. The reputation and circumstances of his successor tended to strengthen his conviction, for Lord Botetourt had attempted a bit of finance, more clever than honourable, and not succeeding in it, had lost both his fortune and his good name. (Channing's *History of the United States*, iii.)

His pecuniary status was as notorious as it was critical, and it is small wonder that Amherst thought that he had been turned out of office in order to provide a place and a salary for a bankrupt nobleman. However, the general quite overlooked the real state of affairs in Virginia. If he had viewed the transaction coolly, and in the light of recent events in America, it would not have assumed such an ugly appearance.

In the previous April Francis Fauquier, the gay and disreputable lieutenant-governor of Virginia, died in Williamsburg. At about that time the Assembly of the Old Dominion alarmed the Ministry by applauding and seconding the sentiments of a circular letter from Massachusetts, which set forth the importance of making a united stand against parliamentary taxation. The obnoxious missive was drafted by Samuel Adams, and though couched in dignified language it was by no means ambiguous. Soon after its receipt the Virginians framed a petition to the king, a memorial to the Lords, and a remonstrance to the House of Commons, stating their grievances and insisting that internal taxation was unconstitutional. (*Journals of House of Burgesses,* April 14, 1768.)

These were sent off to England, where they seem to have caused as great a stir as would have been occasioned by a declaration of independence. Clearly such a rebellious colony must not remain long without a governor, and Hillsborough, for one reason or another, thought of the impecunious Baron Botetourt who, according to the Secretary at War, was "a man every way fit for the business." (*Barrington-Bernard Correspondence.*) But why could not Botetourt have been made lieutenant-governor to succeed Fauquier, leaving Amherst in undisturbed possession of his sinecure? Apparently, the Ministry felt that the presence of "a *governor* and a man of great distinction" (*ibid*), would do more to restore order in Virginia than the appointment of a comparatively obscure lieutenant-governor.

Amherst was just the man to go to the province, but in case he declined to do so, Hillsborough had a substitute in mind. When Sir Jeffery's negative answer was received the Secretary tendered the office to Lord Botetourt, who snapped it up so quickly that the general felt sure Hillsborough and the penniless courtier had made the whole arrangement beforehand. To show his indignation at what he chose to consider an affront, Amherst threw up his military appointments outright, and, encouraged by Lord Albemarle and other malcontents, did his best to create a state of public opinion hostile to Hillsborough and the rest of the Administration. (*Grenville Papers*, iv.)

By the year 1768, England had become restive under the system instituted by George III for the restoration of personal monarchical government. Parliament was controlled by neither Whigs nor Tories, but by a venal band of political adventurers who sat in their midst. These men held the balance of power and swung the vote whichever way their royal master directed. They were well paid for their services, so well paid in fact that George III found it necessary to practise every economy in the ordering of his household affairs. Other than this the employment of these hirelings, who won the title of "the king's friends," had no drawback from His Majesty's point of view. Thus, was brought about the temporary destruction of party government and the re-establishment of an active kingship.

As soon as the results of the new regime became apparent, many of the English people felt a not unnatural hostility towards such a government, in which they were not fairly represented; and when the Ministry and Sir Jeffery Amherst fell out, they were quick to make the general's grievance their own. An ill-used soldier is sure of popular sympathy, and this one found an able champion in the mysterious author of the *Letters of Junius*. The affair was aired with much vituperation. Amherst was as lavishly eulogised as his enemies were mercilessly assailed until all London was heartily sick of the quarrel. (*Stopford-Sackville Manuscripts*, i.)

Meanwhile Sir Jeffery took care to make capital out of the alleged wrong he had suffered; his resentment changed to a spirit of bargaining. Realising what prestige his reconciliation would lend to the none-too-secure Administration, the general named the terms upon which he would forget his troubles and return to the ministerial fold. His demands were indeed surprising for one who had so slight a grievance. First and foremost, he asked for a peerage which should descend to his brother in case he himself had no heirs. Secondly, there must be a compensation equivalent to the loss of his salary as Governor of Virginia. The objection to a pension seems to have quietly disappeared.

As if this were not enough, the general also stipulated that he and his heirs should enjoy the exclusive right of working the coal mines at Louisburg. This grant would doubtless bring in sufficient funds to enable the prospective baron to live in a manner befitting his elevation. Fourthly and fifthly, Sir Jeffery demanded land in America, and pre-eminence among American peers in case the King saw fit to establish such an order. (Woodfall's *Junius*, iii.) This was the modest bill for damages which Amherst presented to the Prime Minister as the grounds of accommodation, and it quite justified Horace Walpole's comment that Sir Jeffery, the newest saint in the Martyrology, had acted too little like a saint. (*Horace Walpole to Sir Horace Mann*, August 24, 1768: the text of this passage as it appears in the various editions of Walpole's letters is obviously misprinted.)

If the erstwhile Governor of Virginia expected that all of these preposterous demands would be granted by the frightened Administration, he was quite mistaken. The Duke of Grafton went to him and answered his requests in the following manner. A peerage required an opulent fortune to enable the bearer to support its dignity; this Amherst lacked, and consequently he could not expect to join the aristocracy. As for a recompense equal to his salary, he had been assured of that from the first; but political and commercial reasons forbade the working of the Cape Breton coal mines at all. He might, however, have a grant of almost any amount of land in America when and where he pleased.

The fifth item was out of the question, because there was not the slightest reason to expect that there would ever be an American peerage. (Woodfall's *Junius*, iii.) So, the dispute went on. The resignation of Amherst's military appointments was accepted, although the Ministry, reluctant to see Amherst bite off his nose to spite his face, stipulated that his successor in the colonelcy of the Royal Americans should give up his office whenever the general chose to make peace with the Government. (*Belvoir Castle Manuscripts*, vol. ii, in the Historical Manuscripts Commission's *Report XII,* Appendix, part v.)

All summer and well into the autumn the miserable affair dragged on, until the approaching session of Parliament doubled the desire of the Administration for a settlement of the case. Just how or why the altercation was terminated no one knows, but finally, in early November, the general was suddenly and mysteriously restored to royal favour, and the reconciliation was cemented by his appointment as Colonel of the Third Regiment, familiarly known as the Buffs.

At the same time, he was re-instated in command of the Royal Americans. A few months later a grant of twenty thousand acres in the province of New York removed the last traces of hard feeling between the soldier and the king. (Acts of the Privy Council—Colonial, v.)

In passing judgment upon Amherst's unpleasant relations with the Ministry, it is difficult to say who was in the right and who was in the wrong. Clearly Hillsborough acted too hastily in appointing his successor; also, Lord Botetourt's disordered finances cast an ugly dye upon the transaction. On the other hand, Sir Jeffery's bill for damages suggests an opportunist and a social-climber rather than a man who merely wished redress for injured feelings. One bit of evidence in the general's favour has yet to be considered.

When William Pitt, now Lord Chatham, racked with the combined tortures of gout and neurasthenia, resigned from the Cabinet in October, 1768, he took pains to lament "the removal of Sir Jeffery Amherst," (Taylor and Pringle's *Chatham Correspondence*, iii), implying that this event had much to do with his decision to leave the Government. Under normal conditions one might be guided by Chatham's sentiments in the case and deduce from his displeasure that Hillsborough was more at fault than Amherst, but considering the state of the man's health and his probable inability to take a rational view of the situation, it seems quite as well to leave out of account his attitude towards the quarrel. Pitt's principal reasons for resigning were his shattered nerves and a recognition of the fact that he was no longer at the helm of the ship of state.

Although Amherst's timely reconciliation enabled the Administration to face the opening of Parliament with some degree of equanimity, his financial status remained practically unchanged by the settlement of the quarrel. It is evident, however, that he intended to avail himself of the first opportunity to increase his income. Shortly before his return to England, he had received a letter from Sir William Johnson, in which the latter remarked that he hoped to procure for a friendly tribe of Indians some of the land, claimed by the Society of the Jesuits in Canada. "And I am of the opinion," he wrote, "that the affair may be made very easy to them, now that the Society is broke in France and can consequently hold no lands as a body—their grant becoming void." (Brodhead's *New York Colonial Documents*, vii.)

If it were easy for "the Cohnawageys" to obtain a part of the Jesuit estates, why would it not be easier, and far more appropriate, for the conqueror of Canada to secure a grant of all the rest of that confiscated property? After some such manner must Amherst have reasoned in the year 1770. The Jesuit estates were indeed a tempting morsel, for they included seven hundred and twenty-five thousand acres of the most fertile country in the St. Lawrence Valley, almost one-eighth of all the granted lands. (Munro's *Seignorial System in Canada*.)

From the beginning of the colony the French government had been lavishly generous in its efforts to encourage the propagation of the gospel and to increase the prosperity of the Reverend Fathers of the Society and Company of Jesus. As land in America was more abundant than money at Versailles, in the days of Louis XIV and Louis XV, the result had been a Jesuit monopoly of the best territory in New France. By a fortunate coincidence, the Society was condemned by the Parliament of Paris just before the signing of the Treaty of Paris, and suffered a general confiscation of its property. (J. B. Perkins' *France under Louis XV*, ii.) This unlooked-for development, coupled with the cession of New France, threw all the Jesuit holdings in Canada into the possession of George III in 1763, to be disposed of as he might see fit.

Aware of this royal windfall, Sir Jeffery Amherst petitioned His Majesty to grant him the estates outright as a mark of his favour. The king received his plea and turned it over to a committee of the Privy Council for consideration. All this occurred in May, 1770. (*Statutes of the United Kingdom, 43 George III, C.*) The committee passed the matter on to the Board of Trade, which was always consulted when any business affecting the colonies was under discussion. (*Acts of the Privy Council—Colonial*, v.) At first everything went along merrily from Amherst's point of view, the only reservation to the forthcoming grant being that the colleges, chapels and other buildings of the followers of Loyola should be retained by the Crown for public uses.

But alas! in the spring of 1771, at the very time when the attorney and the solicitor-general were busy draughting the instrument, Sir Jeffery's great expectations went the way of many of the best-laid schemes of mice and men. A petition from the inhabitants of Quebec to have the Jesuit estates devoted to the support of education in Canada arrived most inopportunely, and so reasonable seemed their plea that Amherst's request was laid upon the table. (*Colonial Office Papers*, 42, Vol. 30, C. 27, in the Public Record Office.) The matter fell into abeyance temporarily, but the prize at stake was too precious to allow this obstruction to end the game. On the contrary, the contest for the possession of the coveted lands had only begun.

While the pursuit of the Jesuit estates in America occupied the general's attention, another source of revenue presented itself much nearer home. Sir Richard Lyttelton, a brother of Baron Lyttelton and a cousin by marriage of Lord Chatham, died about this time, leaving the sinecure governorship of the Island of Guernsey without an incumbent. The office was singularly like that which Sir Jeffery had so recently enjoyed as titular executive of Virginia, and it is not strange that the post was offered to him in the autumn of 1770. The actual government of the island was in charge of a lieutenant-governor who led a forlorn and uncomfortable existence in residence, (*Calendar of Home Office Papers, George III*, iii), while his superior supervised affairs from Whitehall.

Amherst accepted the office, which must have had a sentimental as well as a pecuniary interest for him, for his old chief and early patron, Sir John Ligonier, had been Governor of Guernsey for a year or two in the quiet interval between the Peace of Aix-la-Chapelle, and the outbreak of the Seven Years' War. It is interesting to note that Ligonier, who had been deservedly raised to the peerage, died in 1770 at the ripe old age of eighty-nine years and that Amherst was one of the executors of his estate. (*Autobiography and Correspondence of Mary Granville*, iv.)

Military appointments of higher and higher rank continued to be conferred upon Sir Jeffery. In October, 1772, he succeeded the disgruntled Henry Seymour Conway as Lieutenant-General of the Ordnance, in which capacity he superintended the distribution of guns and ammunition to the various regiments and ships. The promotion brought with it membership in the Privy Council, (*Acts of the Privy Council—Colonial*, v), although not a seat in the Cabinet. George III, like his more soldierly predecessor on the throne, was heartily averse to having any one of his subjects commander-in-chief of the British Army; but feeling the necessity of having some responsible head to the military, from this time on he recognised Amherst as the actual *generalissimo* of the forces in England.

Almost a decade had now elapsed since Sir Jeffery returned from America, and in that period, he had received both smiles and frowns from His Majesty.

After his rehabilitation in the autumn of 1768, the general was more careful in his attempt to walk the tight rope of royal favour, a feat in which practice was fast making him perfect. One example of his proficiency is particularly characteristic. In February 1773, the Duke and Duchess of Gloucester were in town for a while, and on account of the strained relations existing between His Royal Highness and his brother the king, London society-folk were much perplexed whether or not to pay court. If they went to Gloucester House, they would be identified with the Opposition and would probably fall from grace. On the other hand, one could not be sure that George III would not resent any slighting of his unconventional brother.

The duke's offence had been his marriage with the super-beautiful Maria Walpole, the daughter of Sir Edward Walpole and of Mary Clement, a pretty seamstress. It was a true love-match on both sides, and except for birth, the duchess lacked none of the qualities befitting her station, (Trevelyan's *Early History of Charles James Fox*); indeed, if she at all resembled the many portraits of her by Sir Joshua Reynolds her graces must have dazzled and charmed even the most critical of beholders. When the duke and the duchess appeared in London, the leaders of the Opposition hurried to wait upon them, and some of the Court went too. Among the latter was Sir Jeffery Amherst; but he took care to have it understood that he came to see His Royal Highness only, and when asked to see his hostess, he replied that "he had not the honour of knowing the duchess, and therefore desired to be excused." (Horace Walpole's *Last Journals*, i.)

In spite of such meticulous circumspection, the general had a narrow escape from falling between two stools, for when the king heard of his attendance at Gloucester House "he bade Lord Hertford desire his brother, General Conway, to whisper to General Amherst that His Majesty disliked his going to the duke." (*Ibid.*, i.) Such was the precarious life of a courtier under George III.

About the time of this social dilemma a letter from Sir Jeffery provoked a very significant remark on the part of the king. The subject-matter of the epistle was of little importance, but its style irritated the monarch. In speaking of it to Lord North he observed that although "coutched (*sic*) in civil terms," it was "not without that commendation of his own services, which, though very great, would not be lessened if he left the appreciating them to others." (Donne's *Correspondence of George III and Lord North,* i.) His Majesty's words were well chosen. The general certainly did not wear gracefully the distinction he had achieved, and it is probable that the king's sententious remark expressed an opinion of Amherst held by more than one of his contemporaries in the years just preceding the outbreak of hostilities between Great Britain and her thirteen long-suffering colonies on the continent of North America.

CHAPTER 13

The American Revolution

The decade following Amherst's return from America witnessed a serious change in the relations between England and the colonies that had helped her to humble France in the Seven Years' War. The trouble began in 1764, when George Grenville in his endeavour to be an efficient chancellor of the exchequer inaugurated a commercial and military system not approved of by the American colonists. The "New Policy," as it came to be called, comprised three fundamental changes—the strict enforcement of the trade laws, the permanent establishment in America of a portion of the British Army, and the maintenance of the soldiers in those parts by direct taxation. There is much to be said on the side of Grenville and his coadjutors to justify this departure from the old imperial order. In the first place England was weighed down with debt as a result of the late war, and every economy must be practised in order to keep the ship of state off the rocks of bankruptcy.

As the customs service in America cost the British Government *per annum* from four to seven times as much as it yielded in revenue, it was time that steps were taken to remedy whatever leakage might be found there. (Lecky's *England in the Eighteenth Century*, iii.) Pitt had unearthed an amazing amount of illicit trade during the war, and from the fact that many revenue officers resided in England, leaving their duties to good-natured subordinates, it seemed probable that evasion of the payment of duties was very general. The first measure of reform, therefore, provided for a strict enforcement of the existing trade laws, and to make assurance doubly sure, certain additional money-yielding restrictions were placed upon the commerce of the colonies. (Channing's *History of the United States*, iii.)

The proposal to quarter ten thousand British regulars in America was equally distasteful to our ancestors, who felt that inasmuch as they had defended themselves successfully against the French and Indians for almost a century, there was no need of an unwelcome standing army in their midst now that they had beaten their foes to a standstill. But either the Pontiac War or the gloomy prospect of half-pay on the part of many officers made a deeper impression upon the minds of the Ministry than did the logical remonstrances of the Americans. It is possible, too, that the moral support which the presence of the military would lend to the customs service was another item in favour of this part of the plan.

Unreasonable as was the resolve to establish permanently an army in the colonies, the proposed method of supporting it was even more so. It was hoped that the invigorated commercial laws would not only pay for that branch of the government, but would also contribute somewhat towards the support of the military imposition. The latter institution, however, was to rely for its maintenance chiefly upon direct taxation. This was to take the form of a stamp tax—unless the colonists could devise some more acceptable and yet equally efficient method of raising the money themselves.

As the Americans were inclined to exert their ingenuity more in denying the constitutionality of parliamentary taxation than in contriving a less disagreeable impost, the year of grace given them by Grenville for consideration was gone before any satisfactory substitute was found. The colonists were so burdened with their provincial taxes, which the debt of the Seven Years' War had necessitated, that they could not see any justice in this additional load. Very naturally they questioned the right of Parliament to tax those whom it did not represent, and were easily convinced that the proposed Stamp Act was unconstitutional. Whatever its legal status was, the hated piece of legislation went through both houses of Parliament with scarcely any opposition, and received the assent of George III on March 22, 1765

Although Sir Jeffery Amherst was not a member of Parliament, the radical element in New York believed that he not only approved of the Stamp Act but also proposed an increase of the military forces in America in order to insure its execution. The Sons of Liberty on Manhattan Island gave vent to their feelings by bearing an effigy of the general at the head of a procession, and afterwards burning it with conspicuous disrespect. (*Montresor's Journals*.)

This was one of the least disreputable demonstrations against parliamentary taxation. Throughout the length and breadth of the colonies, objection took the form of riots, personal indignities, and the destruction of property. In Boston a mob demolished the house of Lieutenant-Governor Hutchinson and made a bonfire of his furniture, books, and papers.

In all parts of the country those who had been appointed stamp-distributors hastened to resign, and it became very evident that the Stamp Act could not be executed in America. Less noisy, but more effective, was the protest of many colonial merchants who refused to import any goods from England as long as the measure was even nominally in force. Others declared that they could not meet their obligations because of the new order of things. These actions produced great distress among British traders and manufacturers in every part of the kingdom, and led them to petition Parliament for the repeal, or at least the modification, of the New Policy.

In the meantime, George Grenville and his colleagues had fallen from royal grace. The succeeding ministry was headed by the Marquess of Rockingham, a Whig, who naturally opposed the policies of his predecessor, and the repeal of the Stamp Act became the burning question. Pitt threw in his lot with the Rockingham Whigs, although he doubted their sincerity, while Benjamin Franklin preached to the House of Commons upon the hopelessness of trying to enforce the Stamp Act, and upon the probability of a rebellion if soldiers were employed for that purpose. As an antidote for Dr. Franklin, the legislators turned to Amherst, whom they considered equally well-informed, and perhaps less prejudiced. The suspicions of the radical New Yorkers were now confirmed. Sir Jeffery gave his advice in no uncertain terms, the Stamp Act must not be repealed. (*Grenville Papers*, iv.)

In taking this stand the general was in accord with his friend Lord Temple, George Grenville's inconsistent brother, although his ideas did not at all coincide with those of Pitt who bent every effort in favour of the colonists. Temple and Amherst were on the best of terms, however, and the latter was a frequent visitor at Stowe, where he mingled to his heart's content with lords and ladies, dukes and duchesses, and even with members of the royal family. (Campbell's *Lives of the Lord Chancellors*, vi.)

In spite of Amherst's opposition, the Stamp Act was repealed, and a lull in the storm of colonial hostility followed. But Parliament still maintained its right "to make laws and statutes of sufficient force and validity to bind the colonies and people of America, subjects of the crown of Great Britain in all cases whatsoever," and acting upon Pitt's suggestion passed a Declaratory Act to that effect. The Americans had based their protests against the stamp duty upon a distinction between Parliament's right to lay taxes for the regulation of colonial trade, and its newly assumed power of laying direct taxes, a distinction upheld by even so thoughtful a statesman as William Pitt, but now they unconsciously came to the decision that parliamentary taxation in any form was unconstitutional.

Their new contention asserted itself when Parliament substituted a tariff for revenue in place of the repealed Stamp Act. All might yet have gone well if Pitt, who had now become Lord Chatham, had been physically able to control the course of politics. As things were, his health received more attention than did the affairs of state, and while Chatham sought rest and recreation at Bath his colleagues had things their own way at Westminster. Tax after tax was laid upon American imports, and rigorous measures of enforcement made evasion of the laws impossible. The Americans remonstrated in vain, and when the lawless part of the population expressed their sentiments by making merry with the Commissioners of Customs in Boston, two regiments were sent to Massachusetts Bay to intimidate the citizens of that unruly province.

After the arrival of the British soldiers at Boston in the autumn of 1768, it mattered little in what form Parliament tried to disguise the pill of unwelcome legislation; nothing short of a complete reversion to the old order of things would be acceptable to the colonists. The events which followed were not of a kind to improve the disposition of His Majesty George III, or to make firm his somewhat unstable intellect. A bloody fray with the soldiers in March, 1770, kept alive colonial animosity towards the Administration, and, on the other hand, the famous Boston Tea Party, three years later, convinced the king and Lord North, his prime minister, that the time for discipline had come.

A series of repressive acts, which were sure to cause rebellion, were passed against the province of Massachusetts Bay, and particularly against the port of Boston. To quell any disturbances that might arise from the execution of the new laws, General Thomas Gage, Amherst's successor as commander-in-chief of the British forces in America, was sent to Boston with four more regiments, while a threatening fleet of warships blockaded the harbour.

Gage was appointed governor of the province, but in spite of this combination of civil and military authority in one person, he failed to check the spread of rebellion. Indeed, he had not been in Massachusetts very long before he advised the suspension of the legislation of 1774 until more troops were available, for according to Gage's reckoning, the conquest of New England could not be safely undertaken without twenty thousand men in the field. (Historical Manuscripts Commission's *Various Collections*, vi.) This estimate was quite different from one he had hazarded a short while before, when he personally assured the king that four regiments would be sufficient to produce submission, and George III did not like his general's revised version.

When nearly a year had passed since his arrival and he had apparently accomplished nothing, except to seal hermetically the port of Boston, and to unite the colonies in their common cause, General Gage decided that it behoved him to do something, although just what did not particularly matter. In April, 1775, he sent an expedition of about a thousand men to Concord to seize the military stores of the Americans in that quiet town. Gage succeeded in his effort to do something, but his men failed to disarm the rebellious colonists. On the nineteenth of April a skirmish at Lexington was followed at Concord by "the shot heard round the world," and the British Army received its first drubbing at the hands of the embattled farmers.

While Gage was endeavouring to reduce the Americans without committing any aggression that would cause actual hostilities, Lord Dartmouth, Secretary for the Colonies, and Lord North, decided that the command ought to be given to a general of more activity and decision. John Pownall, a member of Parliament, whose brother had been governor of Massachusetts-Bay during some of Amherst's most brilliant campaigns, recommended that Sir Jeffery should be sent to Boston to supersede Gage, and that two major-generals should accompany him. North and Dartmouth both approved of the scheme and in November, 1774, they made up their minds to effect the change. (*Ibid.*; Hutchinson's *Diary of Thomas Hutchinson*, i.)

When the matter was broached to the king, however, their plans were quite upset, for George III "asked who could have thought of doing so unjust a thing to General Gage." But as time went on, His Majesty changed his mind. In January, 1775, he wrote Lord Dartmouth that if matters across the ocean became serious, he was prepared to give the command to Sir Jeffery Amherst, whose presence in New England would both inspire the British soldiers and reassure those colonists who still wished well to the English government. General Gage's feelings would be saved from injury by his continuance as Governor of Massachusetts-Bay and by elaborate explanations on the part of the Ministry. As the king, for some reason, expected that Amherst would beg to be excused, he decided to make his wishes known to him in person, "and take myself the task of obtaining his submission to what I think so essential to perhaps preventing the effusion of blood in that deluded part of my dominions." (Historical Manuscripts Commission's *Report 13,* Appendix, part iv.)

On the last day of January, the general went to the palace and listened to the wishes of George III, who, in a private interview, was "the finest gentleman ever seen," if we may believe Doctor Johnson. (Trevelyan's *American Revolution,* vol. iii; Boswell's *Life of Johnson.*) But all His Majesty's graces were in vain when it came to persuading Sir Jeffery Amherst to go to America. With real regret the king announced his failure to Lord Dartmouth:

> My negociation proved fruitless. I stated very fully the intending to send him with an olive branch in one hand, whilst the other should be prepared to obtain submission, but the ground first taken was never quitted, that nothing but retreat would bring him to go again to America. I am much hurt at not succeeding, as I think it bore a prosperous aspect of bringing those deluded people to due obedience without putting the dagger to their throats. I see he cannot be persuaded; we must do what is next best, leave the command to Gage, send the best generals that can be thought of to his assistance, and give him private instructions to insinuate to New York, and such other provinces as are not guided by the madness of the times, what the other would have been entrusted to negotiate. (Historical Manuscripts Commission's *Report 13,* Appendix, part iv.)

For Amherst's refusal to assume this important trust, various reasons have been assigned. The general's gossiping contemporary, Horace Walpole, sneeringly wrote that "his wife dissuaded him, and he gave answer that he could not bring himself to command against the Americans to whom he had been so much obliged," and upon this evidence, apparently, Sir George Otto Trevelyan has based his assertion of Amherst's grounds for declining the command. (*The Last Journals of Horace Walpole,* i; Trevelyan's *American Revolution,* i.) On the other hand, George Bancroft maintained that Sir Jeffery objected to going to America because the Ministry would not give him an army of twenty thousand men with which to undertake the business of reconciling or subduing the rebellious colonists. (George Bancroft's *History of the*

United States, iv; but this author gives no authority for the statement.)

Friendly as Amherst's relations with the Americans may have been in the past, it is to be feared that lack of military support was quite as influential as sentiment in determining him to keep out of active service in the approaching war. Probably more potent than either of these reasons was his disinclination to give up his comfortable leisure at "Montreal" and the congenial atmosphere of London.

It was General Gage who boasted that four regiments would be sufficient to restore order in New England; but the Americans heard another version of that well-known slur upon their fighting qualities, and whatever love they still cherished for the name of Amherst must have been speedily killed by a report that the general "had said that with 5,000 English regulars he would engage to march from one end to the other of North America." (*Pennsylvania Packet,* June 12, 1775.) It is well-nigh incredible that a soldier who depended so completely upon a large force at his command, should have made such a rash statement; yet the newspaper reporters were not content with letting the story end there.

The sequel to this gasconade was an equally improbable tale that when Colonel Washington heard of it "he declared that with 1,000 Virginians he would engage to stop Sir Jeffery Amherst's march." (*Ibid.*) Whether our ancestors gave any credence to these rumours one cannot say, but it is clear that they knew that the command of the ministerial army had been offered to Amherst, and that for one reason or another it had been declined. (*New England Chronicle,* December 7, 1775.)

With Jeffery Amherst discretion was ever the better part of valour. It is possible, therefore, that a recognition of the futility of attempting to conquer the Americans by a land war was responsible for his refusal to supersede Gage. If so, he was not alone in his conviction, for General Harvey, the adjutant-general and hence the highest administrative military official in England, declared that the conquest of America "with our British Army" would be an impossibility. In fact, he deemed any attempt to subdue the colonists by land campaigns "as wild an idea as ever controverted common sense." (Fortescue's *History of the British Army,* iii.) Harvey's prediction of calamity was based upon the geographical arrangement of the American provinces and upon the spirit of the colonists. The rebellious parts of the empire extended in a thin line along the Atlantic seaboard from Maine to Florida. They were sparsely populated and contained no capital city the capture of which would give a great moral blow to the insurgents.

The British occupied successively Boston, New York, and Philadelphia; but their visitations in these seaport towns were generally more hurtful to themselves than to the Americans, who merely surrounded the hostile army and made any further invasion of the country highly dangerous. Lacking control of the agricultural regions, the English forces, horses as well as men, had to be supplied almost exclusively from England. When an exasperated army advanced inland with the hope of foraging in American fields and pastures, the farmers, as a rule quite indifferent to the course of the war, rose up as one man and gave the enemy a whipping which was not soon forgotten. The fight at Bennington is perhaps the most striking example of this constantly recurring form of disaster. As these forays, or any other attempts to march into the heart of the country, always endangered the British communications, each English general in turn tired of attempting active campaigns in America.

Foreseeing these formidable difficulties) the Secretary at War, Viscount Barrington, advised that the operations should be almost entirely naval, believing that as soon as the foreign and coastwise trade of the Americans was destroyed the discouraged colonists would be right glad to listen to almost any proposals for conciliation. Lord Shelburne of the Opposition appears to have held the same views, (John Adams' *Works*, iii), while Chatham, a few years later, graphically presented the hopelessness of a land war by exclaiming in the House of Lords:

> You would conquer, you say! Why, what would you conquer— the map of America? I am ready to meet any general officer on the subject (looking at Amherst). What will you do out of the protection of your fleet? In the winter, if together, they are starved; and if dispersed, they are taken off in detail. You have got nothing in America but stations. (Cobbett's *Parliamentary History*, xix.)

The truth of these prognostications and statements was more clearly proved in each succeeding year of the colonists' struggle for independence, and whether or not Amherst held such sound views in 1774, it is certain that he did at a later date.

Although Sir Jeffery's scruples, his wife, or his military acumen forbade his taking the field against the Americans, he continued in his office at the Ordnance and despatched arms and ammunition for the British forces across the ocean. (Donne's *Correspondence of George*

III with Lord North, i.) As the American Indians had been the bane of his existence in the Seven Years' War, so now the American privateers, who swarmed the seas, exasperated him by playing havoc with his attempts to supply the army at Boston or elsewhere. One day Thomas Hutchinson, the exiled royal governor of Massachusetts, met the general in the Park, and when the conversation turned to war news, Amherst gloomily announced the capture of an ordnance-vessel, whose cargo he valued at £10,500. (Hutchinson's *Diary of Thomas Hutchinson*, ii.) This was but one of many melancholy events of like nature which made Sir Jeffery's duties interesting, and also aided Washington in driving the British Army out of Boston. Irving's *Life of Washington*, ii.)

In eighteenth-century England the conduct of foreign and colonial affairs was entrusted to two or three secretaries of state, each of whom had a given geographical jurisdiction, in which, in time of war, he was responsible for the movements of armies and the progress of campaigns. Thus, the real helmsman of the British Army in the American war was first the gentle and well-meaning Lord Dartmouth, who resigned his uncomfortable office in the autumn of 1775, and after his time Lord George Germain. The latter gentleman, who began life as Lord George Sackville, deserves more than passing notice, for among the negative causes of American independence none is more conspicuous than he. Born within a mile or two of Jeffery Amherst's birthplace, he was the youngest son of Lionel Cranfield Sackville, the Duke of Dorset.

He fought well in the war of the Austrian Succession; but in the French War his military career came to a sudden and inglorious end, for at the Battle of Minden in 1759, when ordered to advance with the British cavalry, Sackville acted in such a peculiar manner that he was dismissed from the service. His demand for a court-martial only made matters worse, for the judges, finding him guilty of disobedience, declared that he was "unfit to serve His Majesty in any military capacity whatever." George II completed the disgrace by ordering that his name and sentence be given out in public orders "not only in Britain, but in America, and every quarter of the globe where British troops happen to be" as a horrible example of the way of the transgressor. It seems as if these events ought to have been the last the world ever heard of Lord George Sackville—but it was not so to be.

Changing his name to Germain in 1770, in order to inherit the lands of an aunt and £20,000 in money, he suddenly became conspicuous in Parliament by his contempt for the American colonists,

MONTREAL IN 1778

and, in 1774, by his advocacy of extreme measures against Massachusetts. (Channing's *History of the United States*, iii.) This attitude won for him the favour of George III, who made him Secretary of State for the Colonies, and hence it came about that one who had been judged "unfit to serve His Majesty in any military capacity whatever" directed the movements of the British troops in America from 1775 to 1782.

As Amherst was the Nestor of English generals at that time, Germain, who was nine years his junior and much less experienced as a commander, turned to him for consultation at almost every stage of the war. In this way Sir Jeffery came to be the recognised military adviser of the Cabinet, a part which he played well. He recommended this man's promotion and that man's leave of absence, delay here and reinforcement there, until it seems as if the Administration never took a step without first discovering Amherst's opinion of the proposed move.

★★★★★★

Amherst's activities as consulting engineer of the American War may be gleaned from the Historical Manuscripts Commission's Report on American MSS., Vols. i–iv; *Report on Various Collections*, vi; *Additional MSS*. (British Museum); *Colonial Office Papers*; and the *Miscellaneous MSS*. of the Ford Collection in the New York Public Library.

★★★★★★

Some of his deductions were remarkably good, considering his distance from the seat of war. In 1777, for instance, he assured the king that Washington had never had above 10,000 regular troops in the campaign of that year, although including the militia his army might have amounted to a couple of thousand more, an estimate which proved to be astonishingly accurate. (Donne's *Correspondence of George III with Lord North*, ii.) These services bore fruit for Amherst, if not for the British arms, for in the spring of 1776, Sir Jeffery was granted the peerage which he had long coveted. By this elevation he became Baron Amherst of Holmesdale in the county of Kent, and henceforth took his seat among the peers of the realm. In the meantime, the war against the colonists dragged on with no immediate prospect: of conclusive victory for either side.

In 1776, the United Colonies declared themselves free and independent states, and in the following year the surrender of Burgoyne at Saratoga gave the Americans their first tangible encouragement. Since the very beginning of colonial troubles Amherst had served two masters, Pitt and George III, and although that feat is proverbially difficult, he succeeded for many years both in preserving the friendship of his great patron and in being of much use to the king. The great test came in the autumn of 1777, when His Majesty strongly supported the employment of Indians against the Americans as the mode of war best calculated to distress the rebels and to end the contest. (Lecky's *England in the Eighteenth Century*, iv.)

When these violent measures were proposed in the House of Lords, Chatham arose in wrath and demanded, "Who is the man that has dared to authorise and associate to our arms the tomahawk and scalping-knife of the savage?" This question was but the prelude to a terrific denunciation of the Ministry which had debased the army by infecting it "with the mercenary spirit of robbery and rapine" and familiarising it with the "horrid scenes of savage cruelty," until it could "no longer boast of the noble and generous principles which dignify a soldier," nor "sympathise with the dignity of the royal banner, nor feel the pride, pomp and circumstance of glorious war 'that makes ambition virtue.'" (Cobbett's *Parliamentary History*, xix.)

The speech was one of the most dramatic that Pitt ever delivered, but it was also the most ill-considered, for not many minutes after its conclusion Earl Gower remarked sarcastically that it was strange "that they who had the conduct of the last war should forget the means by which it was conducted, and now condemn the measures they had formerly authorised." Indians had been employed on the British side in the Seven Years' War and, if he remembered rightly, treaties and presents had cemented the unholy alliance. (*Ibid.*) For Chatham the situation was decidedly embarrassing.

After floundering about in a vain effort to make a distinction between the use of savages as scouts and their unrestricted employment "for murder and massacre," the orator assured the peers that his administration had never justified or authorised either of those measures. For confirmation he called upon Lord Amherst. The requested testimony was something of a surprise, for the general rose and confessed that he had received aid from the Indians in his campaigns. He was careful, however, not to impute any sanction or knowledge of this practice to the ministry of that time. (*Ibid.*)

If Chatham had acted wisely, he would have let the matter drop then and there, but within three weeks he again asserted, and this time with noticeable petulance, that he had never known of Indians being used as auxiliaries of England in the Old French War. Once more he called upon Amherst to corroborate his statement or to explain what use, if any, had been made of the savages in the conquest of Canada. With evident reluctance the general arose and declared that the English had followed the example of the French in resorting to this expedient, but he was sure he never would have ventured to do so if he had not received orders to that effect.

Amherst denied his lord, but under the circumstances how could he have done otherwise? He knew that Pitt had been perfectly cognisant of every detail of the campaigns in America, and that he had specifically commended the conduct of "the faithful Indian allies" upon at least one occasion. (Kimball's *Pitt Correspondence*, ii.) In taking the side of the king against his best friend, Amherst was actuated not by subservience to His Majesty, but by the truth. The Earl of Shelburne, ever Chatham's friend, came to the rescue by suggesting that the general had received his instructions in this particular from the Board of Trade and not from the Secretary of State. Chatham grasped at this straw and requested that Amherst would put an end to the altercation by telling the Lords of his orders and whence they emanated. The response was brief, but not specific.

"I was desired to make treaties with the Indian powers. I was charged with it in my instructions," said the general, and that was all he would vouchsafe. Pitt still persisted in declaring his ignorance of any such orders and assured his hearers that the papers had never passed regularly through the office of the Secretary of State. Since further argument was futile until the evidence was presented, Chatham subsided, with a final request that Amherst would produce the disputed instructions. (Cobbett's *Parliamentary History*, xix) It is significant that nothing more of them was ever heard in the House of Lords: "the great oracle with the short memory" was probably more than content to let the matter sleep.

Burgoyne's surrender and the apparent apathy of General Sir William Howe revived in the Cabinet the once dashed hope that Amherst would assume the American command and bring the dull war to an early and brilliant close.

Such a happy expectation, however, was soon conclusively disappointed; for in a royal interview about the middle of January, 1778, the general declined the honour in such emphatic terms, "though with every expression of duty," that even George III could entertain no serious thought of a possible change of mind on the part of his disobliging subject. The king wrote Lord North:

"Though out of decency, on being strongly pressed, he took time to consider, he gave no room to expect he will accept. Thus, I have done all I could to effect what the Cabinet unanimously thought the most desirable step." (2 Donne's *Correspondence of George III with Lord North,* ii; Hutchinson, *Diary of Thomas Hutchinson* ii.)

The American struggle soon assumed a new aspect in the eyes of Englishmen, for the success of the colonists at Saratoga persuaded Louis XVI to throw in his lot with the rebels with the hope of humbling all-powerful England and of restoring some of the Bourbon glory which France had lost in the last war. Rumours of such a development were at large in England in the winter of 1777 and 1778 and did not tend to increase the equanimity of Lord North and his colleagues; but until the attitude of France was definitely known in London, the Ministry devoted its time to the discussion of plans for a more efficient campaign against the Americans.

At a cabinet meeting on January 18, 1778, Amherst's sentiments on the conduct of the hostilities were presented by one of the ministers—views which he may have held as far back as the beginning of the struggle, and which were certainly strengthened by the unproductive military operations of 1777. The general believed, so it was stated, that it would be impossible to reduce the colonies effectually without an addition of thirty or forty thousand men to the forces already in America, and that under the circumstances a naval war was the only wise plan. (Historical Manuscripts Commission's *Report 10,* Appendix vi.) He had previously expressed this opinion to the king, with an explanation "that the preventing the arrival of military stores, cloathing and the other articles necessary from Europe, must distress them (the colonists) and make them come into what Britain may decently consent to." (Donne's *Correspondence of George III with Lord North,* ii.)

While the ministers were cogitating the proposed change in tactics, Lord North, made uneasy by the probability of a Franco-American alliance, introduced bills of conciliation which granted practically everything the colonists had demanded in 1774, and appointed commissioners to negotiate a peace with the Continental Congress. Among those who, because of their "conciliatory manners," were suggested as bearers of the tardy olive branch across the seas, was Lord Amherst, (B. F. Stevens' *Facsimiles of Manuscripts;* Rowland's *Charles Carroll,* i), but the appointments were given to men of less reputation, who coaxed the American insurgents in vain. (Lecky's *England in the Eighteenth Century,* iv.)

On the thirteenth of March, 1778, the French ambassador in London delivered to the Secretary of State a note announcing the treaty of friendship and commerce recently signed by France and the United States, and from that moment the wind of England's war policy blew from a different quarter. Almost instantly the ill-defined plans for the year took shape and were placed on the road to execution. George III at once sent for Amherst to ask his advice upon the conduct of hostilities under the changed conditions; "for," as he wrote to Lord North, "we have not a minute to loose." (Donne's *Correspondence of George III with Lord North*, ii.)

The general had done some earnest thinking in the last few days, and when he appeared at Queen's House on the morning of March 17, 1778, he had reconstructed his plan of war. His advice was as follows: Withdraw immediately the troops from Philadelphia (where they had spent an idle and enjoyable winter), and station them at New York. Despatch to the Floridas as many of their number as may be deemed necessary for the security of those provinces. Make New York the rendezvous for the navy, and employ the fleet in the destruction of all vessels in American harbours. (This measure was doubtless to prevent the rebels from fitting out an expedition against the British insular possessions in the Caribbean.)

Finally, if the peace commissioners find that the colonists are resolved to continue their alliance with France, then evacuate New York and Rhode Island, and turn those troops against the French West Indies. (Donne's *Correspondence of George III with Lord North*, ii.) In short, the United States henceforth were negligible; a great war was to be fought with France.

The effect of these recommendations and of the new aspect of the conflict was almost electrical. General Howe was recalled, and Clinton, his successor, was ordered to move the army from the Quaker metropolis to New York as soon as possible. Before long the seaboard towns of New Jersey, Virginia, and Connecticut felt the result of Amherst's advice, in the destruction of their shipping, although it is doubtful whether the general would have countenanced the inland forays which followed these drastic preventive measures. For two years after the battle at Monmouth, the entrance of the French into the sphere of conflict was distinctly reflected in the absence in the New World of military or naval events of any consequence. England's chief problem during that period was one of readjustment to the new war, which was far more complex than that which had baffled her from 1775 to 1778.

Most striking of all the results of the French Alliance was its effect upon Lord Chatham. Up to this time he had distinguished himself as a consistent champion of the Americans, first in the Commons and later among the Peers. Now his change of front was as impressive as it was spectacular. In the spring of 1778, the Rockingham Whigs proposed that the King recognise the independence of the United States and thus avoid the impending conflict with the House of Bourbon, a struggle for which England was conspicuously unprepared. When the Duke of Richmond made this wise though humiliating suggestion, Chatham was at Hayes, recovering from a fit of the gout and still very weak; but he determined to return to his seat in the House of Lords and oppose the measure at any cost. Against the advice of family and friends he did so.

On the seventh day of April, leaning on the arm of his son William, and supported by his son-in-law Lord Mahon, the venerable statesman appeared before the assembly for the last time, and delivered a stirring appeal to English patriotism. Surely the nation was no longer what it had been if at the mere threat of war, it bowed to the will of hated France and gave up half of its possessions. If France meant war, let Britain fight and "if we must fall, let us fall like men." American independence was out of the question, the empire must be preserved intact—not because he loved America less, but England more. Thus, Chatham protested against the dismemberment of that "ancient and most noble monarchy" which he had raised to the summit of its glory. Then, exhausted by his efforts to save Britain from herself, the speaker fell back in a swoon; and a few weeks later William Pitt, Earl of Chatham, was no more.

★★★★★★

In his celebrated picture of this stirring moment, Copley has incidentally given us a portrait of Amherst. When the Duke of Kent was in America in the early part of the nineteenth century, he remarked to Abiel Holmes, the father of the Boston humourist, that this particular likeness of the general was excellent. Holmes' *Annals of America* (Cambridge, 1829), ii, 413, note 2.

★★★★★★

The dramatic element in the great statesman's last speech is only equalled by its poetic justice in relation to Jeffery Amherst. Although the two men had differed from the outset in their views concerning the proper administration of the colonies, the French alliance swept them together again, and probably no words of the generals could have better expressed his sentiments in 1778 than those uttered by his dying patron and friend. At last, Amherst, Chatham, and George III were at one in their attitude towards the American War.

CHAPTER 14

The Bourbon Armada

The prospect of war with France afforded the Duke of Gloucester an opportunity to show his brother, the king, that although guilty of an unconventional marriage he was none the less a valiant warrior when his country was in danger. Coming up to London quite unexpectedly, he offered his services to George III and awaited developments. Probably nothing could have been more annoying to the Ministry, for on the preceding day they had decided to force the king to appoint Lord Amherst commander-in-chief of all the British forces in England. The duke, although a soldier only in name, doubtless expected that the office would be given to him, and consequently his appearance on the scene was anything but welcome. (Walpole's *Last Journals*, ii.) Gallant as was the offer of His Royal Highness, George III had not yet entirely forgiven his brother for marrying the Countess Waldegrave. Consequently, he ignored the duke's letter, and gave the command to Amherst on March 24, 1778. (*Gentleman's Magazine*, March, 1778.)

As commander-in-chief of all British forces in England Amherst's duties were much the same as they had been during the last six years; but the fact that the king at last recognised him as the head of the military establishment restored to some extent the spirits of the army officers and of the people in general. James Murray, who was leading a tranquil life as lieutenant-governor of Minorca, thought that Providence had prevented Amherst's accepting the American command in order that he might save England in this hour of distress, and declared that he was "the fittest person for the great task" to which he had been called. (*Stopford-Sackville Manuscripts*, i.)

Lord Barrington was less sanguine, however, and in an amazingly frank interview with the king he told the latter that there was "not

DEATH OF CHATHAM

one general in whom His Majesty, the nation, or the army would place confidence in case of the invasion of Great Britain or Ireland." To remedy this deficiency the outspoken Secretary suggested that Prince Ferdinand be induced to come to England to take charge of military affairs until the crisis was passed. (Shute Harrington's *Political Life of William Wildman, Viscount Barrington*.) Lord Chatham had entertained the same idea, and if his strength had held out after his speech on April 7, he would have proposed this very measure to the House of Lords. (Walpole's *Last Journals*, ii.)

Lord North even made a gloomy little joke about the general officers, saying that he did not know whether they would frighten the enemy, but he was sure they frightened *him* whenever he thought of them, (Barrington's *Life of Barrington*); and it is very clear that in spite of Amherst's appointment, all England was shaking in its shoes in the spring of 1778. (*Ibid.*)

As affairs became more serious, the king and his perplexed ministers became correspondingly more dependent upon Lord Amherst for advice and encouragement, and the general, as commander-in-chief, became a very important member of the Privy Council. The meetings of that body in the reign of George III were as uninspiring affairs as one might have expected from a collection of subservient, second-rate politicians, who could never quite make up their minds to tell the king of the folly of his autocratic system, nor to resign when they knew that they were clogging the wheels of England's progress. At one of these sessions, which was held in the face of a critical juncture in international relations, Lord North fell asleep as soon as the business was opened; another minister followed suit, while Lord Hillsborough nodded and dropped his hat. Sandwich, First Lord of Admiralty, who was described by one of his contemporaries as—

"Too infamous to have a friend;
Too bad for bad men to commend"

—dozed at first, but later rubbed his eyes and seemed attentive. Amherst, be it said to his credit, "kept awake, but said nothing." Indeed, only Lord George Germain and two of his colleagues paid any attention to the reading of important despatches, while the rest, when they awoke, merely approved of what was proposed.

★★★★★★

Historical Manuscripts Commission's *Report*, "Various Collections," vi.

Another contemporary wrote, "Even at the Cabinet dinners, which were held weekly, I have heard Lord Sackville say that, though he (Amherst) usually gave his decided affirmative or negative to the specific measures proposed, yet he always did it in few words, often by a monosyllable, but never could, without great difficulty, be induced to assign the reasons or to state the grounds of his opinion." Wraxall's *Historical Memoirs*, i.

★★★★★★

Sometimes the king sat at the head of the table and presided over the meetings, asking his counsellors, one by one, for their advice. On such occasions Amherst as the youngest member present usually spoke first, and it is to be suspected that in the presence of His Majesty more attention was paid to the affairs of state than when the Cabinet Council was left to its own devices. (*Ibid.*, vi.)

Much as Amherst may have enjoyed the doubtful distinction of being one of the inner circle of the king's advisers, he was obliged now and then to listen to harsh words of criticism from some of his contemporaries. Once when George III went to see a fleet depart for America, Admiral Keppel was embarrassed by the fact that the ships were not ready, and he "spoke out very plain English before Lords Sandwich and Amherst upon naval equipments, the state of the fleet and the supply of ordnance, stores, and supplies." (B. F. Stevens' *Facsimiles*.) For the ordnance, at least, the general was responsible and as the king gave "all possible attention to Keppel's sentiments, facts, and ideas," His Lordship was "not absolutely happy at quite so much openness," and with good reason.

In spite of an occasional display of carelessness or incompetence, Lord Amherst continued in high favour with His Majesty. Evidence of this blessing was given in the autumn of 1778 when the king and queen, on their way to the camp at Cox Heath, stayed overnight at "Montreal." The royal pair and their attendants were escorted by detachments of dragoons, and when the cavalcade arrived at Lord Amherst's lodge about two o'clock in the afternoon, "a very great concourse of people" was there, "to see Their Majesties as they passed." In the evening illuminations at "Montreal" and throughout the neighbourhood, "together with the ringing of bells, and other public demonstrations of joy, testified the happiness of the inhabitants of all ranks" upon this dazzling occasion.

Nor were the efforts of the citizens to impress His Majesty with their loyalty in vain; on the morrow the king "was pleased to give a sum of money to be distributed to the poor and distressed families of the parish of Sevenoaks, and for the bell-ringers." When the king and queen resumed their journey, Lord and Lady Amherst accompanied them, and as they passed through the village, the procession halted in front of the school, while the master made a short address to George III. (*Universal Magazine,* November, 1778.) So gracious was the sovereign that it seems as if a presidential candidate in the United States could hardly outdo him in his efforts to win popularity by flattering his constituents in this trite but ever successful manner.

Now and then Amherst was used as a royal whip in disciplining those of "the king's friends" who showed dangerous signs of negligence. George Ill's language was very elegant when he wrote to Lord North that the attention of certain members "must be quickened," but the result of the marshalling would do credit to the most autocratic political boss of today (1916). (Donne's *Correspondence of George III with Lord North,* ii.) Amherst wrote letters to this member and to that, reminding them of their duty to His Majesty, and thus made possible the "handsome majorities" which carried England further and further towards destruction. These services were rewarded by another military appointment calculated to increase Lord Amherst's income without adding to his duties. On April 21, 1779, the commander-in-chief became also colonel of the Second Troop of Horse Grenadier Guards. (Cannon's *Third Regiment of Foot.*)

England's fears of a French invasion in 1778 proved groundless; but when Spain joined hands with her Bourbon neighbour in June of the following year and declared war upon Britain, renewed and redoubled trepidation took possession of the English people. What the Spanish Armada had failed to achieve two centuries before was surely going to be accomplished now by a Bourbon fleet, for the French navy had grown rapidly in recent years and in combination with that of Spain its large ships outnumbered the British men-of-war by almost two to one. (Channing's *United States,* iii.) In the face of so great a peril the government exerted itself strenuously. Vigorous measures of defence were obviously necessary, and to supply them a scheme of drafting 30,000 men was proposed.

This was a part of the Militia Bill of 1779. It passed the House of Commons with comparative ease, but in the Lords the radical Whigs violently assailed it. The Duke of Richmond was as usual the chief leader of the Opposition, and his remarks led Amherst to break his accustomed silence, and to make one of the few speeches he ever attempted. The general pronounced the nation so situated that it would be impossible for England to carry on an offensive war with success. As for defence, if Britain had ten to one more than the enemy it behoved her to make the ratio twenty to one. (Almon's *Parliamentary Register*, xiv.)

No words could have been more characteristic of the slow and steady soldier. When Richmond asked for arguments to support such a contention Lord Amherst replied that recent attempts to recruit the army had not been so successful as formerly: England needed more fighting men at once, and as the measure under discussion was a certain means of obtaining them, he was for it. His sentiments, however, did not prevail among the peers, and this part of the Militia Bill had to be dropped, although correspondingly extreme measures for manning the ships of the navy went through both Houses and received the royal assent. (Mahon's *History of England*, vi.)

A wave of patriotism and military zeal swept over England. A large encampment of militia companies was made at Cox Heath, near Maidstone, where many counties were represented, while members of the aristocracy and other individuals offered to raise, at their own expense, regiments or smaller bodies of soldiers for the defence of their threatened country. (Donne's *Correspondence of George III with Lord North*, ii.) Plymouth Harbor was closed to navigation, and at Portsmouth a line of batteries bade defiance to the enemy. On the ninth day of July a royal proclamation was issued charging all officers, civil as well as military, to cause horses, cattle and provisions to be driven or conveyed inland from the coast in case of actual invasion. To use his own words, George III intended that if the French landed troops on English soil they should "have thorough reason to repent of their temerity." (*Ibid.*, ii.)

While Britain's activities recalled the days of 1588, formidable offensive preparations were being made on the other side of the Channel. A French Army of about fifty thousand men was marching to the west coast, with the prospect of being transported to the shores of England as soon as the Bourbon fleet cleared the way. French men-of-war left Brest and soon united with those of Spain: together they numbered sixty-six sail of the line, not counting the train of frigates and small vessels which attended them. For several weeks they cruised off the English coast, appearing most often in front of Plymouth and keeping the inhabitants in a constant state of apprehension.

Against this naval Goliath England sent out Sir Charles Hardy with a fleet of only thirty-eight ships of the corresponding type. The odds against Britain were far greater than they had been at the time of the Spanish Armada, yet the invaders on this occasion were destined to meet the same disappointment as in 1588. The English admiral handled his ships well, drew the enemy away from before Plymouth and successfully avoided an engagement with the superior force. Dissensions between the Bourbon commanders also tended to prevent the success of the attack; and before harmony prevailed in their councils, sickness rendered the Spanish crews unfit for service. The ships of his Catholic Majesty were withdrawn, leaving the crestfallen French admiral with no choice but to make his best way back to Brest, which he did without more ado. The result of the boasted Bourbon invasion had been the capture of a single British ship of the line.

England breathed freely once more, but with her relief came a disconcerting consciousness of the peril that had so recently confronted her. A tumult was raised over the defenceless state of the southern coast, a tumult in which as usual the obstreperous Duke of Richmond made himself heard above the rest. He attacked Amherst in the House of Lords and called the attention of the peers to a few startling facts about conditions existing at Plymouth in the previous July and August. Only four or five thousand troops had guarded the exposed seaport, when it required at least twice that number; the intrenchments were most unskilfully planned; and as for the ordnance, Amherst's particular department, there were guns and shot, but no small stores like handspikes, wadding, rammers etc., without which the former were useless.

Had the enemy seen fit to attack it, Plymouth must certainly have fallen, and it was His Grace's opinion that whoever had been neglectful of his duty, or unequal to the proper discharge of it, ought to be brought to the most exemplary punishment. This invective brought Amherst to his feet in an instant; but his defence was very weak. He declared that he had gone down to Plymouth early in the summer and had observed the state of affairs there. The place ought to have had ten thousand men to insure it against a land attack, but that number could not then be supplied.

He assured the House that there was an abundance of gunpowder and balls, but, conscious of his negligence, he also blurted out that if the latter did not fit the cannon, it was not his fault! The works were admittedly insufficient, but they were the best that could be constructed on the spur of the moment, and were intended to impede rather than to repel the prospective invaders. On the whole, Amherst's explanations were anything but convincing. When the duke merci-lessly ridiculed them, the general's only reply was that he was perfectly willing to submit to an investigation and was ready to abide by the judgment of the country. There, for the time being, the matter rested. (Cobbett's *Parliamentary History*, xx.)

In case of an inquiry into Amherst's supposed negligence George III declared himself neutral, for, as he said:

> The affair relates to him and the Ordnance; if they can defend themselves, I do not see any evil can arise; if they have not done their duty, it is right it should be known. (Donne's *Correspond-ence of George III with Lord North*, ii.)

If we emulate the king's judicial state of mind in trying to form a proper estimate of the merits of the case, we must find the assertion of Sir David Lindsay strong evidence against the commander-in-chief. According to Lindsay, who was in command at Plymouth during the precarious months, the government had neglected the defences to such an extent that the Bourbon allies could have taken the dockyards in six hours. (Fortescue's *History of the British Army*, iii.) On the other hand, it should be remembered that the Duke of Richmond was ever careful to twist facts to suit his arguments.

In the latter part of April, 1780, the wretched business was again dragged into the House of Lords when Richmond went so far as to move that the assembly resolve itself into a committee of the whole to inquire into the state of defence of Devon and Cornwall in the previ-ous August, and to place the responsibility for their lack of security. After a great deal too much had been said on both sides, the peers defeated the duke's motion by a gratifying vote of ninety-two to fifty-one. (Cobbett's *Parliamentary History*, xxi.)

Almost at the moment when Amherst was so vigorously attacked by the Opposition, an opportunity to vindicate himself as a worthy commander-in-chief was fortunately and unexpectedly afforded by a series of anti-Catholic demonstrations known as the Gordon Riots. Logically this reign of terror should have occurred in 1778, when Parliament passed an act relieving Papists of certain unreasonable dis-abilities on condition of their taking oaths which the Protestants con-sidered necessary to the safety of the realm. (Lecky's *England in the Eighteenth Century*, iii.)

The measure applied only to England, but it was generally known that its provision would be extended to Scotland in the following year, and in anticipation of such a calamity the men to the northward made known their sentiments by riotous proceedings in Edinburgh and Glasgow. The lives of Roman Catholics were in constant danger, and liberal Protestants were also attacked. The spirit of unrest spread to England, where the fanatical party found a leader in the unbalanced Lord George Gordon, a young man whose violent anti-Catholic speeches had received only ridicule and contempt in the House of Commons. Outside its walls, however, the fanatical Scotchman easily gathered about him a party, called the Protestant Association, which held a great meeting on May 29, 1780, and decided to petition for the repeal of the Relief Act.

On the afternoon of June 2, thousands of men, bearing the petition, poured in upon Westminster and attempted to frighten Parliament into executing their wishes on the spot. When the legislators objected to recognising this informal display of what we call the right of initiative, the demonstrations of the multitude developed into a riot of alarming proportions. Members of the Commons were seized and insulted, and venerable peers on their way through Palace Yard were subjected to unpardonable outrages. Those who got safely within doors were imprisoned there until, after several hours of suspense, troops arrived upon the scene and dispersed the crowd.

This was but the beginning of anarchy, however, for the rioters, once excited, threw discretion to the winds and turned London into Pandemonium. The scenes that followed in the next five days and nights have been vividly described in *Barnaby Rudge*, but even the pen of Charles Dickens could not exaggerate the horrors of that frightful cataclysm. Not only was the property of Roman Catholics ruthlessly destroyed in every part of the metropolis, but also the houses of the leading ministers were assailed by the all-powerful crowds.

At Lord North's the mob was beaten back by a party of light horse, but Lord Mansfield, the aged Chief-Justice, was obliged to witness the demolition of his mansion in Bloomsbury Square and to see his noble law library consigned to the flames. A still more desperate deed was the burning of Newgate, the greatest prison in London, which belched forth about three hundred convicts as its contribution to the forces of the rioters. So, outrage followed outrage until an attempt was made to capture or burn even the Bank of England.

That such a rebellion could have taken place in London when England was at war with three nations is a commentary upon the unpopularity of the North Ministry, but the reason for the long continuance of the reign of anarchy is found elsewhere. Apparently, the municipal government was paralyzed with fear, but actually its helplessness was due to the provisions of the Riot Act, which tied the hands of the military and gave the rioters full sway. Today (1916), the police system of London commands universal admiration, but in the eighteenth century the metropolis lacked any such institution worthy of the name.

To make matters worse the Riot Act of 1715, in an attempt to safeguard Englishmen against the abuse of military power, dictated that in case of lawlessness a specified proclamation must be read to the mob by a justice or other magistrate, and that the offenders must be given an hour in which to scatter before troops or a *posse comitatus* might make arrests or fire upon them. (*Statutes at Large,* 1 George I, Cap. 5.) These restrictions were of great advantage to the rioters; in the first place, a justice was apt to keep out of the way when dangerous disturbances occurred; and secondly, a mob could do an infinite amount of harm in the hour of grace accorded it before the soldiers might fire a shot. Under such conditions it is not surprising that in 1780 London was at the mercy of the rioters for almost a week.

As things went from bad to worse, George III decided that something must be done to restore order. On June 7, he called a meeting of the Privy Council and questioned his advisers upon the wisdom of longer observing the provisions of the Riot Act. At first the councillors hesitated to take a definite position one way or the other; but when Wedderburn, the attorney-general, declared that under present conditions the reading of the Proclamation was wholly unnecessary, his colleagues readily came around to his wholesome, though perhaps unconstitutional, point of view. (Campbell's *Lives of the Lord Chancellors of England,* viii.)

The king then declared that as chief magistrate he would see their advice carried into effect; and he did. At no other moment in his long reign did George III so nearly approach greatness. His willingness to nullify the Riot Act in order to save London suggests President Cleveland's conduct in 1894, when the chief executive of the United States, under somewhat similar circumstances, ordered federal troops to Chicago without an application from the legislature or governor of Illinois. (Rhodes' *Historical Essays.*) Wedderburn drew up an order authorising the military to use force without waiting for form; the King signed it, and Amherst, as commander-in-chief acted upon it the same day. (Hamilton's *History of the Foot Guards,* ii.) When this measure went into execution, London was quickly restored to order, although in the process over two hundred people were shot dead in the streets.

What Bonaparte did for the Directory in 1795, Amherst did for London at this time; and such uncompromising treatment of lawlessness has ever proved most effectual. Nevertheless, the smoke of conflagrations due to the Gordon Riots had hardly disappeared when the Duke of Richmond was once more on his feet in the House of Lords, fulminating against the commander-in-chief and moving that a parliamentary inquiry be made into certain methods employed by him in suppressing the recent disturbances. (Cobbett's *Parliamentary History,* xxi.) His ground for complaint was not the infraction of the Riot Act, but an order Amherst had issued disarming the inhabitants of the city of London, which, according to the duke, was "contrary to the positive privilege of the subjects of this empire as declared in the Bill of Rights."

In the ensuing investigation, it appeared that one Colonel Twistleton had seen suspicious persons going about with firelocks, and being in doubt as to the proper way of dealing with them, he wrote to the commander-in-chief for instructions. As the riots had only just subsided at the time the letter was written and another outbreak was feared at any minute, Amherst replied that any arms found in the hands of unauthorised individuals were to be delivered up and kept in safety until further notice. (*Ibid.,* xxi.) Although this edict directly contravened one of the provisions of the sacred Declaration of Rights, (I William and Mary, Second Session, Cap. 2—*Statutes at Large,* iii), memories of the recent outrages happily outweighed reverence for the English constitution in both Houses of Parliament, and after much debate Richmond's attempt to censure Amherst for overstepping the law was emphatically rejected. (Journals of the House of Commons, xxxvii: Journals of the House of Lords, xxxvi.)

In the winter of 1780, the Netherlands joined in the war which the United States, France, and Spain were waging against Britain, and after that time almost any hard blow the Americans could inflict must have proved decisive for their cause. Therefore, when Cornwallis surrendered to Washington at Yorktown, on October 19, 1781, the independence of the erstwhile colonies was practically assured. This final catastrophe to British arms was at least partly attributable to Lord George Germain's unfortunate habit of undermining the efficiency of the commander-in-chief in America by encouraging insubordination in his second. (Channing's *United States,* iii.)

In this case he had given Cornwallis an almost independent command and had sent him off on an attempt to conquer the southern states, much to the displeasure of Sir Henry Clinton. Although Amherst did not approve of the operations which Lord Cornwallis proposed, he preferred him to Clinton as a man, and therefore gave him his support. (B. F. Stevens' *Clinton-Cornwallis Controversy*, i.) The result was the surrender at Yorktown, and if Clinton's observations on that disaster were just, Amherst must share in the responsibility for it. According to Sir Henry the loss of the campaign was attributable "to the Cabinet's having given a preference to the plans of a second in command," and he did not hesitate to declare that "to Lord North, Lord G. Germain, Thurlow Lord Chancellor, Lord Sandwich, Lord Amherst, Lord Gower the last not least" the thanks of the nation were due in great part for the loss of America. (B. F. Stevens' *Clinton-Cornwallis Controversy*, i.)

Thus, the conclusion may not be too far-fetched that whether or not Jeffery Amherst's sentiment kept him from taking the field against our ancestors, nevertheless, through his ill-starred advice to Lord George Germain on this occasion, he was a negative factor in the accomplishment of American independence.

The North Ministry, which had too long tottered on the brink of collapse, could not survive the news of Cornwallis's surrender. It is a familiar story how Lord North, upon hearing the fatal tidings, exclaimed, "Oh, God, it is all over!" and although the king was slow to comprehend the significance of the event, his Prime Minister was right. On March 20, 1782, North resigned, and with him fell all his colleagues. Lord Amherst at once gave up the office of commander-in-chief as well as his high post at the Ordnance and retired to the pastoral shades of "Montreal."

But Lord George Germain, the "master marplot" of them all, was not content to retire from office so quietly. As a younger son of a well-known duke, he very much desired a peerage as a token of the king's appreciation of his doubtful services, and in order to outrank Amherst, who had started his career as a page in his father's household, Germain asked to be created a viscount. (*Dictionary of National Biography*.) His request was granted, but the new title brought humiliation as well as glitter in its wake; for when the metamorphosed Lord George Germain essayed to take his seat in the House of Lords as Viscount Sackville, that august body disputed his right to the honour. Unpleasant memories of the Battle of Minden were revived and paraded to prove that the admission of "the greatest criminal this country ever knew, would be a disgrace to the House," (*Parliamentary Register*, xxv), and only after much discomfort was the new peer allowed to enjoy his ill-gotten elevation.

Chapter 15

Last Years

To offset the losses Amherst sustained as a result of the fall of the North Ministry, the king appointed him colonel of the Second Troop of Life Guards, a position which traditionally brought with it certain honours and duties known as "the Gold Stick in Waiting." The incumbent was held responsible for the safety of the royal person, and had to provide a sufficient guard to attend His Majesty, especially on occasions of state. (Cannon's *Historical Record of the Life Guards*.) Thus, the office which Lord Amherst held for the rest of his life was not wholly a sinecure, (*Myers* MS. No. 1453, in the New York Public Library); for the most part, however, the general was once more at leisure and could give much of his time to social life and to the more satisfactory enjoyment of his friends.

Jeffery Amherst was now a man of sixty-five years or more, whom his contemporaries found "grave, formal, and cold." In person he was tall and thin; his complexion was florid and his most striking feature, excepting a large wart on the left cheek, was a conspicuously aquiline nose. Although his intelligent face was an index to the sound judgment and solid understanding which characterised His Lordship, Amherst lacked the cultivation that would have made him more at ease in the society to which his title had raised him. (Wraxall's *Historical and Posthumous Memoirs*—edited by H. B. Wheatley, i.) Most of his friends were military men with whom he had been associated in his various campaigns, but among those whom he found congenial without the common background of the tented field was Governor Thomas Hutchinson, the exiled executive of Massachusetts-Bay.

Hutchinson was a gentleman of refinement and culture, a graduate of Harvard College, and an historian whose work has stood the test of time; yet he and the general seem to have found singular pleasure in each other's company. From the moment of his arrival in England in the summer of 1774, until he died of homesickness and a broken heart six years later, the governor was a frequent visitor at Amherst's town-house or countryseat, as the season might dictate. Oftentimes they walked together in the Park and discussed the course of the war in America, both hoping against hope that peace would soon be restored and that the British Empire would be once more what it was at the close of the Seven Years' War.

Doubtless the fact that the general had been in Boston and had gazed more than once upon the Blue Hills of Milton, made Hutchinson feel doubly drawn to the stolid soldier; but apart from that bond there seems to have been a certain friendly understanding between the two men which helped to alleviate the American's lonely suffering during those last sad years of his life. (Hutchinson's *Diary of Thomas Hutchinson*, i, ii: also, *Egerton MS.*, No. 2659, in the British Museum.)

Another acquaintance often to be found at Lord Amherst's was Lieutenant-General Sir Frederick Haldimand, who had commanded a battalion of the Royal Americans in the expedition against Montreal in 1760, and whom Amherst had appointed governor of the district of Three Rivers, after the conquest of Canada. Haldimand was a Swiss by birth and never spoke English with any degree of success. During the latter part of the American Revolution, he was governor of Canada, whence he returned to England in the autumn of 1784.

From that time on he was in constant attendance at Lord Amherst's where he dined or played cards to his heart's content. Her Ladyship entertained much company during these years, and although Haldimand was always ready to accept her invitations and eat and drink at Amherst's expense, he was equally ready to record his unpleasant impressions of his host in a private diary, which has since been made public.

This was poor taste, but the entries give one an interesting picture of Lord Amherst. At one time Haldimand complained of the general's evasive answers, of his unwillingness to use his influence to do anyone a good turn, and of his dislike of foreigners, (*Private Diary of General Haldimand, April 11, 1786, in the Report on Canadian Archives, 1889*); on other occasions Amherst's receptivity for flattery distressed the diarist, or he "exhibited his usual fussiness." Perhaps the most extraordinary entry is that describing a military dinner at the Amhersts' where Haldimand deliberately "asked for a bottle of old Madeira because it was offered to us with bad grace." (*Ibid.*, Jan. 18, 1787.) From his record for the following day one would judge that the disgruntled guest would have been just as well off without the stimulant which he extorted from his reluctant Lordship. Horace Walpole was another occasional visitor at the Amhersts', and he likewise never lost an opportunity to take a dig at his host, for whom he had a deep-seated aversion; but his remarks on the whole were not so unfriendly as were those of General Haldimand. (*Horace Walpole to Miss Mary Berry*, March 27, 1791.)

Probably Amherst found another form of social activity more enjoyable than his wife's series of routs and receptions: this was the American Club, a congenial group of officers who had seen service in the New World and who had banded themselves together for the sake of auld lang syne and the enjoyment of good dinners. The organisation was formed at the close of the French and Indian War, its first president being the notorious Colonel Charles Lee, (Richard E. Day's *Calendar of the Sir William Johnson Manuscripts*); but at this time Amherst was its head and continued to be so until 1787, when he yielded the honour to Admiral Lord Howe, the brother of Sir William Howe of American Revolution fame. (*Haldimand Diary*, January 30, 1787.)

Although Amherst was disappointed in his attempt to procure for himself a grant of the Jesuit estates in Canada in 1771, he by no means abandoned hope of adding those rich lands to his share of this world's goods. He had come so tantalisingly near winning the prize—the draught of the instrument apparently lacked only the approbation of the king in Council—that after a few years of discreet silence he renewed his petition to the Crown. (*Acts of the Privy Council—Colonial*, v.)

The second plea produced no more satisfactory results than the first, but when Amherst once more presented his request, seven years later, his persistency was rewarded with the prospect of success. An order in council was issued creating a commission to ascertain the extent of the lands, their value, and their nature, and in the spring of 1787, it was common talk in Canada that at last Lord Amherst was to achieve his purpose: the patent was already made out and awaited the action of the Governor and Council of Quebec. (Michigan Pioneer and Historical Society's *Collections*, xx.)

Indeed, so certain did the outcome seem that one Captain Genevay, a friend of General Haldimand, took time by the forelock and sought the position of curator of Amherst's prospective estates. But fate decreed otherwise. In November, just at the time when everything indicated Amherst's long-deferred success, a counter-petition, signed by almost two hundred Canadians, was presented to Lord Dorchester, the governor of Quebec. (Kingsford's *History of Canada*, vii.) In this document and the memorial which accompanied it, the inhabitants argued that the greater part of the Jesuit estates originated in private donations made expressly for educational purposes, and for that reason, they should be regarded as public property and be devoted to the support of a college which was very much needed. (*Report on Canadian Archives*, 1890.)

The legality of their claim was dubious at best, but the virtue of the cause of education gave strength to the suit of the Canadians. Furthermore, Lord Dorchester, who was an army man and had served under Amherst at Louisburg, had a strong dislike for his one-time commander (Donne's *Correspondence of George III with Lord North*, ii), and doubtless did all in his power to prevent the realisation of the latter's mercenary aspirations. While His Majesty's commissioners were busy with the survey and report which were intended to prelude the Amherst grant, the governor gave access to all persons who could advance claims or remonstrances against it, and took pains to impress the adverse sentiments of the Canadians upon the Home Secretary in England. (*Report on Canadian Archives*, 1890.)

The result of his efforts was an unsatisfactory *status quo* that lasted until 1803, four years after the death of Lord Amherst. Then Parliament settled the case by voting his heirs a perpetual annuity of £3,000 in lieu of the long-sought estates in America. As the annual revenue of the Jesuit lands in 1787 was not more than $5,000 it is evident that Amherst's immediate heir was no loser by the $15,000 annuity substituted for the other source of income. (Kingsford's *History of Canada*, vii.) By the end of the nineteenth century, however, the Canadian property would have eclipsed the pecuniary gift as a remunerative asset.

After 1781 Lord Amherst found himself the last leaf of his generation upon the family tree, and he had no children to cheer or comfort his declining years. His brother John, an admiral in the navy, died in 1778, his sister Elizabeth in the following year, and in May, 1781, William, his companion in war and peace, also departed this life. Since the days of Louisburg and Montreal William Amherst had rivalled his more distinguished brother in the acquisition of honours and profitable sinecures. From being deputy-governor of a fortress on the southeast coast, he rose to be a member of Parliament, and finally, governor of Newfoundland, the island which he had recaptured from the enemy towards the end of the Seven Years' War.

In the army he was made lieutenant-general, and although there was talk of his going to America in the War of Independence, (*Stopford-Sackville Manuscripts*, ii),he stayed in England and fought the king's battles in the House of Commons. Like his brother, he was a firm adherent of George III, and belonged to that useful, if not respectable, army known as "the king's friends."

When General William Amherst died in 1781, he left two children, Elizabeth and William Pitt Amherst, aged twelve and eight respectively. Their mother, who was "a very pretty and accomplished woman much beloved by her brothers-in-law," had died five years earlier, and Lord Amherst naturally took his niece and nephew under his wing. William's home in the Isle of Wight was sold, and the children came to "Montreal" to live with their uncle and aunt, who treated them as if they were their own offspring. The boy, it is needless to say, was named for the great statesman, during whose administration his uncle and father had won reputations for themselves in America; indeed, Lord Chatham was one of his godfathers. Lord Amherst sent his nephew to school at Westminster and thence to Christ Church, Oxford, where he received the degree of M.A. in 1797, the year of his uncle's death. (Ritchie and Evans' *Lord Amherst*.)

Two years later he was recommended to the Secretary of State for Foreign Affairs as a young man of exceptionally high character, a reputation which he more than justified during the next thirty years. After a brief mission to China, he was appointed Governor-General of India, and for his conduct of affairs in that part of the empire William Pitt Amherst was created an earl in 1826.

Of course, Jeffery Amherst could not foresee the brilliant career of his favourite brother's son, but he considered his nephew none the less worthy of inheriting the honours which he had won during his long life, and in 1788, he definitely named him the heir to his title and estate. In order to bring this about legally the general procured a new patent of peerage wherein he was styled Baron Amherst of Montreal, and which stipulated that William Pitt Amherst and his heirs male should succeed to the coronet and to the property. (*Gentleman's Magazine*, September, 1788.) When this was settled, Lord Amherst took care to enlarge his domain in Sevenoaks whenever there was an opportunity to do so, and in other 'ways increased and concentrated his nephew's heritage. (*Journals of the House of Lords*, vol. 39.)

In February, 1793, the Revolutionists of France, fresh from the murder of Louis XVI, and drunk with the success of their efforts to overturn the existing order of things, declared war upon England. Foreseeing this event, the British government had already called upon Lord Amherst to take command of the army in Great Britain as in 1778. Although His Lordship was really an old man, he forgot his seventy-five years and cheerfully assumed the task imposed upon him. A task it certainly was, for in the last ten years the British Army had degenerated to a point never reached before or since.

For this decline there were many reasons. In the first place when the North Ministry went out of office Amherst was succeeded as commander-in-chief by Henry Seymour Conway, an ardent Whig who could not get along with the younger Pitt and who consequently resigned his position in March, 1784. From that time on there was no commander-in-chief until Amherst's appointment in 1793. (Fortescue's *History of the British Army*, iii.)

Although that lapse must have been decidedly hurtful to the service, it was not the basic cause of the wane of England's military establishment. The main responsibility must rest upon the shoulders of the prime minister; for, great as was his genius, William Pitt the Younger had his limitations when it came to the administration of the army, the very department in which his father had so pre-eminently excelled. At the end of the American War all soldiers whose terms of service were up had made haste to leave their regiments, and recruits to fill their places had not been forthcoming. (*Ibid.*, iii.)

The fact that it was almost impossible to persuade men to enlist, and those who did so constantly deserted, should have suggested to the ministers that conditions of life in the army needed an investigation and a remedy, but the government dodged the issue and relied upon the purchase of Hessians rather than upon a reconstruction of the English Army to supply the needed soldiers in time of stress. (*Ibid.*, iii.) As a subterfuge this practice might be temporarily economical, but England could not long afford to make her military service as unpopular as it was from 1783 until 1797.

The great evil in the army was the lack of a living wage, and the unfortunate privates found themselves forced to choose between starvation and desertion. The Secretary at War and the adjutant-general were quite aware of the grievous state of affairs, but Pitt, as Chancellor of the Exchequer, declined to do anything until 1792. Then a reformed financial basis assured the soldier a net annual income of only eighteen shillings ten pence half-penny. (*Ibid.*, iii.) Such was the false economy of the younger Pitt. What wonder, then, that Amherst upon resuming his command found the army completely demoralised and fast dying of inanition?

These facts are important, because after His Lordship's death Henry Dundas, Secretary of State for War, spoke of the late commander-in-chief as "a worthy and respectable old man," but one who had done "mischief" that would not be repaired "but by the unremitting attention of many." (Historical Manuscripts Commission's *Report on the Manuscripts of J. B. Fortescue, Esq.*, iv.) By placing the responsibility for Pitt's misdeeds upon Amherst, Dundas was guilty of gross injustice, for the general merely took over in an emergency the hollow framework of an army and did the best he could with it in the two years during which he held the chief command. One could hardly ask that a man of more than seventy-five years should reform a rotten military system suddenly thrust upon him, and those who lament that Amherst "allowed innumerable abuses to grow up in the army" must produce their grounds for such a grave and unjust charge.

In February, 1795, the general was relieved of his burdensome office by the Duke of York, a son of George III. It is said that Lord Amherst was then offered an earldom, which he declined, (*Gentleman's Magazine*, September, 1797); but that any such elevation was proposed is doubtful, not only because the king made no mention of it to the gentleman whose duty it was to inform the general of the change, (*Life and Correspondence of the Rt. Hon. William Windham*, i), but also because if the proposal had been made, Amherst, in all probability, would have snapped up the prize in an instant. Be that as it may, in the summer of the following year he was given the rank of field-marshal, the highest military office in the British Army and an eminence which no man in England deserved more than he.

After his retirement from the chief command His Lordship's health began to fail, and he found himself scarcely able to attend to his duties as Gold Stick, much less to take any part in the conduct of the war which still continued with the French revolutionists. From his retirement at "Montreal" Lord Amherst watched the tedious course of the hostilities and the rise of Bonaparte, little dreaming that the Corsican was soon to become the terror and scourge of all western Europe. On August 3, 1797, the end came, and a week later His Lordship's remains were interred in the family vault in Sevenoaks church. The funeral service was performed by the rector and was attended with little display: plain black velvet covered the coffin, upon the plate of which were inscribed the name, age, and title of Jeffery Amherst. (*Gentleman's*

Magazine, September, 1797.)

In reviewing the general's life, one is struck by certain peculiar features in his career. The first is its division into two distinct parts, which might be respectively labelled obscurity and prominence. Singularly enough the abrupt line of demarcation divides Amherst's life into two periods of forty years each. From 1717 until 1757 he was first growing to manhood and later fighting on the Continent, with almost no prospect of distinction and fame. Suddenly, in the spring of 1758, the unknown colonel was despatched to North America, where he won immediate and enduring glory that surpassed the most fanciful dreams of his youth. The perihelion of his orbit was reached in September, 1760, when, by a triple combination of armies upon Montreal, Amherst achieved the conquest of Canada.

Horace Walpole's zealous devotion to his cousin, Henry Seymour Conway, who in many ways was Amherst's natural rival, almost always distorted his regard for the general; but the dilettante of Strawberry Hill was not far from right when he included Amherst among:

> Those men who, in particular instances in one period of their life, not only have performed great actions, but have conducted them with consummate sense and address, and who in the rest of their lives have been able to display no symptoms of genius. (Walpole's *Memoirs of the Reign of George II*, iii.)

Walpole was wrong, however, in concluding his estimate with an insinuation that fortune rather than foresight was the chief cause of his victories. Amherst was from first to last a soldier of extraordinary ability, and his apparent predilection for court favours instead of for military pursuits, after his return from America, was due to other causes than incompetency. Politically and temperamentally the general was a Tory. He possessed the domestic tastes and love of country-life which one invariably associates with members of that party, and after his five years of active service in the New World, years almost unequalled in English history for consistent military achievement, it was but fair that he should enjoy the tranquil delights of "Montreal."

With untroubled conscience he left the conduct of hostilities in the American Revolution to younger officers; but it should be remembered that when his country was in danger in 1779, and again in 1793, he neither lingered in his home nor for one moment shirked the responsibilities which his martial genius imposed upon him.

While in America General Amherst became acquainted with some of the men who were destined to found "a new nation, conceived in liberty and dedicated to the proposition that all men are created equal." Among them was Benjamin Franklin, with whom the general held pleasant converse more than once during his three years in New York. (Smyth's Writings of Benjamin Franklin, iv.) It does not appear that he ever met George Washington, but, as the Virginian modestly expressed it, "that General Amherst may have heard of such a person as I am is probable." (Sparks' Writings of George Washington, ii.)

In England his name is associated with those of William Pitt and George III, and although no sculptured marble preserves his likeness and memory in abbey or public square, Canada, the flower of the British Empire, sweeping from the fertile valley of the St. Lawrence to the towering summits of the Rockies, will ever remain a splendid and inspiring monument to the energy and ability of Jeffery Amherst.

The Last Siege of Louisburg

By C. Ochiltree Macdonald

To check the power of France, safeguard her commerce, and palliate her conduct in re-exposing British America to the peril of Louisburg, Britain founded a naval and military base in the spacious harbour which sheltered the shattered French Armada of *A.D.* 1746. But the armaments of Halifax were not upon the imposing scale of Louisburg; and, if a petition addressed to the Council of Nova Scotia by the merchants and freeholders of the new capital, expressing alarm at its critical situation, and praying for stronger fortifications, especially a proper citadel, as a last retreat in times of extremity, is accepted as reliable evidence, the moneys voted by the Imperial Government for the fortifications of the place were "injudiciously" applied and "miserably mismanaged."

From other points of view the Nova Scotian was inferior to the Cape Breton metropolis; and its growth was so retarded by the superior attractions of its northern rival that Cornwallis complained that there was often a scarcity of provisions in the city, because the New England and New York merchants preferred to trade at Louisburg.

Louisburg was thus an important commercial centre as well as the greatest military stronghold on the northern coasts, and "ships of all nations" rode at anchor in her ample port. In 1751, 150 English vessels traded there, and the commerce of the city was increasing so rapidly that 30 Boston ships could sometimes be counted in the port.

An English traveller who visited the city found 30 sail of English ships loading and discharging there; 20 large vessels from France lay at the quays, discharging wines, oils, cambrics, linens, silks, velvets, and, "in short, an assortment of all the manufactures of France"; and others arrived almost daily from the West Indies laden with rum, sugar, molasses, coffee, cotton, indigo and cocoa. These commodities were purchased on a large scale by the New England and other "Colonial" merchants for the British "Colonial" markets as far south as South Carolina. Most of them were paid for in good silver dollars; and as the trifling commodities the British traders could sell were chiefly lumber, the balance of trade was greatly in favour of France.

Louisburg was also the emporium of a fishing industry, which competed with the fishing industry of New England, employed fully 2,281 vessels, manned by 15,138 men, and is stated to have supported an export of 974,700 quintals of fish *per annum*. The following table indicates its relation to the metropolitan fishing station:—

French Fishing Villages Tributary to Louisburg.	Number of Boats. Decked Vessels.	Shallops
Egmont Bay (near Cape North)	—	30
Niganish Bay and Cove	—	245
Niganish Island	—	30
Port Dauphin or St. Anne's	100	—
Entrance of Great Bras d'Or Lakes	20	40
Petit Bras d'Or	—	60
Spanish River or Sydney	6	—
Indian Bay or Lingan	—	50
Scatterie Island	—	200
Main à Dieu	—	190
Lorambec	—	80
Gabarous Bay	—	50
Fourché	—	50
St. Esprit Island	—	60
Grand Rivière	—	60
L'Ardois	—	14
St. Peter's	100	—
Petit de Grat (He Madame)	—	100
River and Bay of Inhabitants	100	—
Places in Straits of Canso	100	—
	426	1,255
The Fishing Craft hailing from Louisburg itself were	300	300
Total	726	1,555

Louisburg was likewise the *entrepôt* of an active contraband trade, carried on with the French Nova Scotian villages, *viâ* Cornwallis, now McNab's, Island, in Halifax Harbour, by Joshua Mauger, the father of the Halifax lady who, as Duchesse de Bouillon, perished upon the guillotine early in the French Revolution. Mr. Mauger smuggled from France to Louisburg, thence to "Mauger's Beach" and McNab's Island (which he made vast repositories of French goods); and distributed the contraband merchandise among the French Nova Scotians *via* the military road, between the capital and the Acadian villages, through his truck houses at Piziquid, Mines, Grand Pré, and Annapolis. He was believed to be one of the great intermediaries between France and the Indians in Nova Scotia, and the medium through which French manufactured tomahawks and scalping knives reached the Micmacs for use against the British.

Cornwallis denounced him to the Imperial Government as an audacious smuggler, if nothing worse, and unavailingly urged that so dubious a person should not be permitted to act as Agent-Victualler for Nova Scotia. Mr. Mauger at length retired with his accumulated gains to London, whence he had come, and for many years acted as Agent-General for Nova Scotia in the British Metropolis. He died in 1770, leaving a fortune of £300,000 sterling, which was squandered by his aristocratic son-in-law, the Duc de Bouillon, until his reckless career closed upon the guillotine with his unhappy wife; and it may thus be said that the profits of Louisburg's illicit commerce contributed to the provocation of the French Revolution.

In May-June, 1756, the Franco-British War was rekindled from its ashes, and Louisburg became a pressing danger to British America, especially as the Court of Versailles published the following edict to encourage privateers to prey upon the maritime trade of British-America:—

The tenth due to the Admiralty is remitted.

Besides the produce of the prizes, which shall wholly appertain to the captors, the following bounties shall be paid them out of the Royal Treasury, namely: 100 *livres* per gun, from 4 to 12 pounders, taken from merchantmen; 150 *livres* per gun of the same bore, taken from privateers; 200 *livres* per gun of the same bore, taken from men-of-war; 150 *livres* per gun, 12 pounders and upwards, taken from merchantmen; 225 *livres* per gun of the said bore, taken from privateers; 300 *livres* per gun of the said bore, taken from men-of-war; 30 *livres* per head for every prisoner taken out of a merchantman; 40 *livres* per head for every prisoner taken out of a privateer; 50 *livres* per head for every prisoner taken out of a man-of-war.

The same bounties to be paid for every man on board at the commencement of any engagement. The said bounties to be augmented by one-fourth for all such privateers or men-of-war which shall be taken by boarding.

The said bounties shall wholly appertain to the captain, officers and crew, to be divided amongst themselves according to the share they are to have in the produce of the prize, and pursuant to the agreement at the time of entering on board; the money to be paid to the captain or his representative.

The king promises other rewards to such captains or officers that shall behave well, even to their receiving commissions in his Marine, according to the circumstance and strength of the ships they shall have engaged.

Ships of 24 guns or upwards that shall have been built for privateering shall be taken by the government at the prime cost if they be not employed that way, or at the estimated price if they have been so employed, when they shall be no longer authorised to cruise on the enemies. In order to indemnify the owners of those ships, which shall take any privateers or men-of-war, of the damage they shall sustain by such engagements, the following premiums are to be paid to them:—

100 *livres* per gun, from 4 to 12 pounders.

200 *livres* per gun, from 12 pounders upwards.

20 *livres* per head for every effective man on board at the beginning of an engagement.

Privateers shall be exempt from all taxes or duties whatsoever on provisions, artillery, ammunition, and all other necessaries for their construction, victualling, and armament.

The officers and sailors on board privateers, that shall be wounded and disabled, shall receive the sea half pay, and pensions shall be allowed to the widows of those that shall be killed.

The Louisburg privateers put to sea; and in July an indecisive battle was fought off the port between the ships sent out of Halifax to destroy them and M. Beausier's squadron. While returning from Quebec to Louisburg, on July 26th, M. Beausier sighted the British three leagues southward of Louisburg, and bore down on them before a northerly gale. But they tacked in order to stand off and, fearing to fall to leeward of Louisburg, into which he was carrying provisions, Beausier went into the harbour to land them, and started in quest of the English at 5 o'clock next morning, with the *Héros*, 74; *Illustre*, 64; the frigate *Syrene*, 36; and a 36-gun frigate. Sighting the *Grafton* and *Nottingham*, 70 guns, and a Jamaica sloop, about noon, he crowded all sail to come up with them, and the *Syrene* briskly attacked the sloop; but the *Grafton* and *Nottingham* beat her off.

M. Beausier bore up to her support under press of canvas, and opened fire upon the *Grafton*, leaving the *Nottingham*, which lay upon his quarter, to the *Illustre*; but a calm coming on at the moment, the *Illustre* could not support him, and the *Héros* lay exposed to the guns of the *Grafton* and *Nottingham* until the *Illustre* came to her assistance at 7 o'clock in the evening, before a rising gale. The dusk falling upon the sea terminated the combat, and the French bore off the *Héros* to Louisburg, where she arrived next morning, with two hundred shot in her hull and masts, others between wind and water, 18 of her crew killed and 48 wounded, the tattered flag of France still flying triumphantly at her mast head.

Shortly after this affair Lord Loudoun proposed the reduction of Louisburg, and the Imperial Ministry consented to this prudent measure. The Governors of North Carolina, Virginia, Maryland, and Pennsylvania were immediately assembled at Philadelphia by His Lordship, and entrusted with the common defence of the frontiers during the absence of the Imperial forces in Cape Breton; a general embargo laid upon outward bound tonnage and a hot press at New York, on May 20th, supplied transports for the army and seamen for the fleet; the 22nd, 42nd, 44th, and 48th Regiments; 2 Battalions of the 60th, 500 Rangers, and 100 Boston Carpenters, totalling 5,300 men, were embarked; and on May 25th, 1757, ninety transports convoyed by the only available squadron, consisting of the:—

	Guns
Sutherland	50
Nightingale	20
Kennington	20
Vulture	16
Ferret	14

. . . . .under Rear-Admiral Sir Charles Hardy, fell down to Sandy Hook.

There Lord Loudoun learned from the prisoners taken in a French prize that 5 French sail of the line were *en route* from the West Indies to Louisburg. An express from Boston confirmed this, and stated that these ships had been seen off Halifax; but two sloops of war, despatched to reconnoitre the coast, encountered no French ships, and on June 5th the expedition proceeded to Halifax to join the 2nd Battalion of the 1st, the 28th, 55th, 17th, 46th, 43rd, 27th, detachments of the 40th, 45th, and 47th Regiments, a company of artillery, and an imperial fleet *en route* from Cork, under Admiral Holburne.

The day the British left the Hook, M. de Beaufremont reached Louisburg with the ships which had been sighted off Halifax. M. du Revest had entered the port the preceding day with 4 ships of the line from Toulon; and 24 days later, M. Bois de la Mothe arrived with 9 ships of the line, 4 frigates, troops and stores from Brest.

These accessions brought the military strength of Louisburg up to 7,000 regular troops, supported by 18 ships of the line and 5 frigates, *viz*: —

	Guns		Guns
Le Duc de Bourgogne	84	*Le Défenseur*	74
Le Tonnant	80	*Le Diadème*	74
Le Formidable	80	*Le Superbe*	74
L'Hector	74	*Le Glorieux*	74
L'Héros	74	*Le Célèbre*	64
Le Dauphin Royal	70	*Le Bizarre*	64
L'Achille	64	*La Brune*	36
Le Vaillante	64	*Le Bien Acquis*	38
Le Sage	64	*La Comète*	30
L'Inflexible	64	*La Hermoine*	26
L'Eveillé	64	*Le Fleur de Lys*	36
Le Belliqueux	64	*La Fochine*, flute	36

Ten days later (July 9th), Admiral Holburne, seriously delayed by adverse winds, bore into Halifax, and despatched several ships to reconnoitre Louisburg, while he organised his fleet for the siege.

Lord Loudoun utilised these delays by instructing the army, which now consisted of about 11,000 men. A facine fort was erected on the north side of the citadel, and the proposed siege of Louisburg was rehearsed "with great firing, in the presence of a multitude of spectators." His Lordship also laid out a large vegetable garden for the benefit of the sick or wounded likely to be sent to the base during the siege, and by this prudent measure preserved the health of his troops, while many of the French perished at Louisburg for lack of similar foresight.

On July 31st, three weeks after Holburne's arrival—a reasonable day for the organisation of a naval expedition against Louisburg which Boscawen claimed the following year—the army prepared to embark, and Major-General Lord Charles Hay was placed under arrest for insinuating that Lord Loudoun was expending the nation's wealth in sham fights and planting cabbages.

By August 2nd the troops were on board, the masters of the transports received their instructions, and a grand rendezvous was appointed in Gabarous Bay; but on August 4th an express arrived from the Governor of Newfoundland divulging the naval and military force assembled at Louisburg, and this proved to be so unexpectedly imposing that the departure was deferred. A council of war was immediately held, and it was finally very properly resolved:

> That, considering the great strength of the enemy, and the advanced season of the year, it was expedient to postpone the attack upon Louisburg.

The regiments allotted to the Halifax garrison debarked, and others, assigned to the Bay of Fundy, proceeded under convoy to Annapolis and Beauséjour. The remainder were conducted by Lord Loudoun to New York; and Admiral Holburne, mindful, perhaps, of the fate of Byng, sailed for Louisburg in the following line of battle:—

The *Kingston* to lead with the starboard, and the *Defiance* with the larboard, tacks on board. Frigates to repeat signals.

	SHIPS	GUNS	DIVISION
Hunter	Kingston	60	Sir Charles Hardy, Rear-Admiral of the White.
	Captain	64	
	Invincible	74	
	Nassau	64	
	Sutherland	50	
Port Mahon	Tilbury	60	Francis Holburne, Vice-Admiral of the Blue, Commander-in-Chief.
	Northumberland	70	
	Newark	80	
	Orford	66	
	Sunderland	60	
	Centurion	50	
Ferret	Nottingham	60	Charles Holmes, Commodore.
	Bedford	64	
	Grafton	70	
	Terrible	74	
	Defiance	60	

. . . . and challenged the French to come out by firing a gun and hoisting the standard of England between the ensign staff and the mizzen shrouds. An Englishman imprisoned in the city, who watched this powerful British fleet in battle array off the harbour, says that M. du Bois de la Mothe, the commander of the French fleet, returned the challenge by hoisting the "bloody flag" of France at the main top gallant masthead and firing one gun, but never stirred an anchor.

The British stood off and on for two days; but as the French did not come out, Holburne returned to Halifax. There he was reinforced by 4 ships, and on September 19th he re-appeared so close into Louisburg that the batteries opened fire. The fleet remained off the port challenging the French to come out—a glorious spectacle, it is said, of Britain's naval power—until it was almost destroyed by an autumnal gale, which drove the ships towards the inhospitable coast. The *Tilbury*, becoming unmanageable, struck heavily upon the St. Esprit reefs, and foundered with her captain and half the crew, and the remaining ships tossed for hours upon the mountainous seas "like straws on a mill stream," watched from the shore by crowds of people, who saved about 200 of the *Tilbury's* crew.

Fortunately for Britain, the wind at length shifted off shore, and, although the fleet lay for hours in a desperate plight, none of the other ships were lost. The casualties were, however, disastrous, and the list of them is sufficiently extensive to show that this severe Cape Breton storm was more destructive to the Royal Navy of England than both sieges of Louisburg.

Thus, defeated by the elements, Holburne stationed 8 ships at Halifax, and conducted the remainder to England.

The refusal of the French admiral to give him battle was no reflection upon the honour of France. The masters of Cape Breton could afford to treat a naval demonstration against Louisburg with comparative indifference at so tempestuous a season of the year, and their determination to do so, in Holburne's case was especially wise, as a gaol distemper in Louisburg had seriously weakened their fleet.

When M. du Bois de la Mothe left Louisburg for Brest, in October, leaving two ships on the station, his fleet carried with it this virulent malady, which had destroyed 1,500 seamen, 150 English prisoners, and numbers of the inhabitants of Louisburg during the summer; and the dreadful disorder rapidly increased as the fleet approached the coast of Europe.

Anxious to annihilate the squadron which had prevented the reduction of Louisburg, the Imperial Ministry despatched the:—

	Guns		Guns
Ramillies	90	*Burford*	70
Royal George	100	*Alcide*	64
Neptune	90	*Essex*	64
Namur	90	*Intrepid*	60
Barfleur	90	*Prince of Orange*	60
Royal William	84	*Rochester*	50
Princess Amelia	80	*Hussar*	28
Magnanime	74	*Shannon*	26
Torbay	74	*Biddeford*	20
Dublin	74		

... under Admiral Hawke and Vice-Admiral Boscawen, from Spithead, on October 22nd, to attack it before it reached Brest; but the unpropitious elements which had shattered Holburne's fleet drove them off their station, and before the weather moderated the enfeebled French squadron got into Brest. The crews were then so deplorably weak that the King's Hospital, the City Hospital, the Hospital of Recouvrance, and the Churches of the Jesuits, Carmelites, Seven Saints, Capuchins, Notre Dame, Two Congregations, and La Chapelle du Cimitière were instantly filled with the sick; and, in this painful demoralisation of a powerful fleet which had helped to preserve the key of Canada, France paid a severe penalty for the deplorable neglect of sanitary laws in Louisburg.

The postponement of the second siege of Louisburg provoked great discontent in England.

The loss of Port Mahon in the previous year had maddened the people; and their indignation, consummated in the execution of Byng, had not subsided when Loudoun's decision not to attack Louisburg in 1757 was made public. The disappointed nation construed the delay into fresh evidence of the incompetence of its chieftains; and even Pitt, who had hazarded his power to defend Byng, vehemently censured Loudoun.

The earl did not merit this severe condemnation. When he arrived in America, he had found Colonial military affairs in great disorder, owing to the differences between the Imperial and Colonial executives respecting the defence of the frontiers.

The governors and principal members of the Provincial Assemblies proposed the enactment of Colonial laws and taxes for their own defence, by a Council composed of members of the Assemblies and the

Crown Governors; but their fellow citizens in the British Isles, slow in comprehending the proper methods of administering Colonial affairs, proposed that Colonial defence should be exclusively conducted by the governors appointed in London and one or two members of their Councils; and paid for by taxes levied upon the Colonies by the Imperial House of Commons.

Although the disorder caused by these divergent views was extremely detrimental to the proper organisation of Colonial defence, Loudoun at length succeeded in effecting an arrangement which enabled him to project a blow at Louisburg. But the Imperial Ministry proved incapable of keeping his policy from the knowledge of the Court of Versailles, to which Dr. Henacy, of Arundel Street, a physician, frequenting London society, communicated tidings of the intending expedition, an exact account of the number of ships and transports to be conducted from England to Halifax by Holburne for that service, the troops on board, and the day of their departure; and in January, 1757, despite the vigilance of the British ships on the French coast, a strong squadron left Brest for Louisburg. A second Louisburg squadron from Toulon outmanoeuvred the British in the Straits of Gibraltar; and a third from Brest, even more fortunate, also reached Louisburg to complete the most formidable French armament ever assembled in the capital of Cape Breton.

The imperial authorities, by permitting France to ascertain their policy, and enormously strengthen Cape Breton, thus failed to properly perform their part in the projected second siege of Louisburg.

By a fatality which proves that the elements are not always on the side of the English, the British Louisburg fleet lay wind-bound at St. Helens, while France poured her forces into Louisburg, and Loudoun was delayed at Halifax one month by its tardy arrival. Further necessary delays at Halifax brought a season of the year at which a leaguer of Louisburg could not be attempted unless the city was weakly defended.

This was not the case. A strong army lay behind her walls, a powerful squadron filled the harbour; and, when the strength of the defences was ascertained from despatches forwarded to Halifax by the Governor of Newfoundland, it was clear to the Halifax Council of War that the contemplated siege would last for months.

To invest Louisburg in August under these circumstances would have been bad tactics, imminently liable to cover British arms with disaster. The approach of the wet season would very seriously, probably fatally, embarrass an army besieging a city so guarded landward by swamps; and its necessary dependence upon a fleet exposed to the severe gales characteristic of Louisburg at that season of the year made the enterprise impracticable.

If the foresight of the Halifax Council of War needed confirmation, the disaster to the fleet off Louisburg shortly after emphatically vindicated their judgment. These considerations did not, however, weigh with a distant populace impatient for victory, and they apparently also failed to impress the more temperate Pitt.

The indignation of the nation, inflamed by the reduction of British North America to a "mere strip" along the eastern seaboard by Montcalm, and the recollection of Britain's numerous military failures since the Spanish War (1739) could not be restrained when the news of the postponement of the second siege of Louisburg reached England; and it became apparent that only a speedy return of victory to the standards of the Empire could allay the serious domestic unrest.

An ebb in the tide of French triumphs was, however, at hand. The great Pitt, indignant at the humiliation of the national arms, adopted the politic measures of the general whom he censured; and, taught an imperial policy by New England, boldly advocated the reduction of all Canada.

Sir Charles Hardy was sent out to blockade Louisburg with the ships left at Halifax by Holburne; Commodore Durell repaired to Halifax to make everything ready for the embarkation of an army for Cape Breton immediately Admiral Boscawen reached the capital of Nova Scotia, and a large land and sea force was mobilised. The Court of Versailles, warned by Henacy, the spy-physician of Arundel Street, energetically prepared to defend the threatened Cape Breton capital, and:—

	Guns		Guns
L' Ocean	80	*Le Content*	64
Le Redoubtable	74	*Le Lion*	64
Le Guerricr	74	*L'Hippopotaine*	50
Le Centaur	74	*L'Oiseau*	30
Le Souveraign	74		

. . . . were despatched from Toulon early in December (1757) under M. de la Clue, mainly to proceed into Louisburg at the earliest possible moment in the following spring. But Vice-Admiral Osborn intercepted them with the:—

	Guns		Guns
Prince	90	Guernsey	50
St. George	90	Preston	50
Monarch	74	Ambuscade	40
Culloden	74	Rainbow	40
Swiftsure	70	Lyme	28
Hampton Court	64	Tartar's Prize	24
Monmouth	64	Deal Castle	20
Berwick	64	Gibraltar	20
Revenge	64	Fortune	14
St. Albans	60	Glasgow	20
Princess Louisa	60	Sheerness	20
Jersey	60	Favourite	16
Montagu	60		

. . . .and shut them up in Carthagena. From that *port de la* Clue appealed to the Court of Versailles for reinforcements to extricate his fleet, and, if necessary, to engage the British; and M. du Quesne was sent to his assistance with 5 ships of the line and a frigate.

Two of Du Quesne's ships succeeded in getting into Carthagena; but of the remainder, *L'Orphée*, 64 guns, was captured by the *Revenge* and *Berwick*, sixty-fours, after a gallant engagement, in which the French lost 110 and the British 86 men killed and wounded, and the *Foudroyant* by the *Monmouth* and *Swiftsure*, 64 and 70 guns, after a hot combat, in which France lost 190 and Britain 107 men killed and wounded. The *Oriflamme*, 50 guns, was driven ashore under the Castle of Airglows by the *Monarch* and *Montagu*, 74 and 60 guns, and she would have been destroyed but for the observance of the neutrality of the Spanish coast by Osborne; and the *Piciade* of 26 guns and the remaining ships escaped.

The Louisburg-Quebec squadron mobilised at the Isle of Aix in March was as unfortunate.

On March 11 Admiral Hawke left Spithead with the:—

	Guns		Guns
Ramillies	90	Intrepid	64
Union	90	Medway	60
Newark	80	Hussar	28
Chichester	70	Southampton	32
Alcide	64	Coventry	28

. . . .to intercept it; and at daybreak of April 4th he sighted some French ships, convoyed by three frigates, all of which, however, escaped into St. Martins, Isle of Rhee, except a brig which the *Hussar* destroyed. At four o'clock in the afternoon, when off the Isle of Aix, Hawke sighted the main squadron, consisting of the:—

	Guns
Florissant	74
Sphinx	64
Hardi	64
Dragon	64
Warwick	60

.... six or seven frigates, and 40 transports, which cut their cables and fled in such disorder that many of them ran ashore. At daybreak the men-of-war were seen lying upon the mud almost high and dry, and some, with many of the transports, actually upon their beam ends. But, owing to the shoaliness of the water, Hawke could not destroy them; and, assisted by men sent in launches from Rochefort, the French carried out warps and threw their stores, guns, ballast, and water overboard to extricate themselves before fireships were sent in among them.

By the evening of April 5th some of their warships got up to the mouth of the Charante, but the transports still lay aground towards Isle Madame; and, after cutting away more than 80 buoys laid by the French upon their abandoned anchors and destroying the new military works upon the Isle of Aix, Hawke withdrew his fleet.

Meanwhile the last British Armada against Louisburg had left Spithead for Halifax, and Sir Charles Hardy had commenced the blockade of Louisburg. But, notwithstanding Hardy's vigilance and the vigilance of the British Admirals in European waters, a strong French squadron carrying troops and supplies of every kind, commanded by M. de Chaffant, stole into the harbour. The French commander did not remain long at Louisburg. Dreading to be shut up in the port, and foreseeing its fate he hastened to Quebec, reluctantly leaving 6 of his ships and some frigates to help to defend the place at the earnest request of Drucour.

At Halifax the British Armada swelled to 39 warships, 2 fire ships, 118 transports, and more than 12,000 troops by the accession of the ships on the station, Bragg's Regiment, 200 Carpenters, and 538 New England troops; and, after a stormy passage along the Nova Scotian coast, the whole of the magnificent flotilla dropped anchor before Louisburg.

Many who have travelled from Kennington Cove to Old Louisburg over the ground traversed by the British on June 8th, 1758, and regarded the ruins of the fortress, have doubtless tried to picture the city as it appeared to the victors after the battle. The following extract from a letter written by a British officer on the ground probably gives a fair idea of its appearance as Wolfe studied the fortifications:—

> Louisburg is extremely well fortified all round; it has double ranges of guns, like two tiers of a ship, on the south side, which point westerly, strengthened by double entrenchments about 160 yards from the glacis; besides, they can bring their ships to bear upon almost every post we shall take to cover our approaches, and particularly a valley which we must pass through. The east and north side of the town are defended by their shipping and the Island Battery, besides the fortifications of the town itself, which are not trifling.

Although the sinking of so many fine ships in the mouth of the harbour was an admission that his position had grown critical, Le Chevalier Drucour combated the siege with unshaken firmness, and the fleet and forts poured shot and shell upon the British lines. The continuous musketry fire from the covered way also greatly annoyed the besiegers, and the sorties from the gates grew so formidable that they prevented a general assault upon the city on the 8th of July. That day at sundown the loud booming of the siege artillery suddenly ceased; the French artillery also ceased fire, and the calm of a summer evening succeeded the clanging crash of metal, the clatter of falling masonry, and the hoarse cheers of defiance or triumph from the ramparts and trenches. The clear sky stretched over head like a panoply, but a light mist rolled lazily along the earth, concealing the lower part of the city, whose battlements rose picturesquely above the vapour.

As the darkness deepened the tranquillity of the scene increased. The voices of the seamen on the battleships in the port died away, the hum of the city was hushed; its dark shadows stood out prominently against the sky, and no sound arose from the host that surrounded or the multitude that inhabited it save the hoarse cries of the sentries, telling that all was well in Louisburg.

The first army of England was, however, preparing for a general assault, and the soldiers, wearied of the monotony of the siege and the hardship of the trenches, eagerly received the directions of their leaders.

The French were making similar preparation, and at 11 o'clock, five piquets, supported by seven hundred men, sortied, from the walls, skirted the coast as far as Cape Noir, passed the British lines in dramatic silence, and stormed an important redan held by Forbes' Grenadiers. The unexpectedness of this sortie, the danger of an attack in concert by the Canadians at Mira, and the difficulty of discovering the extent of Le Chevalier Drucour's attempt to destroy the siege batteries, threw the grand army into slight confusion. Major Murray, of the 15th Regiment, immediately besieged the captured redan with Whitemore's and Bragg's Grenadiers. Troops hurried to their support, and after a desperate resistance the French were forced out of the redan to the city walls.

This affair forms a striking instance of the bravery of the defenders of Louisburg. Indeed, it would be difficult to find a better illustration of their courage than this daring venture of a handful of troops into the lines of an enemy nearly 13,000 strong. The statement that most of the sortiers were in liquor is unworthy of belief, both from the courage and system they displayed, and the fact that they arrested a general assault upon the city. They took their lives in their hands and fought gallantly for the city and the glory of the king's arms. Their conduct was in keeping with the traditions of the French Army, and our own annals contain few more dramatic displays of martial courage.

By a curious coincidence, while they were struggling to hold the redan and later retiring not ingloriously into Louisburg, their compatriots at Ticonderoga were celebrating the overwhelming defeat that day inflicted upon the second army of England; and while the British were driving the sortiers back, the largest army ever mobilised in America under the flag of England up to that time was in full retreat from Ticonderoga.

This night affair at the redan cost the lives of Lord Dundonald, captain of Forbes' Grenadiers, a corporal, and three men; and eleven officers and twenty-nine men were wounded, captured, or missing. The French lost a captain and seventeen men, most of whom fell in the redan; four men and one lieutenant were wounded or captured, and many others killed or wounded were carried off in the retreat. At the expiration of the short truce granted the French to bury their dead, the leaguer of Louisburg was resumed with a determination equalled only by the stubbornness of the defence, and the British commanders began to fear that the campaign of 1758 would be consumed in reducing the city.

The Chevalier Drucour's object in opposing the overwhelming

forces that surrounded him with such obstinacy was doubtless, to a large extent, the regard for the glory of the king's arms which had animated him throughout his career. The hope of assistance from Quebec or France also sustained him, although he suffered the mortification of seeing some succour beaten back from the port by Sir Charles Hardy. But the "grand motif" which induced Drucour to expose so many people to the horrors of a protracted siege, the dangers of a general assault, and the risk of harsh reprisals by the victors at the fall of the city was the statesmanlike policy of preventing the British from ascending the St. Lawrence.

Le Chevalier Drucour fully realised the imperial importance of keeping the British out of the St. Lawrence while General Montcalm resisted the second army of England, and, assisted by his intrepid wife, who daily discharged the duties of a gunner on the ramparts to inspirit the garrison, he sustained the gallant defence which still deserves the admiration of the world. The burning and capture of the remainder of the French fleet between July 21st and July 25th interrupted these tactics.

For days expert naval gunners, stationed in the British batteries, tried to ignite the powder magazines of the French ships left in the port, and on July 21st a ball pregnant with fate pierced the powder room of the *Entreprenant*, one of the finest ships in the Royal Navy of France, which immediately took fire and blew up with a concussion that terrified Louisburg. The conflagration spread to the *Capricieux* and *Célèbre*, "64's," and in spite of every exertion to save them, the three ships burned to the water's edge, bombarding themselves with their exploding guns amid the cheers of the Grand Army. The *Bienfaisant* and *Prudent* lay for some time in imminent danger of a similar inglorious fate, but the heroic French seamen ultimately towed them to a place of safety through a storm of British shot.

A few days later Admiral Boscawen determined to cut them out to open the port. The attention of the French was distracted by a vigorous cannonade from all the British batteries, and scaling ladders were ostentatiously displayed at the front to lead them to anticipate a general assault on the land side. By this *ruse de guerre* the French were drawn to the land walls about midnight, while 600 men, divided into two squadrons, commanded by Lefroy and Balfour, stole into the harbour in barges and pinnaces.

Passing close to the Island Battery and within hail of the town, screened by a thick fog, the British dashed for the *Bienfaisant* and *Pru-*

dent; but as the boats ran alongside,, the sentinels at the gangways of both battleships raised a loud alarm.

The French crews rushed tumultuously from below, and the well-known British cheers, the clash of cutlasses, the rattle of musketry, and the confused uproar soon warned Louisburg of what was happening in her fog-bound port. The city was instantly thrown into disorder. Threatened, it seemed, with an assault by land and sea, the consternation of the inhabitants almost developed into a panic, and some artillerymen increased the confusion by turning the guns of the harbour and Point Rochefort forts on the *Bienfaisant* and *Prudent*.

This blunder sealed the fate of the remnant of the French fleet. The crews, finding themselves unexpectedly exposed both to the British and to the guns of Louisburg, gradually surrendered, and the *Bienfaisant* was towed into the north-east harbour by the exultant British seamen. The *Prudent*, which lay so hard aground that she could not be moved, was set on fire after some small craft had been moored alongside for the escape of her crew.

The events of the next few hours were a repetition of those of yesterday; and the spectacle of the *Prudent* burning fiercely on the harbour waters, with her brave seamen pouring over the sides into the vessels left for their escape, affected the French almost to tears. Tongues of crimson flame darting from her ports and hatchways, ascended with incredible rapidity to her lofty masts, blazed through the intricate riggings, enveloped the ponderous yards, and expanded into vivid sheets as the sails burst their lashings and took fire.

Clouds of black smoke pouring from all parts of the ship hung like a pall over the harbour; her guns exploded, hurling destruction into the city; and the blackened ruins of the *Prudent* soon disfigured the sparkling waves. Flames burst intermittently from the hull until nearly eight o'clock; but at that hour the beautiful battleship was reduced to a mass of charred timber, and in her smouldering ruins expired the last hopes of Louisburg.

The "town party" now loudly clamoured for the surrender of the city, and the "military party" was as sensible that the end had come. The forts were shattered and the walls breached by the accurate fire of the British artillerymen; the reinforcements despatched by France and the Viceroy of Canada had been beaten back, and not even the remnant of a fleet existed. The wisdom of an immediate surrender was clear to the humblest habitant; and as the British could be seen preparing a general assault, a drummer beat the *chamade* at 10 o'clock in the morning, and a flag of truce was hoisted on the Cavalier Battery.

The town major then went out with offers from Drucour to surrender the city on much the same terms as the French had allowed the capitulating English at Port Mahon in 1756; but General Amherst, exasperated at a long defence which had disorganised his plan of campaign in the St. Lawrence, told the town major that rather than grant the honours of war to the garrison he preferred to carry the city by assault.

The Chevalier de Drucour was so incensed at this reply that he decided to defend the city to the last extremity. But, when this heroic decision became known, the civic authorities, headed by M. Prevot, the *intendant*, hastened to the palace and implored him to spare the inhabitants the horrors of an assault. They pointed out that the city would be ravaged with fire and sword, urged that the Highlanders and Rangers would spare neither age nor sex, and intimated to His Excellency that the responsibility for the horrors of the event would rest solely upon himself. While the civic and military parties held high debate the people surrounded the palace, murmuring at the obstinacy of the military, and crying out that the governor was more solicitous for the glory of the king's arms than for the welfare of the king's subjects.

The tumult increased when the truce conceded by the English expired and the British Army prepared for the assault. The citizens appealed to General Whitemore, who commanded the troops nearest the city, for an extension of the armistice; and when, on his own responsibility, he granted fifteen minutes more, they surrounded the governor's palace and implored him to surrender the stronghold. The increasing unrest of the populace moved Drucour; and, after a dignified resistance to their importunities, he at length agreed to capitulate on the hard terms of the besiegers.

When the town major reached the camp of the Grand Army, he found the troops preparing for a general assault on the city. His opportune arrival arrested their advance; and after some discussion the following terms of capitulation were mutually agreed upon:—

(1) The garrison of Louisburg shall be carried prisoners of war to England, in the ships of His Britannic Majesty.

(2) The artillery, ammunition, and provisions, as well as arms of all kinds in the town of Louisburg and on the islands of Cape Breton, St. John, and their appurtenances, shall be delivered, without damage, to Commissioners appointed to receive them

for the use of His Britannic Majesty.

(3) The governor shall order the troops on the island of St. John, and its appurtenances, to embark on the ships sent by the admiral to receive them.

(4) The gate called Port Dauphine shall be surrendered to the troops of His Britannic Majesty tomorrow morning at 8 o'clock, and the garrison, including all those that carried arms, shall be drawn up on the Esplanade at noon, there lay down their arms, colours, implements, and ornaments of war, and then embark upon the ships prepared for their reception.

(5) The same care shall be taken of the sick and wounded in the hospitals, as of those belonging to His Britannic Majesty.

(6) The merchants of the city, and their clerks, that have not carried arms, shall be sent to France in such manner as the admiral shall think proper.

(7) No terms to be allowed to deserters, Canadians, or Indians.

The articles of capitulation were signed under circumstances not since paralleled in the history of Cape Breton. On the neighbouring sea lay the fleet, on the green hills the triumphant first army of England, and between them, circumvallated by British guns, stood the key of Canada; its scientific walls shattered by the long cannonade; its hospitals, churches, nunneries, public buildings, and dwellings injured by explosive shell, and its picturesque port disfigured by a ruined fleet.

The flag of France still fluttered at the citadel staff, but the intimidated citizens heeded it not. Their eyes were turned towards the spot where the signatories to the capitulation had assembled; and, as a group of French officers was seen slowly returning to the gates, a sigh burst from the multitude. The accumulated power, wealth, and military science of France had tottered to a fall in Cape Breton, and a hated rival again held the key of her Colonial Empire.

The difficulties under which Le Chevalier Drucour defended Louisburg for seven weeks have not received generous, or even proper, prominence in narratives of the siege by British authors. But to less partial students of the event Drucour appears a heroic figure in his leaguered city, hemmed in by 41 warships and about 13,000 men; weakened by disloyal mercenaries, who could, not be allowed to mount guard or converse together; and dismayed by the repulse of the succour sent to him—vigorously harassing the British, directing the sortie, frustrating the intended assault, sinking his ships in the harbour mouth, and, accompanied by his intrepid wife, diligently superintending the whole complicated system of defence.

The end came only when the city was *in extremis,* and under circumstances in which no soldier need feel ashamed. As he later wrote from Andover:

> The captain of a ship strikes when his vessel is dismasted, his riggings cut to pieces, and several shot received between wind and water. A governor of a town surrenders a place when the breaches are practicable and when he has no resource.

Such, said Drucour, was the case at Louisburg, and he had no alternative but surrender. He naturally tried to make the best possible terms for the King of France, and a condition upon which he laid the greatest stress, therefore, was:

> That the honours of war should be granted to the garrison on their surrender, such as the right to march out with their firelocks on their shoulders, drums beating, colours flying, twenty-four charges of ammunition for each man, etc., etc.

These terms had been granted by Marshal Richelieu to Governor Blakeney and his garrison at Port Mahon in 1756, with the observation that:

> The noble and vigorous defence which the English have made having deserved all the marks of esteem and veneration that every military person ought to show such action; and Marshal Richelieu being desirous, also, to show General Blakeney the regard due to the brave defence he has made, grants the garrison all the honours of war that they can enjoy.

Amherst's refusal to grant these terms was a diplomatic mistake. The French fought well, and deserved an acknowledgment of their defence of the city. The concessions solicited by Le Chevalier Drucour would not have dimmed the prestige of the British arms, and they might have spared England the reproach that she hated the valour of her foes.

The conduct of the French admiral has been severely censured by Sir John Bourinot, who states that De Gouttes effected nothing for the defence. The views of this Cape Breton historian receive some support from the subsequent treatment of the admiral by the French

Court; but they are not supported by the testimony of the grandfather of "Chinese Gordon," who erected the last two batteries against Louisburg. This eye-witness kept a diary of the siege, which is now one of the most valuable accounts of the last leaguer of Louisburg, and the following review of the conduct of the French fleet is from this authentic source:—

The landing of heavier guns, ammunition, stores, etc., for Wolfe's batteries, in a cove to the eastward of the lighthouse, was jealously watched by the Marquis de Gouttes, who endeavoured to prevent the landing of these munitions of war by towing a sloop armed with two 32-pounders as near the cove as possible, under cover of the Island Battery.

The duel between this armed sloop, supported by the powerful armament of the Island Battery, and the British warships was a creditable affair, and cost the British frigate *Diana* at least six men killed and wounded. The warm participation of the French fleet in the subsequent spectacular artillery duel between Battery Island and Wolfe's "Lighthouse" Batteries is further evidence of the admiral's activity. On June 27th Gordon recorded a constant fire from the French ships on the British working parties, on June 29th the killing of a grenadier of the 40th Regiment in his tent by a shot from one of them, and a very hot bombardment of the British works, which rather abated towards evening, owing to the explosion of a 13-inch shell in the most active ship.

Her crew were thrown into great confusion by this accident, and used all despatch to save the ship by throwing her powder overboard. The work on the epaulement, then under construction by the British, was much interrupted by this naval bombardment, particularly by the broadsides from the *Aréthuse*, which was stationed as high up the harbour as the depth of water would permit, with her guns trained upon a low pass by which the British were obliged to advance.

On July 1st, although Drucour had reduced the strength of the fleet by sinking a number of ships in the harbour mouth, during which operation the *Aréthuse* went out and extremely annoyed the British, the French admiral kept up a hot fire on the British all night. On the 2nd the tediousness of making the epaulement, exposed to the incessant fire of the *Aréthuse*, was noted by Gordon. On the 3rd the violent cannonade of the British lines by the decimated French fleet lasted all day; and a combined hot bombardment by the ships and the town took place the following day. The fire of the French ships on the

5th was "very smart" all day; and on the 6th they briskly returned the fire directed upon them by the British batteries, although the *Aréthuse* was in a damaged condition.

Two days later the French ships engaged the British batteries, and on the 9th, they bombarded them without intermission. On the 11th the fire of the French ships was very hot, but on the 13th, it slackened, continued slack through the 14th, and on the following night the *Aréthuse* escaped.

The escape and pursuit of this gallant frigate was an exciting incident of the blockade of Louisburg.

She passed safely through the British lines, and arrived in European waters; but shortly afterwards (May 18th, 1759) she was captured by the *Thames* and *Venus* between Rochefort and Brest, after a sharp engagement, in which she lost 60 men, and the *Thames* 15. Her capture was hailed as a signal event in England, as she was the fastest, and one of the most formidable, frigates in the French navy; and the Lords of the Admiralty acknowledged the intrepidity of her officers by releasing them on parole.

After the escape of the *Aréthuse* the French fleet continued to annoy the British, and on the 20th one of the ships was partially dismasted by the siege batteries. On the 21st a shot from the British marine battery destroyed the *Entreprenant, Capricieux*, and *Célèbre*. On July 23rd the remaining ships bombarded the British lines, but on July 25th they were captured by Admiral Boscawen's cutting-out expedition, and the French fleet was extinguished.

With these facts before us it is impossible to believe that the French admiral contributed nothing to the defence of Louisburg.

Louisburg was not interfered with on the day of the capitulation. The grand army remained within its lines; Sir Charles Hardy's ships hovered off the harbour mouth; others rode at anchor along the coast or moved towards the horizon, and stillness reigned over the theatre of strife until the pealing of melodious bells announced the hour of vespers in the fallen city. The religious services on that memorable evening were doubtless marked by a solemnity which impressed the humiliated citizens; and the officiating priests might have exclaimed, in the language of the author of the Book of Lamentations.

At the close of the services the people promenaded the streets up to a late hour; others wandered curiously over the huge fortifications that had once more failed to uphold the majesty of France; and many of the refugees shut up in the city seized an opportunity of escaping through the breach into the interior.

The demeanour of the people was in general orderly, but towards midnight the lower orders mingled with the soldiery that thronged the cabarets, and repeatedly disturbed the peace of the city. Some shops and store-houses were plundered, and the restlessness of the Indians increased the alarms of the night. The Micmacs, for whom no terms had been made at the capitulation, justly dreaded the entry into the city of a conqueror who had objected to any consideration being shown them; and both Drucour and Prevot, the *intendant*, were greatly relieved when nearly five hundred of them made their escape around the Island Battery in canoes.

The churches of the city remained opened all night for the hasty marriage of the girls who could be induced to take husbands to protect them from the feared licence of the British occupation.

Many fair Acadians modestly availed themselves of the opportunity for matrimony, and some interesting Cape Breton romances reached a hymeneal stage at the altars of Louisburg before the British grenadiers appeared at her gates.

At eight o'clock in the morning Major Farquhar led three companies of grenadiers to the West Gate, and occupied its approaches until noon. Few of the inhabitants witnessed the humiliating ceremony; but at noon the entire population flocked to points of vantage to witness the surrender of the city. The French troops were marched to the Esplanade, where Le Chevalier Drucour and his staff, Admiral Boscawen, Sir Charles Hardy, and Philip Durell, Amherst, Wolfe, Whitemore, Lawrence, the Governor of Nova Scotia, and a distinguished assembly of military and naval officers awaited them. After formal salutations had been exchanged, the governor and the military officers of high rank surrendered their swords, the civil Governor delivered up the keys of the city, and the garrison reluctantly resigned their standards and arms to the conquerors.

The 58th Regiment and the 3rd Battalion of the 60th then camped on the glacis, and the fleet entered the harbour, followed by a long train of transports. The French flag was left flying on the walls, as after the first capture by the New England Militia thirteen years before; and five Dutch ships, laden with provisions for the French, entrapped by this *ruse de guerre*, rewarded the tactics of the conquerors. The *Countess of Claremont* and a richly laden French merchantman were also secured.

Three days after the capitulation Captain Amherst, the general's brother and *aide-de-camp*, left for England in the *Shannon*, Captain Edgecumbe, with despatches and all the captured standards; but the *Shannon* had hardly disappeared on the horizon with the tidings of victory when a vessel from Halifax beat into Louisburg with the tidings of the defeat of the second army of England at Ticonderoga.

A council of war was immediately held on the flagship, and General Amherst proposed that, after providing for the defence of Louisburg, the armada should ascend the St. Lawrence. But the defence of Louisburg by Drucour had consumed so much time that it was too late for a military expedition to ascend the river; and Amherst discovered that he could only assist Abercrombie through Boston. This he undertook as promptly as possible with the 2nd Battalion of the 1st Royals, the 17th Regiment, the 47th Regiment, the 48th Regiment, and the 63rd Regiment, convoyed by the *Captain*; but he arrived too late to retrieve the misfortunes of the second army, and his troops were sent into winter quarters.

By keeping the British before Louisburg so long that they dare not ascend the St. Lawrence to assail Montcalm's rear, Le Chevalier Drucour thus rendered good service to France; and it may be said that his defence of Louisburg temporarily preserved French Canada.

As affairs settled in Louisburg, detachments of troops occupied the Morien and other collieries in the neighbouring coalfield—a rich district destined to be the scene of industrial activity which would revive the commercial importance of Louisburg. St. Anne and Sydney (Espagnol) were also occupied, and on August 8th Lord Rollo issued from Louisburg with the Light Infantry of his own (the 22nd) regiment, the 40th and 45th Regiments, and some other forces, to occupy Prince Edward Island—the island of St. John—upon which Quebec to some extent depended for supplies of food.

The lieutenant-governor of the island refused to acknowledge the articles of capitulation, and resisted every attempt the British made to land. Lord Rollo then drew up his forces, and threatened to destroy the forts by general assault. The resistance of the French could not under the circumstances be effective; but the lieutenant-governor appears to have considered that the glory of the king's arms and a proper regard for his own reputation demanded some formal opposition to the British. The defence of St. John's (Prince Edward) Island lasted, however, but several hours; the British pressed with accumulated weight on Port la Joie (Charlottetown), and the garrison of 500 men at length surrendered as prisoners of war.

Meanwhile the first army of England remained encamped on the glacis of Louisburg or behind its original lines. The late governor was treated with respect, and Madame Drucour, who received high consideration, enjoyed the personal friendship of Wolfe and Amherst, whom she had probably met through her capture on the *Écho*, and to whom she had sent "pyramids of sweetmeats" or fresh butter made by her own fair hands during the siege. She turned her popularity to account, humanely devoted herself to increasing the comforts of the captives, and endeavoured to reconcile them to their humiliating lot. Her good offices were needed, for the French did not conceal their dislike of the English, and openly rejoiced on July 31st, when an exaggerated rumour of the defeat of the second army of England at Ticonderoga spread through the city.

This, and the suspicion that the funds of the Royal Exchequer had been secreted before they entered the city, irritated the British, and the relations between the conquerors and the conquered were unfriendly. The tension was at last relieved by the despatch of the French combatants to England. The garrison and invalid soldiers were embarked by the grenadier companies of the 40th, 47th, 48th, and 63rd Regiments on the 9th of August; the sailors of the annihilated fleet went on board the transports during the next day, and four days later they left the harbour in six vessels, convoyed by the *Dublin, Devonshire, Terrible, Northumberland,* and *Kingston,* amid the feeble cheers of the citizens.

From the quarterdeck of the last ship that glided through the Narrows, Madame Drucour and the ex-governor gazed at Louisburg, and the sentinel on the Lighthouse Battery caught a glimpse of the white flutter of the scarf with which Her Excellency waved farewell to the city where she had won so high a position among the bravest of her sex. The first army of England then marched into Louisburg.

ALSO FROM LEONAUR

AVAILABLE IN SOFTCOVER OR HARDCOVER WITH DUST JACKET

AN APACHE CAMPAIGN IN THE SIERRA MADRE *by John G. Bourke*—An Account of the Expedition in Pursuit of the Chiricahua Apaches in Arizona, 1883.

BILLY DIXON & ADOBE WALLS *by Billy Dixon and Edward Campbell Little*—Scout, Plainsman & Buffalo Hunter, *Life and Adventures of "Billy" Dixon* by Billy Dixon and *The Battle of Adobe Walls* by Edward Campbell Little (*Pearson's Magazine*).

WITH THE CALIFORNIA COLUMN *by George H. Petis*—Against Confederates and Hostile Indians During the American Civil War on the South Western Frontier, *The California Column, Frontier Service During the Rebellion* and *Kit Carson's Fight With the Comanche and Kiowa Indians*.

THRILLING DAYS IN ARMY LIFE *by George Alexander Forsyth*—Experiences of the Beecher's Island Battle 1868, the Apache Campaign of 1882, and the American Civil War.

INDIAN FIGHTS AND FIGHTERS *by Cyrus Townsend Brady*—Indian Fights and Fighters of the American Western Frontier of the 19th Century.

THE NEZ PERCÉ CAMPAIGN, 1877 *by G. O. Shields & Edmond Stephen Meany*—Two Accounts of Chief Joseph and the Defeat of the Nez Percé, *The Battle of Big Hole* by G. O. Shields and *Chief Joseph, the Nez Percé* by Edmond Stephen Meany.

CAPTAIN JEFF OF THE TEXAS RANGERS *by W. J. Maltby*—Fighting Comanche & Kiowa Indians on the South Western Frontier 1863-1874.

SHERIDAN'S TROOPERS ON THE BORDERS *by De Benneville Randolph Keim*—The Winter Campaign of the U. S. Army Against the Indian Tribes of the Southern Plains, 1868-9.

GERONIMO *by Geronimo*—The Life of the Famous Apache Warrior in His Own Words.

WILD LIFE IN THE FAR WEST *by James Hobbs*—The Adventures of a Hunter, Trapper, Guide, Prospector and Soldier.

THE OLD SANTA FE TRAIL *by Henry Inman*—The Story of a Great Highway.

LIFE IN THE FAR WEST *by George F. Ruxton*—The Experiences of a British Officer in America and Mexico During the 1840's.

ADVENTURES IN MEXICO AND THE ROCKY MOUNTAINS *by George F. Ruxton*—Experiences of Mexico and the South West During the 1840's.

AVAILABLE ONLINE AT **www.leonaur.com**
AND FROM ALL GOOD BOOK STORES
07/09

LEONAUR

ALSO FROM LEONAUR
AVAILABLE IN SOFTCOVER OR HARDCOVER WITH DUST JACKET

THE FALL OF THE MOGHUL EMPIRE OF HINDUSTAN *by H. G. Keene*—By the beginning of the nineteenth century, as British and Indian armies under Lake and Wellesley dominated the scene, a little over half a century of conflict brought the Moghul Empire to its knees.

LADY SALE'S AFGHANISTAN *by Florentia Sale*—An Indomitable Victorian Lady's Account of the Retreat from Kabul During the First Afghan War.

THE CAMPAIGN OF MAGENTA AND SOLFERINO 1859 *by Harold Carmichael Wylly*—The Decisive Conflict for the Unification of Italy.

FRENCH'S CAVALRY CAMPAIGN *by J. G. Maydon*—A Special Correspondent's View of British Army Mounted Troops During the Boer War.

CAVALRY AT WATERLOO *by Sir Evelyn Wood*—British Mounted Troops During the Campaign of 1815.

THE SUBALTERN *by George Robert Gleig*—The Experiences of an Officer of the 85th Light Infantry During the Peninsular War.

NAPOLEON AT BAY, 1814 *by F. Loraine Petre*—The Campaigns to the Fall of the First Empire.

NAPOLEON AND THE CAMPAIGN OF 1806 *by Colonel Vachée*—The Napoleonic Method of Organisation and Command to the Battles of Jena & Auerstädt.

THE COMPLETE ADVENTURES IN THE CONNAUGHT RANGERS *by William Grattan*—The 88th Regiment during the Napoleonic Wars by a Serving Officer.

BUGLER AND OFFICER OF THE RIFLES *by William Green & Harry Smith*—With the 95th (Rifles) during the Peninsular & Waterloo Campaigns of the Napoleonic Wars.

NAPOLEONIC WAR STORIES *by Sir Arthur Quiller-Couch*—Tales of soldiers, spies, battles & sieges from the Peninsular & Waterloo campaingns.

CAPTAIN OF THE 95TH (RIFLES) *by Jonathan Leach*—An officer of Wellington's sharpshooters during the Peninsular, South of France and Waterloo campaigns of the Napoleonic wars.

RIFLEMAN COSTELLO *by Edward Costello*—The adventures of a soldier of the 95th (Rifles) in the Peninsular & Waterloo Campaigns of the Napoleonic wars.